Chicken Soup for the Soul.

The Power of Forgiveness

D0451450

Chicken Soup for the Soul: The Power of Forgiveness
101 Stories about How to Let Go and Change Your Life
Amy Newmark, Anthony Anderson

Published by Chicken Soup for the Soul Publishing, LLC www.chickensoup.com

The publisher gratefully acknowledges the many publishers and individuals who
granted Chicken Soup for the Soul permission to reprint the cited material.

Front cover photo courtesy of iStockPhoto.com/danielschweinert (© Daniel Schweinert).
Interior photo courtesy of iStockPhoto.com/3dsguru (© 3dsguru).
Photo of Anthony Anderson and Amy Newmark courtesy of Issac Brekken/Getty Images.

Cover and Interior Design & Layout by Brian Taylor, Pneuma Books, LLC

Distributed to the booktrade by Simon & Schuster. SAN: 200-2442

Publisher's Cataloging-in-Publication Data
(Prepared by The Donohue Group)

Chicken soup for the soul : the power of forgiveness : 101 stories about
  how to let go and change your life / [compiled by] Amy Newmark, Anthony
  Anderson.

    pages ; cm

  ISBN: 978-1-61159-942-8

  1. Forgiveness--Literary collections. 2. Forgiveness--Anecdotes. 3. Anecdotes. I.
Newmark, Amy. II. Anderson, Anthony, 1970- III. Title: Power of forgiveness : 101
stories about how to let go and change your life

BF637.F67 C45 2014
158.2/02   2014952873

PRINTED IN THE UNITED STATES OF AMERICA
on acid∞free paper

24 23 22 21 20 19 18 17 16 15 14   01 02 03 04 05 06 07 08 09 10 11

Chicken Soup for the Soul®
The Power of Forgiveness

101 Stories about How to Let Go and Change Your Life

Amy Newmark
Anthony Anderson

Chicken Soup for the Soul Publishing, LLC
Cos Cob, CT

Chicken Soup for the Soul

Changing your life one story at a time®

www.chickensoup.com

Contents

3

~Learning to Live with Family-through-Marriage~

4

~Patching Up Rifts with Siblings~

5

~When Bad Things Happen in Love and Marriage~

❻

~Forgiving Friends and Colleagues~

❼

~Lessons from the People You Meet~

❽

~When a Crime Has Been Committed~

❾

~The Importance of Self-Forgiveness~

~A Poem that Says It All~

~Bonus Stories about the Power of Forgiveness~

Introduction

Self is the only prison that can ever bind the soul.
~Henry Van Dyke

This is a life-changing book. The fact that you are reading it means you are at least *thinking* about using the power of forgiveness to change yours. We hope these 101 personal, revealing stories will motivate you to let go and get on with your own life.

It's astounding how many of the contributors to this book talk about the freedom they feel after forgiving someone. They hadn't realized how much they were holding themselves back by holding on to the resentment, plotting revenge, and staying angry! Many of them lay out the steps for you—exactly how you, too, can analyze your situation, come to grips with what happened, and then forgive and move on. It's empowering and it's freeing to leave those resentments behind, to put them in the past. And many of our contributors eventually realize that the only people they're hurting by not using the power of forgiveness are themselves.

These stories cover just about every kind of human relationship and all the different ways that things can go wrong, so you will undoubtedly find some good advice in these pages. In Chapter 1, you'll read about people forgiving their fathers. Anthony Anderson, coauthor of this book, talks about forgiving his biological father right before he died, and how right it was to do that. He says, "I sleep peacefully at night knowing that I was able to release my father from a burden of guilt as well as Robert releasing me from the burden of anger I had towards him." And he passes on some great advice about how you can take the first step, whether you feel it's your responsibility or not. Someone has to be the strong one, right?

You'll also read a fascinating story by Kara Sundlun in Chapter 1. It was only when her biological father was running for political office that she discovered who he was. Eventually, when he became governor of Rhode Island, and after she filed a paternity suit, he accepted her as his child and even had her come to live with him. She didn't start a relationship with him until she was in her late teens, but she forgave him and he passed away at the age of ninety-one in her arms. Kara says, "Forgiveness is the closest thing I have found to a fairy godmother. Its energy has the magical power to transform us and create the happy ending we so badly want."

In Chapter 2, you'll read about forgiveness between mothers and their children, including a very moving story by Ruth Logan Herne. Ruth was raised in abject poverty by a depressed, alcoholic mother. One day Ruth came across her mother's poetry from when she was a teenager, and that was her wake-up call—she saw her mother as the talented, thoughtful girl she had been. And when her mother stopped drinking, Ruth embraced the relationship with her again and was thankful to be her daughter.

And then there are the in-laws and the "steps" and the "halfs" and all the other family relationships we add to our lives through marriage. In Chapter 3, we read stories about learning to live with family-through-marriage, including an uplifting story by Helen Colella that is sure to make you smile. Helen's brother married a widow and became the stepfather to a wonderful, loving teenage son. Their relationship was fabulous but the stepson became increasingly unhappy with his stepfather, until one day he opened up and told him that he wanted to be described as his son, not his stepson. Of course the stepfather had always viewed him as his son but didn't want to look like he was trying to replace the boy's late father. It's a great example not only of the power of forgiveness but also of speaking honestly and openly.

The occasional fights between siblings are a normal part of growing up. But when things go wrong between adult siblings, it really hurts. In Chapter 4 you'll read many stories about patching up rifts with siblings, including a fascinating one by Mark Rickerby, whose brother was a drug addict. After his brother died, Mark needed to forgive him for what he had done to the family. Mark also needed to forgive himself for what he viewed as his failure to save his brother. One night, in a dream, Mark's brother appeared and assured him that he hadn't done anything wrong. And Mark forgave him. When he woke up, he says he was "heartbroken that it was just a dream" but also says that he had "a heart lighter than it had been since he died."

Chapter 5 is all about the bad things that can happen in love and marriage. You'll read many stories about affairs and marriages that failed, but you'll also read how husbands and wives learned to see past these transgressions and reconnect with the person they used to love, even if it's only to maintain a civil relationship post-divorce. One such story, by Karen Todd Scarpulla, is about how she and her teenage kids moved back in with her ex-husband when he was diagnosed with terminal cancer. She nursed him through his final year, and she learned to separate his bad behavior from the person she had once loved. She says, "Forgiveness had given me the ability to stop judging him and accept him for who he was. I was finally at peace with our past. It was time to let go of our history, so we could both move on."

There are plenty of people we need to forgive outside our families. Most of us have had a falling out with a friend or work colleague at some point. Unfortunately, we don't have family occasions to force us back together to work things out. In Chapter 6, you'll read stories about a variety of misunderstandings and just plain bad behavior and you'll meet some great role models who show you how to overcome your feelings and use forgiveness to reclaim your lives from these people.

Joe Rector writes about what happened when he resigned as coach of his son's baseball team and the father who took his spot exacted revenge on him by not letting Joe's son play for the rest of the season. Joe remained angry about this for years, and resentful of the father's son as well, until one day his own son said to him, "Dad, it's time to quit being mad. His dad was a jerk, and he hurt me back then, but I'm okay now and don't care." Joe realized he was right and he forgave the other father. He says, "Almost immediately, I felt as if a huge weight had been lifted from my shoulders." And he was able to enjoy baseball again. The only person he had been hurting during all those years was himself.

In Chapter 7, "Lessons from the People You Meet," you'll read inspirational stories that will make you look at strangers in a new light. When Marya Morin moved into a new home, it seemed that her elderly neighbor was determined to make Marya's family miserable, complaining about any noise the young family made, even if they were just laughing. Then one day, when Marya was hosting a barbecue for friends and neighbors, she had an epiphany. She invited her crabby neighbor to join them, and discovered that she was just a lonely old woman who was being mistreated by her own grown son. After that barbecue, Marya reports, "We never heard a harsh word from her again. In fact, we became close friends, forgiving and forgetting our rocky beginning, and embracing our friendship instead." That's a great lesson for all of us. You have to look beyond someone's behavior to see what is motivating it. Sometimes, addressing that unseen motivation will solve the problem for you.

Nevertheless, it's hard to imagine forgiving someone for murder or rape or pedophilia or drunk driving, but our contributors have done it. Chapter 8 contains fourteen stories by contributors who forgave someone who committed a crime against them. We start the chapter with a story by Immaculée Ilibagiza, known worldwide as one of the survivors of the Rwandan Genocide, that terrible, insane civil war that occurred two decades ago when the Hutu majority turned on the Tutsi minority, even killing members of their own families.

Immaculée and seven other Tutsi women spent three months crammed into a twelve-foot-square bathroom, hiding in the home of a local Hutu pastor. When they finally emerged after the slaughter had ended, Immaculée learned that her entire family had been killed except for one brother who was studying abroad. When she was introduced to her family's murderer in a local jail, she said, "I forgive you," shocking the jailer, who expected her to kick the cowering old man who lay at her feet in rags. But Immaculée explained: "Hatred has taken everything I ever loved from me. Forgiveness is all I have left to offer."

She walked out of that prison free of anger and hatred and says she has lived as a free woman ever since.

Perhaps the most important forgiveness of all is self-forgiveness, because we seem to beat ourselves up more than anyone else. So this book ends with a whole chapter on the importance of self-forgiveness, and as an example, you'll read Judythe A. Guarnera's story about the advice she received in a divorce support group. The leader asked the participants to say, "In my marriage I did the best I could." Then they were told to say, "My spouse did the best he or she could." And Judythe came to realize that her husband had done his best, and she had done her best, and it just hadn't worked out. She forgave her ex-husband and herself, and thus faced a better future.

And finally, you'll read a poem by Christina Galeone that we believe is a wonderful way to sum up the lessons we have learned from this book. When she talks about rage "steamrolling good as well as bad" it sounds like she is speaking for every contributor to this collection. Forgiveness brings peace. Rage and anger bring nothing but more of the same.

As Anthony Anderson says in his story, "Life is fleeting. We need to LIVE and LOVE in the moment!" We hope this important new collection of stories from Chicken Soup for the Soul will help you reunite with a loved one, get over a dispute that's keeping you up at night, and shrug off those daily problems and issues that arise, big and small, in all our lives.

The Power *of* Forgiveness

Lessons on Forgiving Fathers

Because forgiveness is like this: a room can be dank because you have closed the windows, you've closed the curtains. But the sun is shining outside, and the air is fresh outside. In order to get that fresh air, you have to get up and open the window and draw the curtains apart.

~Desmond Tutu

The Forgiveness of Robert and Me

We cannot destroy kindred: our chains stretch a little sometimes,
but they never break.
~Marie de Rabutin-Chantal,
marquise de Sévigné

My mom was only a high school senior when she met my biological father Robert Anthony Anderson, who was eight years her senior. Although their relationship was short-lived (less than a year), Robert was already out of her life by the time I was born. Don't get me wrong, I had a father. His name was Sterling Bowman. This was the man that I would call Dad until the day he passed away ten years ago. He married my mother while I was just a baby.

My dad raised me, protected me and comforted me when Robert would break his promises to me. I remember one time being a young kid waiting excitedly for Robert to come by my house. I was excited because it was my birthday and Robert had promised me a new bike. That day had come and gone, but no Robert. I had opened gifts from my entire family but still waited for one last gift to open. I would race to the front of the house every time I heard a car drive by, thinking that it was Robert. Robert never came. Later that evening my father took my hand and walked me to the garage, opened it, and to my surprise there it was, a brand new bike that my dad had bought me because he knew Robert was going to be a no-show. After all, this wasn't the first time Robert had disappointed me.

Even though my mother was married to my dad, she always maintained a friendly relationship with Robert in hopes that he would have a relationship with me. For some reason Robert's relationship with my mother never extended to me. I remember when I was eleven or so, my mother would drop me off at my grandmother Elsie's house. She was Robert's mother. I was dropped off there for three Saturdays in a row hoping that Robert would come by to visit with me. I would be there all day and well into the evening, sitting in a house full of strangers, waiting. That visit never came. My mother would pick me up and ask, "Did he show up?" and my answer was always "No!" During my last visit, my mother saw the hurt and disappointment on my face and said, "You don't have to go back if you don't want to." I never went back.

I never felt that there was a void that needed to be filled. After all, I had my mom, dad, brothers and sister, so I really didn't need or want Robert in my life. I can honestly say that I never harbored any ill will or resentment toward Robert, mainly because I didn't know him. Then one day I really needed some help. I was late on a car payment and my car was repossessed. My dad was giving me some "tough love" and teaching me a lesson in responsibility, so I couldn't ask him for the money needed to get my car out of impound. That left only Robert to call. I had never asked him for anything in life so I was sure that he would help me. By this time I was in my early twenties and Robert had been expressing that he wanted to be a part of my life.

I called and explained in detail what had happened. I had enough money to cover the late payment and repossession but I did not have enough to cover what the impound charges would be at the end of the week when I got paid. I was also gainfully employed but in between paychecks, that's why I needed his help. The impound fees totaled close to $300. I wasn't asking for a handout, I was asking for a loan that would've been paid back in full within the next five days. His reply was, "Sorry. I can't help you." He never gave a reason as to why he couldn't help me, so I said no problem, hung up the phone and had no plans to ever speak to Robert again.

That moment never sat right with me, and years later worsened when I started working as an actor. All of a sudden I was HIS son! He now wanted to have a relationship with me after being absent for the first twenty-five years of my life. Bragging about me to his friends and strangers alike. I often wondered how a man that never held me as an infant, never wiped away a tear or spent time with me could make such a bold claim.

My mother had a recurring joke with Robert about that long ago bicycle promise to me. She said to him, "Why don't you just buy him a bike?" For some reason, Robert couldn't bring himself to do it, but he bought a bike for my son, which was ironic because he had no relationship with my then eight-year-old son. Had he only listened to my mother I would've opened the door to have a conversation with him about "How do we start a relationship and where do we go from here?"

Over the years Robert would call and we would talk about superficial stuff because that's all he knew about me. He never once tried to get to know me nor did I try to get to know him until one day my mother called and said that Robert was sick and he wanted to see me. I just assumed it was the flu; after all it was flu season. But two days later my mom called again and said that Robert had liver cancer and wanted to talk. I rushed over to finally talk to the father that I never had. I believe I did so because I had lost my dad just the year before.

We talked for more than three hours! We talked about everything, but most of all we talked about having a relationship. We both agreed that it was finally time to bury the hatchet and move forward as father and son. He finally said five little words that I had been waiting a lifetime to hear: "I'm sorry, I love you." It moved me to tears. I repeated those words to him. We hugged and called it a night. I saw the joy in his eyes. I told him I would see him on Saturday.

This was Thursday evening. On the ride home my mother shared the news with me that Robert was terminally ill and had a hospice nurse coming to see him the following day. That's why we would be seeing each other on Saturday. I thought to myself this couldn't be happening! I had so many questions that needed to be answered. There were so many questions that I'm sure he had for me, too.

When I returned to my father's home on Saturday, he looked as if he had aged fifteen years in those two days I hadn't seen him. He was hooked up to an oxygen machine and had a morphine drip. He was not responsive and his pupils were dilated. I sat with him all day and night, just talking to him about my life, my wife and children. I let him know that my children were there but they didn't want to disturb him right now, so we would be back in the morning. I leaned over, kissed his forehead and whispered in his ear that I loved him, and it sent a shockwave through his body. He managed to mumble words for the first time that day. Although those words were garbled and hushed I still heard them loud and clear! "I LOVE YOU SON!" I left with my family, only to get a call at midnight that my father had passed away.

Our relationship was the last wrong that my father needed to right before passing on. I believe he held on just long enough to do so. That night I forgave him and he forgave me. We had wiped our slate clean and I was ready to start anew, but unfortunately we were out of time.

I sleep peacefully at night knowing that I was able to release my father from a burden of guilt as well as Robert releasing me from the burden of anger I had towards him. He accepted and forgave me for my faults as I did the same for him. I learned a great deal from that experience. I learned that life is fleeting so we need to LIVE and LOVE in the moment! And that is how I live my life. I no longer hold onto negativity and pain. I tell my loved ones and friends how I feel. I send the flowers for them to smell and enjoy above ground.

The advice I would give to anyone is: You can always take the first step. You can always extend the olive branch whether you feel it's your duty or not. And you can always be the forgiven as you're forgiving!

~Anthony Anderson

Finding Dad

Forgiveness is a mystical act, not a reasonable one.
~Caroline Myss

I was thirteen years old and had never even seen a picture of my father, when suddenly the invisible character of my childhood had a face. I don't know what woke me up on that cold Michigan night, but my eyes popped open with a sense of urgency at the very second a CNN news anchor was announcing the results of the 1988 gubernatorial election in Rhode Island.

"It was a close one in the Ocean State for Bruce Sundlun," she announced. She talked about how this war hero/business tycoon-turned politician almost beat the incumbent, Governor Edward DiPrete.

My mom had always said, "Your biological father is a man named Bruce Sundlun." But now, for the first time, he was real and staring back at me. On TV. My real father was no longer just the faceless man who broke my mother's heart. The news anchor proved his existence to me with a picture and a story. That night, Mom and I were sleeping in a hotel room, bone tired from a long day of moving to a new house, when I reached over and shook her. "Mom, wake up! Is that him?" I shrieked.

Bleary eyed, she looked up and answered me in a scratchy, shocked voice. "He must have gone back to Rhode Island, where he's from."

I wanted to press "rewind" and freeze his picture. Did I really look just like him, like Mom had always told me?

My creators met in the glamorous world of aviation in the 70s when flying was still about the coolest thing you could do on earth. He was the handsome World War II bomber pilot turned airline CEO, and Mom was his chief flight attendant. She fell madly in love with my father, but when she became pregnant with me, there was nothing but turbulence ahead. There was no DNA test in 1975, and he refused to claim me. Mom knew I was his, but she yielded to his big time lawyers and settled out of court for thirty-five thousand dollars to pay for my life, and a promise not to contact him again or let me use his very important surname.

At that moment, staring at him on TV, none of that mattered. I was a girl who had just found her father—or almost. The Universe woke me up in the middle of the night, awakening a primal need to know the other half of me. And nothing was going to stop me.

My quest wouldn't be easy. My father was eventually elected Governor of Rhode Island in 1991, and he ignored the letters I wrote to the State House asking to meet him. Finally, we hired a lawyer, and I managed to get a secret meeting and a DNA test that proved I really was his daughter. I was positive that once he knew I was really his, he would open his heart and welcome me into his life. But, instead, he did nothing. I was heartbroken. Again. How could he do this to me? What happened to my happy ending?

I really wanted him to be a dad, but if he wouldn't, then I felt he should at least help us pay for college since Mom had been struggling to do it all on her own for so long. I filed a paternity suit at the age of seventeen, and a media frenzy erupted. My story started leading the evening news, and the nation's newspapers printed headlines like "Gov Child" above my picture. Even under the scrutiny of spotlights, my war hero dad was still fighting me. Why couldn't he just be a dad? My soul ached for his acceptance.

I could have given up, but somewhere deep inside me, a little voice told me to have faith, that he would come around. "It's all meant to be," I told myself. I'm sure it sounded like wishful thinking, but it wasn't. My dad shocked the world when, in the middle of the media frenzy, he agreed to pay for my college tuition and invited me to come live with him so we could "get to know each other." I didn't know if I could trust him, but I packed my bags and left everything I knew to uncover my other half. I welcomed his offer of acceptance. My identity was worth the risk.

The same part of me that told me to have faith also demanded that I forgive my father for all the rejection, pain, and anger he had caused me. When I showed up on his doorstep to cross the threshold of my new life, I knew I had to choose to forgive if I wanted the happy ending my soul had been yearning for so long. So I did. I gave my father a chance at redemption, and he ran with it.

There was no long, maudlin apology. Instead, we started to heal the past by living in the present. We discovered we were a lot alike, right down to our love of Oreo cookies and chocolate ice cream sodas. The daily doses of love we shared from simple joys together settled sweetly in my core, and I started to heal the cracks of abandonment in my foundation. My wounds gave way to wisdom, and on the journey to find my father I found my true self. I learned that it's never too late to heal; my father became Dad, and then Poppy to my children. I knew my father one year longer than I did not know him when he passed away at the age of ninety-one, in my arms, surrounded by the family I had always dreamed of. Forgiveness is the closest thing I have found to a fairy godmother. Its energy has the magical power to transform us and create the happy ending we so badly want.

We often teach what we have to learn, which is why I wrote the book *Finding Dad: From "Love Child" to Daughter*. My story taught me that forgiveness is truly the greatest gift you can give yourself.

~Kara Sundlun

Gramma's Good China

The truth is, unless you let go, unless you forgive yourself,
unless you forgive the situation, unless you realize that the situation is over,
you cannot move forward.
~Steve Maraboli

For years, every Saturday afternoon my family—Mom, my stepfather and I—had dinner at Gramma's house. We watched sporting events on TV, played *Yahtzee* and enjoyed a home-cooked meal: spaghetti and meatballs, pot roast, chicken and biscuits... you get the idea.

Anna Marie, or Gramma as we all call her, is seventy-nine years old and very set in her ways. She attends church every Sunday, never misses an episode of *60 Minutes*, completes the daily crossword puzzle in the newspaper, makes apple pie for every holiday and refuses to ever take the good china out of the cabinet because her regular dinnerware is "good enough."

However, one Saturday at the end of October things were different. My mom, my stepdad and I stayed home because my father was coming to visit. My biological father, that is, who I hadn't seen since he left town sixteen years earlier. He called asking to visit, saying he wanted to see me.

I was dreading it.

Saturday afternoon when the doorbell chimed, I peered through the blinds at my father on the porch. He looked older, heavier, grayer. For some reason, I expected him to look exactly as he did in the single photo I had of him—the two of us at the lake when I was seven. I kept the picture in my sock drawer.

My father, mom and stepfather were politely exchanging pleasantries when I stepped into the entryway. My father extended his hand to shake mine. "David," he said, smiling. "It's great to see you, son."

I knew what I should do, but I couldn't. My arm, my hand was immobile.

This man had walked out on us. He had never been there. He missed every Christmas and birthday, my basketball games, my college graduation; why would I shake his hand?

I nodded, grunted and sat on the couch.

Mom told him about her job and the vacation cruise that she and my stepdad had taken, then motioned towards me. "David's been busy lately with his job and finishing his thesis, haven't you, honey?"

I nodded. "Yeah, high school, college, getting a job. A lot can happen in sixteen years."

"David," Mom grumbled through clenched teeth.

My father held up his hands. "It's okay. I understand. You're not thrilled to see me. This was a stupid idea, but I wanted to see you."

"You've seen me." I shrugged.

"Why don't we have dinner?" Mom suggested. "I made meatloaf."

"Thanks anyway. I'm not hungry." I got up and headed for the door.

My father called after me. "I'd really like you to stay."

"But, honey, you haven't eaten," said Mom.

I walked out the door.

And that's how I left it. I didn't say another word about it. My father didn't call again. The following Saturday we went to Gramma's as usual.

Secretly, I stewed about my father, daydreamed about him, lay awake at night, replaying the visit. What should I have said or done? Why did he leave? Why did he return? Did he know how much he hurt me? Did he even care? I was angry. I couldn't let it go.

Two weeks after my father's visit, I took Gramma grocery shopping for Thanksgiving. When we returned home, I put the groceries away while Gramma sat at the kitchen table reviewing her shopping list.

"Green beans; got it," she mumbled, checking off items. "Potatoes; got it. What have I forgotten?"

I set the bag of onions on the countertop.

"Oh, the apples," Gramma said. "I forgot apples for pie."

"Okay," I replied.

Gramma reached out and caught my sleeve. "What's wrong, David?"

"I'll get apples tomorrow."

"Not apples," answered Gramma. "What's wrong with you?"

I shrugged. "I'm fine."

"You're not fine," Gramma said. "In this family, food is serious business. If I'm talking about pie and all you say is 'okay', then you're not fine."

"I'm putting groceries away."

"I know what this is about," Gramma announced. "It's about your father."

I turned away and slid two jars of olives into the cupboard.

"Your whole attitude has changed," Gramma said. "Ever since he came to visit, you're not the same."

"This isn't the time," I told her, grabbing another grocery bag off the floor.

"This is the perfect time," she replied. "You finish with the groceries. I'll make coffee."

Ten minutes later we sat at the dining room table, facing each other over a plate of brownies.

Gramma sipped her coffee. "Tell me about this."

"I'm mad," I replied. "He left us and hasn't bothered to keep in touch. Why has he come back?"

"Your father wants to make peace."

"Well, I don't want peace. I don't want to see him."

Gramma pointed at me. "This isn't good. You're tearing yourself up. And you're making life miserable for everybody else being such a grumble-bug."

I couldn't help smiling when she mentioned the name she had called me since I was a baby whenever I got upset. "My father is making me a grumble-bug."

"No." She shook her head. "You're *allowing* your father to make you a grumble-bug. You're making yourself miserable and you know what? Your anger isn't affecting your father a bit. He doesn't know you're a grumble-bug."

I rolled my eyes.

"Look at it this way," Gramma explained. "Anger is like taking that beautiful turkey we bought and leaving it on the counter until it spoils and smells bad. Then, to really show your father how angry you are, you cook the spoiled turkey and you eat it yourself hoping your father gets sick."

"That doesn't make sense," I said.

"Exactly," replied Gramma. "Neither does the way you're handling this situation. Your father goes off to live his life — you stay sick with anger. You're only hurting yourself."

I shrugged. "What do you suggest?"

"Forgive him."

"No way, Gramma." I folded his arms. "Why should I?"

"Forgiveness isn't always something you do for the other person," Gramma explained. "Sometimes you can forgive to help yourself feel better."

"What do I do?" I asked.

"Invite your father for Thanksgiving."

I shook my head. "Do you know how uncomfortable that would be?"

"I never said it would be easy," Gramma answered. "But it's better than eating spoiled turkey the rest of your life."

"Okay," I agreed. "I'll invite him to dinner, but on one condition."

"What condition?"

I pointed to the cabinet in the corner. "It'll be a special occasion. The regular dinnerware won't do. You'll need to use... the good china."

So, the following Thursday, we had Thanksgiving with my father and the good china.

"Are we actually going to eat off it?" Mom asked, stroking a plate with her fingertips.

It wasn't my best Thanksgiving, but it wasn't nearly as bad as I had imagined. We had a good meal and my father joined in the conversations. My father and I played *Yahtzee* after dinner. I discovered we both were Dallas Cowboys fans. After the apple pie, I walked my father out to his car.

"I'd like to get together again sometime, David," my father said. "I have a lot to tell you. And I'd like your forgiveness."

I nodded. "I've got your phone number. I'd like to hear what you have to say. I'll call you."

My father held out his right hand.

This time I did shake his hand. It wasn't easy, but I knew if Gramma could use the good china, I could do this. I was starting to feel better already.

~David Hull

Dad the Perfectionist

When you forgive, you love. And when you love, God's light shines upon you.
~Jon Krakauer, Into the Wild

My dad was a perfectionist. Whatever he did had to be the best. There was no tolerance for anything else. That made it difficult for my sister and me. Our school grades were expected to be all A's, our tests all 100's. It didn't happen, of course. We were ordinary kids trying to figure out the world, making mistakes and learning from them.

I was always good at English, but math was problematic for me. One night, as I struggled with the word problems assigned for homework, I asked Dad for help. He looked at the problems and started asking me questions. I didn't know the answers right away and that annoyed him. The more he demanded that I figure it out, the more I withdrew. His annoyance quickly turned to impatience.

"You're not dumb. How could you not know this?" he asked.

It was as if he had punched me in the stomach. I couldn't breathe for what seemed a long time. At that moment I certainly felt dumb. I finally whimpered, "I just have trouble with math."

Even though I still couldn't really understand the problems, I knew it was a bad idea to continue.

"Thanks, Dad," I said, "but I think I can do it by myself now."

"Okay," he said, and looked relieved as he left the room.

I cried and put away my homework. There was no point in even trying to do it after that. I never again asked for his help.

I buried the incident deep inside. But even though I chose not to focus on my dad's words, they affected much of what I did and how I related to the world. I didn't raise my hand in class unless I was absolutely sure I knew the answer. I wouldn't take the lead in any group in case it would show how inept I was. I hung back from volunteering so that I wouldn't look foolish.

This hesitancy stayed with me through high school, into college, and until I had my first child. Postpartum depression sent me for counseling. It was then that I brought out the anger I felt toward my father for his putting me in this shrinking-violet position. I was eventually able to work through it and my life changed. I became more positive and more assertive; I was enthusiastic about life at last. Best of all, I no longer felt dumb. If I didn't know something, I could always find out instead of pretending that I knew the answer.

Many years later my father was in an assisted living facility, and my sister and I were caring for him. One of us would visit daily. He and I often sat side-by-side watching TV. He would comment on the shows, sometimes critically, but often just to make conversation. He seemed to have mellowed over the years.

One day we went out for coffee to a local shop. We were chatting about old times and I asked him if he would have done anything differently in his life.

"Yes," he said, turning serious suddenly. "I wish I wasn't so hard on you girls, but that was all I knew. That's how my father was with me."

At that moment I saw the pain that he had been carrying all those years and I knew I had to let go of whatever lingering resentment I had been holding onto.

"I forgive you, Dad," I said. And then, because I suddenly saw that forgiveness goes both ways, I added, "I hope you can forgive me for anything I might have done to distress you."

He looked at me across the table, surprise and love etched in his expression.

"There's nothing to forgive," he said.

As we finished our coffee, I realized that I finally felt peaceful in my father's presence.

On the way home I thought of things I had done with my own children that I would now choose to undo. I hoped that they could forgive me, too.

~Ferida Wolff

Healing from Within

Forgiveness is not always easy. At times, it feels more painful
than the wound we suffered, to forgive the one that inflicted it.
And yet, there is no peace without forgiveness.
~Marianne Williamson

"**I** do love you. You have never done anything to make me
feel otherwise, it's just the way I am," my father would
say. Understandably, this made absolutely no sense to a
child who so desperately wanted a connection with her absent father.
Most of my life I had asked myself, "If he really loved me, how could
he be content to just speak to me on the phone occasionally or write
letters?" He was missing every milestone of my entire life!

Luckily for both my father and me, I had the most wonderful
woman to love, encourage, nurture and support me as I grew and often
rebelled. My mother always saw the best in me and told me as much,
even when others might have said I was at my worst. As I matured,
she taught me many vital life lessons: how to persevere against all
odds and succeed, how to love wholeheartedly and how to trust the
processes of healing and growth that are integral parts of life. Perhaps
most affecting, she taught me that intense anger toward another is a
sure-fire way to break your own spirit and potentially leave you with
deep regret.

After the sudden loss of my stepfather when I was twenty-one,
amidst my sorrow I felt pangs of guilt. What could I have said or done
differently? Why didn't I tell him I loved him more often? He had,

after all, been like a father to me since he had joined our lives more than six years earlier. It was then that I understood the message my mother had tried to convey. I realized I didn't want to live through the pain of "should've, would've, could've"… twice. My father was still here and I had to let go of the victim mentality in order to gain inner peace, if nothing else.

What could I do to make him love me? How could I make him want to have a relationship with me? I initiated phone calls more often, trying to engage him in conversations that would offer some glimpse of the person he truly was. He gradually opened up and shared stories about his life. During our talks, I learned that he too had grown up without his father. He was the youngest child and the only boy in a family of girls. Something in me softened when I learned this. It was not his excuse; it was his reality. Seemingly all at once, my anger changed to empathy. I began to peel back some of the protective layers I had built around me and really connect with my dad. I realized that if I was open to it, I might actually learn something from him.

Our relationship blossomed with my shift in mindset. Our phone calls became more frequent, filled with "I love you" and punctuated regularly with giggles on both ends. I also visited with my dad, which deepened our connection. Needless to say, when he was diagnosed with terminal cancer, I was devastated. I finally felt like I was getting to know him and then the proverbial rug was yanked out from under us. Although he was sick and undergoing various treatments, his determination was inspiring. When I would ask how he was feeling, his response was always, "I can't complain… I saw the sun today!" These words motivated me during some of my darkest days and will continue to reverberate in my mind and heart forever.

Fortunately, I was able to enjoy a few more years of these animated talks with Dad. When he was finally called to leave this earth, I was simultaneously crushed and ecstatic. I would miss him terribly, but I knew that we had both found peace in our relationship. I truly forgave my father for the time he'd missed, and as a result I believe he finally forgave himself. Whenever I think of my father I only remember the advice, anecdotes, giggles, and most of all, the love!

~Vanessa Hogan

Daddy's Little Girl

Grudges are for those who insist that they are owed something; forgiveness,
however, is for those who are substantial enough to move on.
~Criss Jami, Salomé: In Every Inch In Every Mile

Ours wasn't your typical father/daughter relationship. The words "warm and fuzzy" simply didn't apply. I can't remember my dad saying, "I love you." There were no affectionate kisses. No hugs.

What I do remember is a lingering sense of impending doom as I wondered when the next verbal explosion might occur. Most of my memories of my father are of terse exchanges during the week or alcohol-induced outbursts on weekends, of being told on numerous occasions that I was not wanted, that I was an accident.

It's understandable, then, that as I grew up I struggled to find a way to make my father love me, or at the very least make him proud. That struggle happily resulted in high marks in school—so high, in fact, that I was valedictorian of my graduating class. At last, my dad had to be proud of me—he even said so, promising to stand and applaud when I received my award.

Graduation day dawned bright and sunny, made brighter by the knowledge that my dad had not had a single drink in nearly three months. As the biggest moment of my young life approached, my heart sank. My dad had left the house early that morning to run errands. As the minutes ticked by, I realized that the length of his absence likely would be directly related to his degree of drunkenness when he returned. As anyone who has lived with an alcoholic can tell you, we can often tell by that person's facial features whether or not they have succumbed to the "demon drink." As I saw my father pull into the driveway, I knew instantly that he had not only succumbed to the demon, he had completely surrendered. He was falling-down drunk.

The next few hours were a haze of anxiety, disappointment, and fear as I wondered if my big day would end in humiliation if my father decided to become vocal at the graduation ceremony. He didn't.

And that should have been the proverbial happy ending. But when he walked me down the aisle at my wedding a few months later—drunk once again—I couldn't find it in my heart to forgive him. He had cast a horrible shadow over yet another momentous occasion in my life.

We maintained a cordial but "arm's length" relationship for several years.

Then just eight short years after that nerve-wracking graduation day, my dad was gone, dead of lung cancer at the age of fifty-six. I no longer had to dread his outbursts. I also no longer had the opportunity to try to repair an obviously damaged relationship.

Over the next two decades, my thoughts often drifted to my relationship—or lack thereof—with my dad. Surprisingly, even though I still felt saddened, and at times angry, about our dysfunctional relationship, I found myself wondering what had happened in his short life to make him so unhappy.

In 2000, I visited France and the Normandy American Cemetery at Omaha Beach, and I began to understand my father and the man he was—somewhat distant, extremely proud of his service to his country, and stubbornly patriotic. As I stood on that desolate windswept beach in France, I saw the 9,386 cold stone crosses commemorating the soldiers who died there in World War II. I felt closer to my father than I ever had.

At the tender age of seventeen, my father had enlisted in the U. S. Marine Corps by lying about his age. Just sixteen months later, he spent three weeks battling the enemy, up close and personal. Most recall the battle of Iwo Jima as the setting of the immortal "raising of the American flag," etched in our memories by the famous photograph: six war-weary young soldiers struggling to raise the flag of the country they had pledged to serve, honor and defend. I believe my father, however, remembered—though rarely spoke of—something entirely different. Being left on an island filled with the enemy. Hand-to-hand combat. The "kill or be killed" mentality drilled into him for his own safety. Buddies falling dead at his side. The only battle by the U.S. Marine Corps in which the overall American casualties exceeded those of the Japanese.

Some who returned from that fierce battle were able to block out the horror and live fairly normal lives. I don't think my father was one of those "lucky" ones. I now realize that his frequent drunken weekend-long discourses about being a marine and fighting in what was considered one of the bloodiest battles of World War II were an indication of how profoundly those experiences had affected him.

As I reflect on our relationship, I hold firm to the belief that life is about choices.

Perhaps my father made some poor choices while I was growing up—perhaps there was a reason. Will I choose to hold the effects of my father's service to his country against him? His drinking, the verbal abuse, his inability to show affection?

No.

I can choose resentment or I can choose to forgive and be proud of the honorable man that was my father; the man who had integrity, an incredible work ethic and was as generous as anyone I know. I choose the latter.

And now, more than twenty years after his death, I can also choose to be Daddy's little girl.

~Linda Bruno

Change of Heart

To forgive is to set a prisoner free and discover that the prisoner was you.
~Lewis B. Smedes

"I don't care what you say. I will never forgive my parents!" Tears pooled in the eyes of the well-dressed blonde standing before me in a blue silk suit. She had waited patiently in line to say her piece following my presentation.

"As an only child of affluent parents, I never lacked anything nor was I abused," she said. "However, I was deprived of what I needed most. I was never hugged, told I was loved, or praised for anything. The only reason my childish mind could find was that I didn't deserve their love. So I tried to earn it by becoming an overachiever, excelling at everything, until now I'm the youngest attorney in my office. But I've yet to hear the words, 'We love you, honey, we're so proud of you!' I guess I'll never be good enough."

Tears spilled as she concluded, "Robbing a little child of something that would have cost them nothing to give is unforgivable!" Before I could respond, she turned and walked briskly away.

Having spoken for many years on the subject of forgiveness, I'd heard countless heartbreaking stories, but for some reason this one touched me deeply—and prompted memories of my own past resentments. I recalled a bitter time decades earlier when I was challenged to forgive. Angry tears had blurred my vision that day on the church steps when an older woman asked, "Have you forgiven your father?"

At that moment my father was awaiting transport to the state prison for premeditated attempted murder of my mother. Against all medical odds, Mom had survived his numerous blows to her head with a claw hammer—her punishment for taking us children and trying to escape.

I thought that was such an insensitive question. Why on earth would I forgive my father? I wanted him to suffer! I was still outraged that he'd received only three and a half years for his horrible crime. Glaring at her, I hissed, "I'll never forgive him!"

My charismatic father, well respected within our community, had warned us to never divulge what happened in our home and never try to leave. "If you do," he threatened, "I'll kill you all, then plead temporary insanity. Believe me, I'll never be convicted."

That woman's well-meaning question had merely refueled my reasons for hating my father. Flashbacks covering years of abuse and terror—my wounded mother not expected to live, the recent courtroom drama of humiliation and injustice—swept over me anew.

At the trial, the defense had carefully recast my father as a "kind and devoted family man." When he unexpectedly took the stand I wondered what he could possibly say in his own defense. We listened in shock as he lied to a packed courtroom and sympathetic jury, dramatically describing his heartbreak upon discovering that his wife and older daughter were prostitutes. His award-winning performance won him a minimum sentence. My heart shattered. It was so wrong.

Touched by my renewed memories, I watched sadly as the tearful young woman exited. I collected my books and materials, said goodbye to the event leaders and walked to my car. On the outskirts of town, I stopped at a small café to unwind before starting my long trip home. The aroma and taste of the hot chocolate caramel latte soothed my senses and I slowly relaxed.

What if I had never had a change of heart by deciding to do the very thing I swore I'd never do—forgive my father? I'd likely just be another bitter, miserable person with a victim mentality, shaking my fist at God—or fate—for the bad hand I'd been dealt in life.

Yes, deciding to forgive my father had definitely changed the course of my life—but, oh, what a battle! I had thought I'd be free of my father after his imprisonment, but I wasn't. My bitterness kept me chained to him day and night without hopes of parole. And, strangely, no matter how hard I tried, I couldn't block out that conversation between the woman and me on the church steps.

After retorting that I needn't worry about forgiving my father since he'd never ask me to forgive him, the woman had insisted, "But you still need to forgive him." When I argued my father didn't deserve forgiveness, she agreed and countered, "But don't you deserve the freedom forgiveness brings?"

"I'm not the one in prison," I snapped.

After verbally sparring back and forth, I finally demanded to know just who in his right mind would expect me to forgive my father.

She answered softly, "God."

The following months I battled bouts of depression. As I became more irritable and stressed, stomach problems developed. Maybe I was getting an ulcer? No wonder—after all my family and I'd been through! Something else I could blame my father for!

One day while setting out a mousetrap (we couldn't use poison because of our pets), I wondered if my refusal to forgive my father would be like taking rat poison and then waiting for the rat to die. I doubted my father was suffering at all due to my lack of forgiveness, but I did know that my resentment was slowly poisoning me.

In light of this conclusion, I decided the best thing I could do for myself was to forgive my father. How else could I be free of him? I knew this logically, but my emotions remained unconvinced.

I was at a stalemate. Contrary to the idea that forgiveness is a sign of weakness, I discovered the opposite. Forgiveness requires great strength—strength that I didn't have. So I went straight to the One who promised in Matthew 7:7 NIV: "Ask and it will be given to you; seek and you will find; knock and the door will be opened to you."

So I prayed. "God, I'd like to forgive my father, but I have a problem—I don't want to. Can you change my wants—help me to want to forgive him? Then I will." That became my daily prayer.

Amazingly, several months later, I was suddenly overwhelmed with a desire to forgive my father. Where had that come from? Then I remembered my prayer—God had answered it. All I had to do now was keep my end of the bargain. So I whispered, "I forgive you, Dad, for everything." My bitterness vanished and I was free!

Draining the last drop of latte before hitting the noisy freeway, I couldn't help smiling. Had I continued living in the past, chained by its bitterness and pain, I would have never embarked on my thirty-plus-year journey as an international speaker and award-winning author on the subject of forgiveness. All made possible when over half a century earlier I had a change of heart and forgave my father.

My fervent hope now was that the beautiful young lady in blue would have a change of heart, too, and find the strength to forgive her parents soon and move forward with her life.

~Kitty Chappell

Another Point of View

Getting over a painful experience is much like crossing monkey bars.
You have to let go at some point in order to move forward.
~Author Unknown

Forgiving someone can seem like the toughest thing in the world to do. But it became easy once I realized it wasn't the other person keeping me from forgiving; it was myself.

My mother and father divorced when I was five years old. Even though I knew they had problems, and that my father had moved on to be with someone else, I was still a child who wanted his family together. So when my father finally said goodbye to my brother, sister and me, it felt like we were being abandoned. I couldn't forgive him for walking away from our family.

My father was not totally absent as we grew up. For the first year he came to see us once a month and take us out for our birthdays to celebrate. But the more time passed, the less we saw of him. By the time our family moved to California when I was nine, he wasn't coming around much at all. Once we were 1,500 miles away, he wrote once in a great while, then not at all.

Our stay in California came to a close two years later. My mom's company had closed, and jobs were hard to come by. So we moved back to Texas to be closer to family and return to the place that had always felt like home. I have to admit that I hoped our father would come back into our lives. For a short time, he did.

Shortly after he learned we were back in Texas, he contacted us.

He said he had missed us and wanted us to be part of his family. At first we didn't understand, but my mom explained our father had a different family now, a new wife and children, and he wanted us to live with them. Because she loved us so much, our mom left the decision up to the three of us. My brother, sister and I went to my father's house and met his new family. We got along well enough with the other kids and his wife. But we had been a family with our mom for so long, that was where we wanted to be. We told our father, and I knew he was disappointed. Soon after that we didn't see him anymore.

I felt abandoned for a second time, and swore I would never forgive him again. I knew that he had been asking for another chance and we had given it. Although we hadn't chosen to live with him, we still loved him. But when he didn't visit, call or write, I couldn't forgive him for forgetting about us a second time.

Years went by, and we all grew up and started families of our own. Any anger I felt turned into a kind of numbness, and I tried not to think of my father at all. Then one day we were notified that he had passed away from a long illness. Any chance of forgiveness was gone — or so I thought.

One day, while visiting my mom, I mentioned how I felt about things. She smiled and said, "That was so long ago, and maybe it was too hard to try to keep hold of both families at once. You made the decision to be a family with me. Maybe he needed to try to be a family for them."

I thought long and hard about that, about all the anger and resentment I had felt over the years, at my unwillingness to forgive my father for leaving us. Then I thought about what my mom had said, and about all the challenges I had faced with my own family. I realized I really didn't know what had been happening in his life, and what he might have felt he was giving up in letting go of us to hang on to a new family. Maybe it was the hardest thing he'd ever had to do. Maybe he had never forgotten about us after all.

At that moment I let go of my anger and felt a sense of forgiveness in my heart. I knew that I could never walk in his shoes or understand everything about what he might have been going through. I forgave at that moment, knowing my life with my mom and brothers and sister had been a good one, and that being unwilling to forgive my father was only hurting me. The weight that lifted at that moment was tremendous. Since then I have lived with the understanding that the best we can do is the best we can do. That we should give others the benefit of the doubt that they are doing their best too, and forgive them when they seem to fall short. Hopefully, sometime in his life, my father did the same for himself.

~John P. Buentello

Flag Waving for Beginners

Sometimes the poorest man leaves his children the richest inheritance.
~Ruth E. Renkel

A couple of months ago I came into my inheritance. It happened at my mother's house in Laurel Springs, New Jersey as I played on the rug with my daughters. My sister, trailing behind her three teenage sons in a storm of hugs and fist bumps, threw a cardboard box on my lap. "What's this?" I asked, and gave it a shake.

"Open it," she said, and squeezed her nieces' cheeks.

Out popped a laminated nautical map of the San Diego coast. A shotgun casing rattled inside a plastic box. Taking up the most room: an American flag, folded into a thick triangle. Our father, who died this past summer, had made arrangements to be buried at sea. The package came from the Neptune Society, one of many companies that offer cremation services and burials at sea and is often used by veterans.

My father and I had a complicated relationship, and we hadn't seen each other for the past twenty years. My first reaction to this windfall was: What do I do with the flag?

Growing up, I idolized my father, Michael Nester, a Mensa card-carrying teamster from Arizona, which all seemed exotic to a boy growing up in South Jersey. I regarded Dad as a noble savage autodidact and aspired to be like him. Patriotism was how we bonded, even though I only half-understood what he was saying when he assigned me to read Ayn Rand and Voltaire and everyone in between. It was the Reagan era, and my dad was often hilarious expressing his patriotism. "Just give me three thousand G. Gordon Liddys," he'd say, "and this country could take over the world." We sneered at Dick Cavett when he interviewed Liddy on his talk show, and cheered on Ronald Reagan when he defeated Jimmy Carter. I drew stars and stripes on my book covers and notepads, and played with army men in the back yard with firecrackers.

Then things went sour. Dad was laid off, his company a casualty of the great 1980s recession. After years of money struggles, he got his job back, followed quickly by an affair for which my mother could never forgive him. Then he left New Jersey for Tucson, Arizona. I was seventeen, my sister sixteen. He never came back, not even to visit, never sent support checks or birthday cards. I was disillusioned.

In the intervening years, the flag became a vessel for what I would call my father's antisocial feelings. He turned more right wing while I went moderate left. He bought guns and end-times supplies, and I moved to New York to be a poet and, eventually, an English professor. He ignored me; I resented him. Years go by much easier when there's a country's width between two people. Then a flag turns up on your lap.

My sister, who flew to Tucson to help empty his apartment, thought I should get the flag since I "was his firstborn son." Do lines of succession rules still apply? I've never owned any flag, unless Phillies pennants or rainbow gay pride banners count. I'm not what you would call a flag-waver. And now that I had one, I felt more puzzled than partisan. What if I spilled something on it? Burnt it in the fireplace by accident? This debate turned into an allegory for my relationship with my country. Right-wingers like my father revere flags and distrust the government, while lefties like me find flag-waving an empty gesture and place more importance on public trusts. I was of the same mind as Samuel Johnson, who wrote that patriotism is the last refuge of the scoundrel.

Back home, I'd hardly touched the flag outside of moving the cardboard box from pile to pile. Then I took the flag out and discovered something else in the cardboard box: a DVD. I put it in my laptop and was transported aboard the *USS Comstock*, behind a shaky camera. Boxes of sixteen service people's ashes and sixteen flags lay on a table with a purple tablecloth.

This, it should be noted, marked the first time my father was ever out to sea. After he enlisted in 1965, he never served on a ship, didn't go to Vietnam—a juvenile record, so the family story goes, kept him stateside. Instead, he worked at the Navy yards in Philadelphia, where he met my mother on Market Street, and then in Norfolk, Virginia, where I was born.

Though wind gusts had overwhelmed the microphone, I could still make out the words of the officers at the podium, a biography for each veteran whose ashes were returned to the sea. "Two tours in Vietnam." "A chaplain for twenty-six years." "Retired after twenty years." "Dedication to family and friends." "Instilled his love of the military in his children." "Operational specialist World War II, given the Victory Medal." "A gracious, caring and loving grandfather."

My father's turn came last. His dedicatory words were the most brief: "Michael Nester, born June 11, 1947, in Maryville, Tennessee. He treasured his time in the United States Navy, where he was honorably discharged and is proud and humbled to return to the sea." Then, a sentence read very quickly that combined elements from the Navy Farewell with The Order for the Burial of the Dead: "farewell, fair winds and following seas unto almighty god we commit the soul with sure and certain hope of Jesus Christ and eternal life." A whistle, and down the chute the box of my father's ashes went. The ceremony ended with a twenty-one-gun salute. It hit me: this flag was my inheritance.

It's not often when the compulsion to go to the hardware store arises, but recently it happened. Off to the local hardware store I went to purchase a flag bracket and pole. I inexpertly bolted it to the brick at the side of my house. The plan is to run the flag up a pole and let it flap in the wind until sundown this Flag Day. Then I will fold it back into a neat triangle. It won't be that hard to do, and it's the least I can do to make things right with my old man.

~Daniel Nester

Rambling to Forgiveness

Fathers represent another way of looking at life —
the possibility of an alternative dialogue.
~Louise J. Kaplan

I come from a family of tiny people. My mother was Irish, my father Italian, and at 5'2" I towered over both of them. Maybe that was why my father always seemed so angry—all those years of looking up at people, of feeling small, invisible. He had several brothers and sisters, most of whom he had stopped speaking to years before. Minor slights led to major rifts, so I only saw my aunts and uncles at funerals.

When someone passed away, he pushed all the vendettas and hurt feelings aside and marched us off to pay our respects. These gatherings always started out cordially, with the brothers tentatively approaching each other and talking quietly among themselves. By the end of the evening, back at the house, when we were polishing off the last of the cannoli, they were talking louder, standing taller, and slapping each other on the back. My aunts dabbed at their eyes with their silk hankies, wept over the deceased, and murmured about how long it had been since we had last seen each other.

It never lasted. By the week's end the old resentments had resurfaced and we were back in enemy territory. I wouldn't see any of those people again until the next funeral.

All this animosity was largely generated and nurtured by my father. I never knew the Italian side of the family, or what they had done to make him want nothing to do with them. But they were among the many people he never spoke to and refused to discuss. Not welcome in our home, they remained a mystery to me. Sitting alone in the living room, reading the nightly news, my father nursed his resentment like a tall, cool drink; quietly and continuously stirring the ice.

At sixteen I desperately wanted a car of my own, and I begged him to let me drive the old Rambler sitting in the garage next to our new station wagon. He didn't trust my driving, and he didn't particularly trust the boys he envisioned me driving around with. This struck me as absurd, in that I had never had a date, and his images of boys and me were just that, imaginary.

When I was a child he used to joke with me. "You are going to be so pretty when you grow up I'll have to beat the boys off with a stick!" Little did I know he would practically do that. Dating for me was hopeless. When the phone rang, he leapt to answer it. If it was a boy calling for me, he'd yell, "She's not home!" and hang up on him. So much for my social life. I raged and wept; he rattled his newspaper and went back to reading, his feet propped up in his favorite lounger.

I longed to get out, to literally drive away, to listen to my music on the radio, to be free, and yes to ride around with boys; big, tall, handsome teenage boys.

My father kept a wary eye on me from behind the headlines. I was perpetually angry with him.

So we rattled on and on; I was relentless, he resistant. We argued over the car until suddenly, unexpectedly, he agreed to let me drive it anytime I wanted. With one stipulation. He would do some work on it to make the Rambler safer for me.

I was amazed and thrilled. Fine with me. Fix it all you want; just let me drive it.

My father went out in the garage, shoved the driver's seat up to within inches of the steering wheel and blowtorched it in place. Permanently. At five feet, he could drive this car. At 5'2" I could slip in behind the wheel and reach the gas and the brakes too.

But my tall, imaginary, boyfriends would never be able to get behind that wheel.

I was furious. What would all my friends think when I drove this car with my nose pressed up against the windshield? I'd look ridiculous. No one had a car like this. It was like some clown car in the circus, weird looking and stupid. How could he embarrass me like this?

But a car was a car, and although mortified, I grudgingly accepted it.

Later that year my best friend Mary was in a really bad auto accident. Her boyfriend took a turn too fast, spun out and rolled the car three times. She was a quiet girl, a good girl, an A student. Naturally she was attracted to a guy who was a little on the wild side, someone who "really knew how to drive." The car was destroyed; they both made it out of the wreck, but just barely.

When I got home from school the day of the accident, my father was waiting for me in the driveway. He handed me the keys. "You drive; we're going to the hospital." For a reclusive man, this was completely out of character. I don't remember him ever suggesting we visit anyone anywhere, in or out of the hospital. Other than funerals, we didn't seem to socialize much.

My father sat next to me, silently gazing out the window, for once letting me drive without comment.

We found Mary in the ICU, her boyfriend still in surgery. As we stood by her bed, her mother joined us and gently stroked the tips of her fingers. Tears ran down her cheeks as she gazed at her daughter, so bruised and broken.

My father glanced at me. His dark eyes moist, as if he were about to weep. I had never seen him cry and I didn't want to. Under the harsh hospital lights, the creases in my father's face cut deeper than I had ever noticed before. On a face whose emotions were so often obscured by anger, I saw relief that it wasn't me in that hospital bed, and fear that someday it might be.

He drove the Rambler home, sliding easily behind the wheel.

We didn't speak on the way back. He stared straight ahead, following the speed limit, driving carefully.

I looked over at this man who had been so difficult to live with for so many years, and I forgave him, for everything.

~JoAnn Richi

The Self-Help Section
of a Barnes & Noble

Seek truth and you will find a path.
~Frank Slaughter

I t was in the middle of Barnes & Noble sometime in 2009 when I realized what had happened to me. It was a terrifying, sickening, and nauseating experience as my fingers traced the words of a girl retelling her account of being molested by her grandmother. I coughed up tears and vomit. The writer's words caused a revelation; what used to be memories of normalcy turned into nightmares of betrayal.

I always wondered why my other grandma never helped me take a bath. I felt disgusting and guilty. I had been so close with this woman, and I had done nothing to stop her. Tears of pain and confusion ran down my face, collecting on the pages of this book I had discovered in the self-help section. I do not remember the title or the author, but simply the story I had randomly flipped to. I wasn't even there for myself! I went there to find answers for my family... my dad... my brother.

It felt as if I were wavering somewhere between self-pity and self-hate. I felt naïve for not seeing the red flags: the promiscuous behavior, the nudity, the affection... the bathtub... the locked door. My perpetrator was untouchable, so I looked for someone to blame. I wanted to blame organized religion because, coincidentally, she was a preacher's wife whose congregation always marveled at how she "walked the talk." I wanted to blame my father for sacrificing my brother and me to the hands of that sadistic woman. I chose to blame both.

Distancing myself from my father wasn't that difficult since my parents were already separated. I became cold-hearted and numb, convicting this man guilty by association. My respect for him had died along with that innocent little girl, and angry outbursts became more frequent. He still managed to remain in my life, offering meals and shopping sprees as peace treaties. I welcomed his materialistic apology, forcing it to dress my wounds. But it wasn't until recently that he truly attempted to attend to my scars. He opened up to me about his past pains during a summer visit to his then-home in Florida, breaking the dam that held back the years of trauma.

I finally realized that he would have never wished his heartache upon me. He, too, was once a helpless little child. My heart melted as I watched my father crumble, crying out for help in the midst of his emotional shipwreck. It was in this moment that I wholeheart-edly relinquished all blame toward my father. I loved this man, his faults and shortcomings, his mistakes and fears. I understood that his troubled soul was incapable of protecting my brother and me because he was still chained to the burdens of his childhood. I didn't blame him; I couldn't.

Some days it is still hard to live with myself as the product of molestation, but God works in miraculous ways. I never thought that I would be able to talk about it because I was always afraid; maybe no one would believe, or maybe they would make it into a joke, or maybe someone would blame me for what happened. Although I haven't truly forgiven my abuser, I can forgive myself for the pain I inflicted upon my own skin as I dealt with this horrible truth; I can forgive my father for allowing the cycle to continue into the next generation; I can forgive organized religion for sometimes harboring fugitives in their congregations because evil exists everywhere and Christianity isn't well-versed in background checks.

I can only hope that maybe these words are the ones some girl will trace in the middle of a Barnes & Noble self-help section, but this time knowing that she is not alone. I am praying that she salvages freedom and forgiveness from the destruction.

~Kalie M. Eaton

Forgiving the Unforgivable

The things that people in love do to each other they remember,
and if they stay together it's not because they forget,
it's because they forgive.
~Author Unknown

What is forgiveness? Why do we find it so hard to forgive? These questions were hard for me to understand until the events that started one Tuesday morning. Any other day, I would have been waking up to prepare for school, but that day I had a dentist appointment. My mom usually took me, but on this day my dad sat in the driver's seat, my mom nowhere to be found. As I began to wonder what was going on, in a shaky voice he began to talk.

"Your mother has left to go to your aunt's for a couple of weeks," he said. When I asked why, he began to cry as he told me the same story of his affair that he had told her the night before. Only thirteen at the time, I was shocked and devastated at the thought of having to choose between my mom and dad and possibly never being a family again.

Very little was said throughout the next two weeks. It was like time had stopped. Everything was in slow motion. Nothing felt right without Mom there. The middle school drama that had affected me before no longer mattered. I suddenly realized what was really important.

I wanted so badly to hate my father for what he had done to our family! I wanted to shut him out and hurt him the way he hurt us. But when I looked into his eyes, I saw that I didn't have to. I knew he would deal with the guilt for the rest of his life, and it was not my place to judge him or hate him. After all, he was my dad.

I chose to forgive him, not because it was easy, but because he needed it and I knew it was what I needed to do. I wanted him to see that even through his biggest mistakes and failures I still loved him just like he would me. That is what family is all about. I could not handle seeing his tears or the hurt in his eyes.

When my mother finally came home I was very happy to see her, but I was also just as scared as when she had left. I didn't know if she was coming home to stay or coming home to say she was leaving for good this time.

I could tell she had missed me too as she walked through the door and tears flowed down her face. I saw love and hurt at the same time. I had never seen my mother like that and it frightened me. The strong woman she had always been seemed so frail and broken. Nevertheless, she told us she was going to try to make it work. I was relieved, but it was not the end of the story, as I had hoped — it was only the beginning.

I watched her cry for months; I saw the pain in her eyes every day. She had to wear waterproof make-up because the tears became a normal, everyday occurrence. My dad tried and tried to make it right and to show her love, but it wasn't until she completely forgave him that the tears slowly stopped. Carrying the weight of his betrayal was hard on her until she just let it go. It took years to build their relationship back, but it is even stronger now and they have grown from their experience. My dad treats my mother like a princess, even to this day, as she deserves. He has worked to earn her love and trust since the day she came home.

Seeing my mom go through this taught me so much about forgiveness. I cannot imagine the pain of being betrayed by the one person she loved and trusted with all her heart. To have that completely torn apart, but be strong enough to start over and rebuild that trust takes a special person. My mom taught me how strong forgiveness really is by her actions. It's not easy to forgive, but she has shown me it is possible and it is worth it.

~Sheridan Kee

Chapter 2

The Power *of* Forgiveness

Forgiveness between Mothers and Children

How does one know if she has forgiven?
You tend to feel sorrow over the circumstance instead of rage,
you tend to feel sorry for the person rather than angry with him.
You tend to have nothing left to say about it all.

~Clarissa Pinkola Estes

Mary's Girl

Man has two great spiritual needs. One is for forgiveness.
The other is for goodness.
~Billy Graham

I didn't know we were different at first. As a little kid, I was unaware of how circumstances set me apart in our 1960s middle-class, 10th Ward neighborhood in Rochester, New York.

Squalor isn't a word or concept you understand at age five. By age nine or ten, I understood that my life was out of sync with the rest of the community when people referred to me as "one of the Herne girls."

By age twelve I realized that some neighbors shunned us while others allowed me to play with their kids, in their yards, and even hang around for supper now and again. They encouraged me by befriending me.

But not much penetrated the darkness of our home, a long-neglected dwelling of fetid air, dirt-crusted windows, filth, and the smattering of bare-bulb lights that rarely worked. Around age eleven, I took charge of my one room upstairs and scrubbed it from top to bottom. There were no pretty blankets or soft coverlets, but the thin sheets I found to cover my stained mattress were clean, if shabby. The pillow had a cover. I washed the floor weekly, and dusted the broken dresser as if it mattered. And it did matter. It mattered to me.

Sometime after I was born, my mother's brilliance was dimmed by chronic alcoholism and depression. Entire seasons went by that I never saw or heard her. She spent long months locked away in her small room with secret, silent demons. She attempted suicide at least twice that I remember, and she cried over her lack of success.

I must have glimpsed the real person within her as a small child, because during the dark years I waited for that woman's reappearance. During those alcoholic stupors and fright-filled nights when my brother and I dumped her whiskey down a sink, trying to nudge her back to some form of normal, I believed there was another woman within the caricature I called "Mom."

There is nothing fun about a sordid existence, but I was blessed to attend a vibrant, busy Catholic school. My uniform allowed me to fit in. No one knew it was given to us at the Thanksgiving clothing drive. The plaid jumper was clean and tailored like everyone else's with no marks of identification. I was challenged and beloved by numerous teachers over the years, wonderful women who said I bore a true gift for writing. They made me feel special! As year piled upon year, I finally had to move out of my parents' house. I lived with my older sister, guilt-ridden because I left two younger brothers behind in the darkness and filth.

Then one day I came across my mother's poetry. As a teen she'd been instrumental in starting a high school magazine, a reasonably priced form of entertainment in the Depression-era 1930s. I didn't know that when I found her folder, all I knew was the sheer beauty of her words, cadence-strung emotion done with point and pride.

Instantly I saw where my talent came from. For the first time it was clear that whatever I'd seen as a small child, before whiskey dimmed the sparkle in her eyes and slurred her words, was real. I held tangible proof in my hands in the form of her teenage writings.

That book was my turnaround, my wake-up call to forgiveness. God had blessed me with a talent through my mother. While hers may have been scourged by time and circumstance, I realized that the woman I knew personally wasn't the real Mary Elizabeth Logan Herne, because "M.E. Logan" wrote with stunning grace and abandon.

I desperately longed to know that woman someday, but in the meantime I accepted God's grace, my time, and my life. A teenage girl's words on paper showed me what God wanted me to see, the lineage of hope. That day, for the first time, I thanked him for the grace of being Mary Elizabeth's daughter. And I decided then that someday I would use my God-given talent to make other women smile and grab hold of their faith and their lives, no matter what they'd endured. With God lay hope.

My mother quit drinking when I was thirty-three years old. Once in a while she'd lapse for a day or two, but she never fell into the pit of despair again. After three decades of waiting and loving, I finally got to know her. I sensed her old dreams and bitter disappointments, but what I saw and cherished was the bright light within her shining again, somewhat shadowed, but a glow that shone with God's love and humility.

My children never saw their grandmother drink. Their early visits to her were in the morning. Once she stopped drinking, this wasn't a problem, and to this day, the thought of their grandmother as the woman I'd known is alien to them. To my six children, she was the petite, gray-haired "Grandma" that loved to hear their stories and tell her own. Just as it should be.

When she realized she was dying of cancer, she gripped my hand, looked me in the eye and said, "I know you are serious about your writing. On that day when you become published, will you do me the honor of using my name? I want everyone in the world to know that you're mine."

I said yes.

My dream of publication came years after Mom's death, but her words helped me hone the talent she gave me. And when that first book came out, a novel of love, loss and second chances called *Winter's End*, it was dedicated to my mother, Mary Elizabeth Logan Herne, "from whence the talent came."

And the grace of God's fulfillment is in the name I use as I publish my books… Ruth Logan Herne — Mary's girl.

~Ruth Logan Herne

Replacing the Pain

*When you haven't forgiven those who've hurt you, you turn back against
your future. When you do forgive you start walking forward.*
~Tyler Perry

How do you forgive your mother when she is a drug
addict? How do you forgive her when she dies unexpectedly and leaves you all on your own? For eighteen
years I couldn't, I didn't.

I was ten when my mother passed away. I found her in her bedroom on a crisp, Midwestern Thanksgiving morning. It was just the
two of us in the house. Everything was silent, except for the beating
of my heart.

I looked at her and knew she was gone.

Before she died, my life was chaotic. I hid in the corners and in
the shadows while my mother got high and fell asleep on the living
room floor. My brothers, sister and I became forgotten members of
the house. My dad moved out, and my mom boxed up the memory
of us, like she did her wedding dress.

Soon the drugs became everything in her life. She forgot to feed
us, forgot to pick us up from school. Sometimes she would be so
desperate for drugs she would force me to call my grandmother and
beg for money. I was only seven years old. I was already tired of her
games, but I didn't know a different way of life. I assumed everyone
had a mother like mine.

After my mother died, my father moved back in with us. We

tried as best we could to reattach the family, but it was difficult after everything we'd seen throughout the years.

Like survivors, we stumbled wide-eyed every day through the aftermath of the earthquake my mother left behind.

I grew up and moved out. On my own, it was time to take stock of what had happened in my life, and how I could be different than my mother, better.

I had so much anger in me. How could I ever have my own children? How could I love a child when I had never been loved? My mother was absent my whole life. She was missing when I graduated high school, missing when I got married. She was missing every time I needed her.

Slowly, my heart turned to steel. I hated feeling lonely and sad — homesick for a mother I had never known.

As the years passed, I stopped thinking of her. I lived my own life, careful to not make the same mistakes she had. I was careful not to take drugs, careful not to lie, careful not to manipulate people or to let them down. I walked on eggshells.

Then I became pregnant. While I was sad that my mother was missing that too, my mindset shifted with my growing belly. I had a lot of time to spend with this baby blossoming inside me. I spent hours rubbing my stomach and reflecting on the life I had as a child. I was sure I would never treat my son the way my mom treated me. I would make sure he had the life I didn't, full of love, and attention, and understanding.

The day came when my son entered the world, and my world completely changed. His birth healed me in ways I never would have guessed, and healed some of the gaping wounds created by my mom. I knew then his life would be better than mine. But in order to create that happiness for him, I would have to forgive my own mother, let go of the hurt and the heaviness she had left in my life.

I forgave my mother then, after eighteen years of being angry, after eighteen years of hurting. I forgave her so that I could make space in my heart for all that my son had to offer. There was no room anymore for all of the negative emotions I felt when thinking about my mother. I forgave her for my son. So that in place of hatred, love lived instead.

How do you forgive your mother when she is a drug addict? How do you forgive her when she dies unexpectedly and leaves you all on your own? For eighteen years I couldn't, I didn't.

Then one day it became clear that the way to end the pain was to simply let forgiveness take its place.

~Kate White

The Ritual

Forgiveness is the cleansing fire that burns away old regrets and resentments.
~Jonathan Lockwood Huie

The phone rang at 10 p.m. "Is this Diane Caldwell?" an unfamiliar voice asked. I knew this was it. My eyes focused on the weave of the tapestry hanging on the wall by the phone. Noticing for the very first time the way disparate threads of red and blue and black interwove to create the scene.

"Your mother died of liver failure at 9 p.m. She died peacefully."

A wail pierced the silence. What a sound, I thought, and then I realized the sound came from me.

My mother had ruled our home as the Ice Queen. She had only to raise one eyebrow and I froze in fear. There was never a kind word or a gesture of affection from her. In fact, the only words I heard from her some days were: "Be a good girl, Diane," spoken in a tight-lipped snarl.

While other children ran about laughing, I sat in silence, my hands folded in my lap, afraid to do anything. "Be a good girl" became like a mantra. No matter what I did or where I was, I heard it in my head.

"Would you like a cookie, Diane?" Aunt Anne would ask.

"No thank you," I would say, fearing that to accept might be "bad."

For my first fourteen years, I lived as a "good girl," fearing and hating my mother.

And then I rebelled.

I ran away from home at sixteen. Ran off to New York. Panhandled on the dirty, gray streets of New York's Greenwich Village. Hanging out with the weird and alternative. My every act subconsciously calculated in defiance of my mother.

On a rare visit to my mother in her Delray Beach home, she looked at me out of the corners of her eyes.

"I was watching an Oprah show the other day…" her voice trailed off.

I glanced up from the book I was reading.

Mother's eyes turned from mine and studied her long, perfectly manicured fingernails. "It was about something called emotional abuse…."

Again she stopped, ran her thumb over each of her nails in sequence, cleared her throat just slightly.

"Diane," she began in her nasal Philadelphia accent. "Diane… Diane, did I ever say 'I love you' to you?" The last words came out in a breathy explosion, almost a hiss.

Silence. The only sound in the room was the quiet hum of central air conditioning.

"No," I said, holding my breath, waiting for the words I'd never heard my entire life.

The garbage truck rumbled past the edge of the complex. Trash tumbled from containers by the road. Silence hung in the room. Gears engaged and the garbage truck pulled away.

My mother rose like a ghost and walked away.

• • •

Now she was dead and it was too late for us. But not too late for me to try and do whatever was possible to heal the wounds that continued to fester and poison every act of my life.

I knew I had to do something. The "Ritual" was created as an act of healing.

I assembled three of my best friends. Three friends who had also lost their mothers.

I laid the table with salty, sweet, sour and bitter foods: a good cheddar cheese, fresh baked banana bread, sliced lemons, and sliced radishes. Photos of Mom ranging in time from her young adult years to her wedding photo to our family holiday pictures lay in an arrangement at the top of the table.

We munched on the cheese.

Once my parents had a Halloween party. My cousin Shirley won the contest for dressing as a pregnant bride. My mother was roaring with laughter, but I didn't understand what was funny about it at the time. Then my mother invited everyone down into the rec room and they played "pass the orange." People had to pass an orange from under their chin to the next person, and they were arranged man, woman, man, woman. I remember sitting on the stairs watching—amazed. I had never seen my mother act like that before."

We tasted the banana bread.

"At rare moments she could laugh like a little girl," I said. "Every now and then, when I was really young, she'd let me into the bed with her on a Sunday morning and we'd play this silly game called "skinny bones," and we'd tickle each other and she'd laugh like she was no older than me."

The lemons were passed around the table.

"Oh God," I said. "My poor mother. She was the unwanted child of immigrants—born nine years after what her parents thought was their last child. I once heard her talking to her sister about how she had been called 'the accident' and left in bedrooms with tossed overcoats while her parents played cards with neighbors."

"Once she told me that she'd stuck peas up her nose at the dinner table trying to get some attention, but then nobody could get them out. They had to take her to the hospital and her mother didn't speak to her for weeks after that."

Only the radishes remained. We picked up slices and chewed.

"She wore her next oldest sister's hand-me-downs. They were nine years out of style, and way too short. Her sister was really short and Mom was tall. And she wore glasses and used to be called out of class for having head lice. I think she lived in constant shame."

Tears flooded my eyes.

"She never knew love. How was she supposed to give it? She embraced her fancy dresses and material possessions as if they were life rafts saving her from waves of scorn. Each new outfit was a step up out of a childhood in which she suffered daily shame and humiliation. My poor mother," I shared.

When the "ritual" was over, my friends hugged and kissed me and walked out the front door. As soon as the door closed, I broke down and wept uncontrollably—each sob a letting go of the hurt and hatred I had carried all my life. Beneath the hate was pain. Beneath the pain was fear. I let it all go until I felt something shift inside. I was suddenly lighter.

My childhood wasn't so bad, I thought. Mother did her best. I never knew what it was to be looked down upon for my old tattered clothes. She worked hard to provide me with everything possible that a little girl could want.

"I forgive you," I whispered to my departed mother. "I love you," I said out loud, saying the words I had longed to hear my entire life and releasing myself from the hardness that had imprisoned my heart like a metal cage. It's too bad it took death for me to finally let go. But it did.

~Diane Caldwell

Understanding My Mother

Let us forgive each other — only then will we live in peace.
~Leo Tolstoy

I was a mistake. My parents were young South African students studying in England during the era between the two world wars. A baby didn't fit into their plans so I was given to my mother's close friend, Freda, to foster.

My mother paid the occasional visit while my father vanished from my life. It was Freda who loved and cared for me. As I grew older I heard whispers of a brother, but when I asked I was told, "What nonsense" or "Don't ask stupid questions."

Just before I turned five, Freda and my mother fell out so I was sent to boarding school. I spent the holidays in the local orphanage where I was instructed to "Look after the little boy in the bed next to you. Treat him like a brother." He was younger than me but we kept close and turned to each other for comfort and companionship. I was never quite sure if he really was my brother. Nobody spoke the truth.

The year 1939 arrived and with it World War II. Along with millions of children I was handed a gas mask to sling over my shoulder while my name and destination was written on a cardboard label and hung around my neck. I was sent, like a parcel, with other evacuees on the train into the country. The Battle of Britain had begun.

I lived with a family in the New Forest. This was a place of magic and make- believe, so instead of feeling lost and bewildered I became solitary and self-reliant as I explored the streams and woodlands. No school. Life was an exciting adventure.

I was left in this paradise for a year when another bombshell hit. My mother arrived with news. "I'm going to have a baby and we're going home to South Africa," she announced.

"I'm going to have a baby sister," I sang and danced with joy. The little boy in the orphanage was forgotten as I focused on this new baby.

We sailed on the refugee ship, the Capetown Castle. Children crammed every corner, spilling onto the decks and passageways and into the cabins. I was terrified. There was a convoy of battleships protecting us from the ever-present danger of submarines. My mother, wan and sick, retired to the cabin for the entire voyage, which took two weeks. Once again I was alone with my fears.

My sister arrived a few months after our arrival and it was love at first sight. I was no longer alone. My brother continued to fade into the past.

Once in South Africa I was sent to boarding school again. When home for the holidays, I self-righteously felt that my mother neglected my sister, leaving her in the care of an African nanny. I was too frightened to speak my mind but I silently hated her for her neglect. Maybe I was frightened of losing my sister as well. I kept my silence and avoided being with my mother. My hatred seemed all-consuming, a constant pain in my heart.

On leaving school I moved to Cape Town, where I had a job as a nurse, then married and had children of my own. I seldom contacted my mother; no phone calls, no letters. The Cold War remained.

I was twenty-five when fate stepped in. My husband was transferred to Port Elizabeth, where my mother and her new husband lived. I dreaded the move. I was still angry and defiant. I feared another confrontation as I had vowed never to forgive her for her neglect.

On arrival, my mother informed me that she was booked into hospital the following day for a mastectomy as she had breast cancer. She was forty-nine.

I was devastated. Anger, despair, disbelief swept through me, but I kept my feelings in reserve. I had to be the strong one once again.

It was my stepfather, Uncle Johnny, who helped me. He spoke about my mother as a person in her own right. Not the mother I thought she should be.

After her operation he took me to her. I watched as he treated her with such tenderness and compassion; emotions I had never felt for her.

While she recuperated he drew my attention to her creative talents. "Come see the yacht she's building. Look at the sculpture in the garden. What do you think of this portrait?" His admiration of her impressive talents had its effect. A glimmer of a new thought niggled around my rancour. Maybe her overwhelming creative life force and intellect overrode her maternal instincts? It was an idea worth pursuing. I needed a change of heart.

Thus begun my understanding of her needs and ideas rather than being immersed in my own self-centred attitude.

She battled psychologically through convalescence, relying on me for support. Although we never spoke about it, we both sensed that time was against us.

During this time Uncle Johnny purchased a secret hideaway, a place for his family to holiday and a haven for my mother. The Shack, as it was called, comprised a rambling wooden structure that sat precariously amid the sand dunes, a few yards from the sea.

We swam in the natural inlets and explored the pools for sea life as the whales and dolphins swam by. My mother would point to a whale's tail slapping the ocean. "Look, he's swallowed Jonah and is suffering from indigestion." If the dolphins cavorted past, there was always a mermaid amongst them. Wide-eyed and open-mouthed, the children fell under her storytelling spell that diverted mysteriously from the versions I had read.

We crammed a lifetime of enjoyment into a few short holidays. My mother's latent maternal instincts enveloped my brood of children. She'd evolved into the mother I had always wished for. I had changed too. However, the past was never mentioned. My father and brother were nonexistent dream figures.

Uncle Johnny always spoke about my mother in a positive light, commenting on her many achievements, until I felt my attitude change as I understood her through his loving eyes. He never judged, just tried to understand her point of view. I listened and learned.

About eighteen months after her first operation, she was diagnosed with cancer again. This time it had attacked the brain.

I wept until I had rid my soul of its despair. She would be gone and I would be left once more. Slowly it dawned on me that in those few short months we had found each other and my resentment had vanished.

My mother and I had reached out to each other, and my resentment had been replaced with understanding and love.

~Ann Hoffman

Postscript: In 2013, thanks to modern technology, family and friends, my brother and I found each other... but that's a story for another day.

I Can't Give You What I Don't Have

Find the love you seek, by first finding the love within yourself.
Learn to rest in that place within you that is your true home.
~Sri Sri Ravi Shankar

I watched two young boys sharing some candy. It didn't take long for them to eat all of it, and the younger boy asked the older one for more candy. The older boy said, "I don't have any more candy." But the younger boy kept asking for more. Finally the older boy said, "I can't give you what I don't have."

I didn't know the boys and the scene probably took less than two minutes, but it changed my life.

I'd learned an important lesson. People can't give what they don't have. The older boy wasn't being selfish or mean; he wasn't hoarding candy to eat later. He simply didn't have any more candy.

I'd had a very unhappy childhood. My mother hadn't wanted a child and she was cold, indifferent and never displayed any signs of affection toward me.

I spent my childhood trying to be perfect so she'd love me. I was quiet, kept my room clean and was very little trouble. As a teenager I helped with the housework, got good grades in school and never talked back. She admired a necklace in a store one day and I skipped my school lunches for a month to save money to buy her the necklace.

After she got it, she never wore it. I vowed someday I'd be rich enough to buy her gifts she'd like and then she'd like me.

As an adult, I lived in another state but sent her cards and gifts for every important occasion, and because she was on a limited income, I often sent money to her. I called her but she didn't call me. I sent her cards and gifts but she didn't send even a Christmas card.

I was sure eventually, if I was good enough, if I loved her enough, if I did enough, I'd win her over and she'd love me. It was like trying to thaw a glacier with a candle.

And then watching two small boys sharing candy taught me more than I'd ever learned from books, or therapy, or counseling. People can't give what they don't have.

No matter how old I got, when I was around her I felt five years old, begging her to hang my kindergarten drawing on the refrigerator door, wanting praise, wanting acceptance, wanting love. I could go to her every day for the rest of my life asking her to love me, but it would never happen. There was no love to give.

A cousin had been telling me for months that I needed to travel across four states to visit my mother in her nursing home before it was too late. She emphasized the words "too late."

My mother had not asked me to come. In fact she hadn't answered any of my letters for a year.

There was no reason to travel hundreds of miles to be disappointed. She wasn't going to suddenly throw her arms around me and hug me and say she loved me and she was sorry for being cold and distant all these years. No. Nothing had changed, she had not changed.

But I had changed.

I'd blamed her for withholding love from me as both a child and an adult. I'd been hurt, angry, wounded, frustrated, and confused. Why couldn't she love me? Why wouldn't she love me?

The answer was simple. There was no love in her to give. She wasn't withholding anything; it simply wasn't there. She couldn't give what she didn't have.

And now I could let go. I could stop trying. I could stop crying.

I could stop hoping things would change. I could let her go. I was no longer angry, I was just relieved. I could give up.

I wasn't going to make the long trip in hopes of salvaging something that never existed.

I don't have a puzzle to solve, I didn't do anything wrong, I wasn't a bad child. My mother was a woman who, for whatever reason, had no maternal feelings.

The long struggle was over. I could never win her over. I was never going to hear the words, "I love you. I'm proud of you. I'm glad you are my daughter."

I'm letting you go, Mother. You don't have to say anything.

I know you can't give what you don't have.

~April Knight

And Now We Are Love

The decision to forgive touches you to your very core,
to who you are as a human being.
~Robert Enright, Ph.D.

I t is her birthday today and I think of her with love and tenderness, but it was not always so. At six years old I decided I would never need anyone again, and mostly that meant her. And I watched, as if from another plane, as my life careered from one emotional upheaval to another.

At four years old I had tried to tell her that Daddy was "doing things." She called me a dirty little liar. As an adult, long after I had escaped to distant shores in a far-off land the recriminations continued. In letters scrawled in haste she would write: "You always were a daydreamer," "You always had fantasies." Sometimes she used the "lie" word.

Years passed. My career was successful; it was where I poured everything. But I was like an egg, a brittle shell on the outside and soft and runny on the inside. Most people only saw and knew the shell. They said things about me and to me that hurt, but I never answered back. I simply retreated further.

She was old now. The ache got bigger, the hatred deeper. Worse, I despised her. She hadn't protected me, she hadn't saved me, she hadn't stopped it. She was the real reason I lived a life of pain.

The social workers at work told me to discuss it with her and would watch me freeze and recoil in horror. "What's wrong, scared she'll have a heart attack?" I would nod numbly, tears filling my eyes as I closed off more.

In my forties and when she was much older, I moved back across the globe to a place that was in reachable distance, but not too close. At some stage I read Eleanor Roosevelt's perceptive words: "No one can make you feel inferior without your consent." The idea of consenting to the ways in which we are treated finally gave me the impetus I needed to sit up and take notice. The right therapist helped. For two decades I had searched for her and she appeared when my work life went belly up.

I extended love and friendship to my mother. Despite the views of the social workers in the antipodes, I decided not to discuss my childhood with someone who was increasingly frail. Instead, we did things together—walked on beaches, attended church, talked about our beliefs, discovered, to my astonishment, and no doubt hers, that we had much in common.

There wasn't much time. She had dementia. Her short-term memory was fading fast, and the rest of her memories faded in and out. Once she tried to hit me and I calmed her by rocking her back and forth in my arms. Once in tears she looked at me and asked why she couldn't remember things anymore. Her body heaved as she sobbed in my arms.

The daughter who had loathed her mother for so much of her life opened her heart and let in a frail old lady. I cooed, stroked her hair, we talked into the wee hours and, calm at last, she slept.

I sat, looking at my shaking hands, and thought of all the dreadful and negative energy I had wasted over the years in the hatred I had felt for her. People don't understand, of course. They don't understand that the reactions we have about the person who was supposed to protect us can be as strong as those we feel toward the actual perpetrators.

We came close to having the conversation only once. We had taken the train for a day trip to the beach when her mind was still bright. Suddenly, she looked at me and sounding very emotional said, "I sometimes think I should have been more affectionate with your father." She stared at me, her blue eyes willing me to say something.

This was my chance; this was the moment. Her eyes sparkled with tears as she waited. I watched as every part of her body tensed.

Instead, I leaned toward her and patting her knee said, "I am sure you were affectionate enough." I saw thanks in her eyes. Her body relaxed, and she nodded. I felt bathed in the love she felt and had always felt for me. And I knew, as I should have always known, that the only real way to deal with pain or tragedy or abuse is with love. At that moment I loved her back in ways I had never felt before.

These days, more than a decade after she passed over, she still visits me. Sometimes I hear her soft Scottish brogue; sometimes I feel her touch; sometimes something moves; sometimes when I walk in nature I know she is with me.

And now we are love.

~Susan E. Méra

The Cupcake Incident

You don't raise heroes, you raise sons. And if you treat them like sons,
they'll turn out to be heroes, even if it's just in your own eyes.
~Walter M. Schirra, Sr.

"No, you listen to me!" my younger son, Jon, protested. I felt paralyzed — unable to speak — as a
convulsive wave of tears engulfed me. My mom
used to call it "hiccup crying" — gasping for breath between sobs. I
finally had to hang up the phone, unable to listen anymore.

Jon had never used that tone of voice with me — ever! He had
never even talked back to me while he was growing up. He was the
"perfect" son who could do no wrong, and now he was speaking to
me in a "foreign" language! I didn't know who he was or what he was
talking about.

The cupcakes I had been icing with pink peppermint frosting for
the Ladies' Annual Christmas Tea sat on the kitchen table — half-baked
and half iced.

Mark, my husband of thirty-three years, had only seen me that
upset once before in our marriage. "What's going on?" he asked, crossing
his arms against his chest.

In between sobs, I sputtered, "Jon... said..." And that's as far as
I got before another wave of grief stopped me and the tears flowed
again.

Finally, after catching my breath, I recounted the entire conversation. Jon was seeing a lovely young woman while he was attending

Grove City College in Pennsylvania, but he failed to communicate to us that he was in love with her and they were planning on getting engaged. We were absolutely clueless!

While Jon was away at college, his former girlfriend, Justine, had asked to meet me for lunch. As a mom of two sons, I had learned it was always better not to have anything to do with ex-girlfriends; in fact, it was best never to mention their names again. So I was careful to ask Jon's permission before I made plans to see her. He had given me an emphatic "yes."

"Mom, you can do whatever you want! It's fine with me," he said reassuringly.

What Jon had failed to realize was it might not be okay with the woman of his dreams—the one he was going to marry! When Kim got word that I was making plans to see his old girlfriend, there was a "slight" problem in the communication department.

I was caught in the middle. That's when I received the phone call from Jon that blindsided me!

Seeing my distress, Mark called Jon right back and said, "If you ever talk to your mom like that again and in that tone of voice, don't bother setting foot in this house." There was a brief moment of silence and then Mark demanded, "Do you understand?"

I cringed when I heard those words. Now we had two hurting hearts—no—four: Jon, me, Mark and Kim! How were we ever going to patch up things? Would I see Jon again? Would we all reconcile?

The day after Jon's phone call, the doorbell rang and the delivery-man presented me with a white box wrapped in green floral wrap. I thanked him profusely and closed the door before anyone else could see my puffy eyes from a sleepless and tearful night.

When I opened the box, there was a cupcake arrangement made with hot pink carnations and white chrysanthemums. Tucked inside the flowers was a gift card with red hearts. It read, "Please forgive me, Mom. I was wrong and I'm so sorry. Love, Jon." I clutched the card to my chest and heaved a sigh of relief.

It's been five years since the "cupcake" incident that nearly severed our mother/son relationship, but in its place came a deep gratitude for sharing the truth and widening the future for even greater possibilities.

Jon and Kim were married on May 30, 2010. Instead of losing a son, I gained a daughter!

That was the first time I had ever received flowers from Jon, but definitely not the last! There's always room for more "cupcakes."

~Connie K. Pombo

Chapter
3

The Power *of* Forgiveness

Learning to Live with Family-through-Marriage

Let us not listen to those who think we ought to be angry with our enemies, and who believe this to be great and manly. Nothing is so praiseworthy, nothing so clearly shows a great and noble soul, as clemency and readiness to forgive.

~Marcus Tullius Cicero

Role Reversals

It is not flesh and blood but the heart that makes us fathers and sons.
~Johann Schiller

My father died in 1949, leaving my forty-four-year-old mother a relatively young widow with two children to raise on her own. Mom accepted the responsibility without question. She went to night school to improve her chances of getting a better job and earning more money to help her raise my brother and myself.

My brother and I discussed why she never remarried, but respectfully accepted her decision and never challenged or questioned her any further. Years later when my brother decided to marry, that very question arose. "Why didn't you ever take the plunge again?" he laughingly asked.

Mom didn't hesitate. "Honestly, I never wanted to bring a stepfather into the house, to you and your sister," she explained. "I've heard too many stories — kind of like the mean stepmother in Cinderella — only the cruel stepfather."

Millie, the woman my brother planned to wed, was a widow whose husband had been killed in a fishing accident. She had a fourteen-year-old son. Now as irony would have it, my brother was about to become a stepfather, but nothing resembling the image my mother described.

From day one, I knew there would never be a question as to how he cared for and respected his wife and stepson, Michael. There was only one way to go — grow together as a family surrounded by love. I knew my brother would make a great father because in a way he had taken on the father role with me after Dad died. I experienced his kind, gentle and caring spirit and knew he truly and deeply loved his forever family-to-be.

From the get-go, George and Michael hit it off. They were like two peas in a pod. So much so that Millie often wondered how she survived their antics and constant teasing as the camaraderie between them turned to a father-and-son relationship.

When Michael was stricken with nephritis, my brother's concern was one of a real father. He worried about the recovery process, tried to empathize with the suffering and devoted himself to nursing his son back to health. George loved Michael as any father would.

Over the years, when George and Michael were in a social situation that required introductions, neither hesitated to say who the other was and exchange loving stories about their relationship. Every time they introduced one another to someone, I noticed a strange ritual. My brother would always say, "This is my stepson, Michael." And Michael would always say, "This is my father, George."

At one family gathering, Michael seemed out of sorts and a little agitated with my brother. Finally, after some friendly prodding, I discovered he had a "mounting" problem with my brother. This complication, as he explained it, wasn't apparent to anyone but needed to be taken care of immediately. I was devastated and my heart ached for him and his concern.

"Knowing George, I'd have to say there must be a reason behind it, Michael. Go talk to him about it."

"I know," he agreed. "When the time is right."

Shortly after dinner began, Michael decided to propose a toast. He lifted his glass of soda and thanked us for coming, being part of his new family and for loving him. Glasses clinked. Warm fuzzies followed. Then without a warning, he turned to my brother and asked, "George, do you love me? Do you think of me as your son?"

My brother gasped with horror, nearly choking on his wine. "Of course I do, Michael. How could you ever think otherwise?" His eyes filled with tears. "What makes you ask such questions?"

Everyone at the table froze. All eyes focused on Michael, who proceeded. "Can you tell me why you introduce me to your friends and business associates as your stepson when I introduce you to my friends as my father?" he asked.

I watched my brother struggle through the tears. "Michael, you are my son in my heart, in my soul and in all the ways that count. But in all good consciousness I could never bring myself to assume the title of father or presume I had that right without your approval."

By now, all of us witnessing this event were weeping.

George continued, "Since the subject never came up before, I believed it to be an unspoken understanding: I am your father."

"Well," said Michael, "since I consider you my father in my heart, soul and in all ways that count too, I'd like you to officially take on the title. And from now on tell everyone I am your son."

My brother rose, walked over to Michael and embraced him. "Thank you, son," he said.

I watched and listened, beaming with happiness as my brother kept one arm around this fine young man and raised his glass high. "To my son, Michael."

Everyone cheered with delight. I felt great pride, deep respect and unconditional love for my brother who had just imparted the same feelings to his son. At that moment, I saw how love influences life and affirms its own truth.

~Helen Colella

The Challenge

When you forgive, you in no way change the past—
but you sure do change the future.
~Bernard Meltzer

"How dare you read my diary?" I shrieked.

With that outburst, my stepmother slapped me across the face. "Don't you ever raise your voice to me," she snarled.

I had never defied her before and she had never hit me. But for the last week Thelma had questioned, accused and shown disdain for nearly everything I'd said or done.

I was sixteen. Living with her had been a challenge since she and Dad were married ten years earlier. I had tried so hard throughout the years to win her acceptance. Since my birth mother was an alcoholic and never around, Thelma had become "Mom" early on. I so wanted her to like me.

When I was younger, sometimes she and I walked through the woods exploring trails and collecting wildflowers. I would be ecstatic. But, more likely than not, in the evening when I was still jabbering excitedly about our adventure, Mom would look at me with disgust and grumble, "Stop gushing."

Sometimes she sent me off to school with a controversial poem or thought haunting my mind. Lulled into a false sense of camaraderie, I would arrive home babbling about my day, only to be silenced by a frown of impatience or an annoyed, "Must you carry on so?"

Her mood determined my day. She could build me up so easily, and bring me down in a moment. Our rapport changed from day to day, from hour to hour, leaving me in a state of confusion and frustration, never knowing what to expect.

As I matured and began dating, Mom became less trusting and even more critical, her words more cutting. She called me boy-crazy, accused me of wearing my heart on my sleeve, and seemed suspicious of any relationship I shared with the opposite sex.

Now she was reading my diary! Her distrust hurt more than the slap across my face. I suddenly became very tired of trying to cope with the challenge of living with Mom. I went to Aunt Katherine in tears to ask if I could live with her.

Aunt Katherine listened patiently while I poured out my anger and frustration. When I finished, she sat quietly in thought. "Of course you can stay here for as long as you want," she said finally. "But maybe it would help if you knew more about Thelma."

I knew very little. Mom was a private person, never close with anyone and never showing affection. Before she entered our lives, I hugged and kissed my daddy each night at bedtime. But when Mom arrived, she scoffed. "Don't you think you're a little too old to be kissing your father goodnight?" I was only six, and I treasured those moments. But her disapproval ended that sweet luxury.

"When she was little," Aunt Katherine began, "her mother was very sick. She died when Thelma began grade school. Thelma's brother died a few years later when he was a teenager. I don't know how he died, and I don't know what happened to her father. But I do know Thelma grew up in an orphanage."

"An orphanage? Mom lived in an orphanage?"

"Yes, but when she was in high school, she worked for a lovely family who gave her room and board and later put her through teacher's college. That's where she met Walter, her first husband."

Aunt Katherine smiled. "They were very much in love. But in those days women teachers weren't allowed to be married, so Thelma and Walter had to keep it a secret and live apart."

"They were married and couldn't live together?"

"Yes, but that wasn't the worst of it. Thelma got pregnant and lost her job. Then Walter became ill. He was diagnosed with cancer and died shortly after their baby was born."

Aunt Katherine stroked the back of my hair and rested her hand on my shoulder. "She had a hard life, honey. She was left with large medical bills and no job. She was young, and heartbroken, and alone with her baby—your brother, Duane."

I shook my head in wonder. "She's never said a word."

"Maybe her memories are too painful," Aunt Katherine said quietly.

I reflected on what a sad, lonely life Mom had known. As some of the pieces to the puzzle of her personality began to fit together, my anger began to wane.

Aunt Katherine, in her kind, caring way, convinced me to go back home that night. From then on I tried to be more understanding and forgiving. It wasn't easy, because Mom didn't change. But now when she accused or belittled, I figured it was because she was still hurting from her past. So instead of being angry, I felt sorry for her.

Most of the time I still got very frustrated, but I didn't feel like a victim anymore. The problems were hers, not mine. Understanding that helped me feel more in control of my life. I could choose to be angry, or I could choose to be forgiving. I chose forgiveness.

The challenge from my youth remained as I struggled through college, marriage, and children to show Mom I loved her in spite of her indifference toward me. And she tried, equally, to convince me that my tolerance and affection were signs of weakness.

Sometimes I wondered if she would go to her grave showing contempt for me. But one day, shortly before she died, Mom removed the shield that had closed me out.

"Mom," I implored, "tell me about your parents. What were they like?"

She gazed at me strangely, then stared into nothingness. Finally after several minutes she began slowly. "When I was little, my mother became ill with tuberculosis. She had to remain in bed and I was no longer allowed to go near her… to feel her arms around me… to kiss her goodnight.

After a long pause I asked, "And your father?"

"My father… was…" Mom looked into my eyes and squared her shoulders, taking in a deep breath. As though fortified, she continued matter-of-factly. "My father was a child molester."

I stifled a gasp.

Mom clenched her teeth and jutted her chin upwards, as though swallowing hurtful memories.

"There was a trial. My father was sent to jail and I was sent to an orphanage." She paused, then continued slowly. "Years later, when I came home from college, my father told me he loved me 'in a different way than a father loves a daughter.' Then he kissed me… on my lips. And I felt… so…" Her voice trailed off.

Mom was entrusting her deepest secrets to me, the one person she had always rejected. I was finally given passage to her world.

At that moment I knew that through all those years of struggle my choice to forgive had not gone unnoticed or unfelt. It was a sad victory—the end of a hard-fought, painful challenge.

I took her hand in mine and, remembering days of long ago, said softly, "It's okay, Mom. Everything is okay now."

~Kay Conner Pliszka

22

The Wedding Gift

At the end of the day, a loving family should find everything forgivable.
~Mark V. Olsen and Will Sheffer, Big Love, "Easter"

The alcove in the church where my fiancé and his best man stood with the pastor was trimmed with polished oak panels and white walls. The last rays of light from the setting sun shone through the stained glass windows. Members of my bridal party milled about. Their chatter about tomorrow's events drowned out whatever the pastor was saying.

Tomorrow was the big day and I was sure to be nervous, but for now I felt relaxed. The church door opened with a squeak and light from outside flooded in. Everyone's attention turned to the new arrivals. I stiffened. This was the part I feared the most.

I greeted my father and stepmother as they took a seat in the last pew. My mother had an amused expression on her face. My parents had been divorced for twenty-one years. They had the type of divorce where they communicated with each other as little as possible, and there had been no communication at all for the last six years.

My mother had promised me she would be kind, knowing how important it was for my father to be a part of my wedding. It was my stepmother I worried about. We had our struggles as a stepfamily in the six years we lived together. I struggled to accept her role in my life and resisted her attempts to teach me responsibility and account-ability. I felt she favored my stepbrother over me, as all the chores were dumped on me. Despite old feelings, I wanted her included in the festivities and even politely insisted that she be escorted down the aisle to be seated with my father at the wedding.

The rehearsal at the church went without a hitch and the dinner that followed went just as well, even though my parents somehow ended up seated across from one another. Still, I slept in spurts that night as unanswerable questions haunted my thoughts. Would family photos at the church be awkward? Would my parents end up seated near each other at the reception because there was no assigned seating? Would my father leave the reception early?

The next day brought a flurry of activity and rushing around. Before I knew it, I was standing in the doorway of the little church with my father by my side and a full audience awaiting our walk down the aisle. He gave my hand a squeeze and we both started to cry. I knew then that everything about that day was going to go just right.

After the ceremony, my husband and I stood by the doorway greeting our guests. My mother and stepfather stood with us, thanking everyone for coming. I braced myself as my stepmother approached. How was this going to play out?

What I got instead was the best wedding day gift—forgiveness. Smiling from ear to ear, my stepmother embraced my mother in an enormous hug and told her what a beautiful wedding it was. I was speechless. My mother was dumbfounded. Everything about the gesture was genuine. Twelve years of hurt melted away as I watched her reveal her true self in an act of humility.

Forgiving her for every injustice I felt as a kid and filling my heart with love allowed me to let go of the past and embrace my future with my new husband. That chapter in my life ended on a good note.

The family photos turned out great. My parents sat at tables next to each other, and it wasn't a problem. And my father stayed to the end.

~Valerie D. Benko

23

High Hopes

A stepmother might have to rise above a little more than everyone else to make everything go smoothly and for everyone to feel comfortable. It's one of the nicest gifts they could give.

~Elizabeth Howell

"Y ou're not my mother. I'm not calling you Mom!" he shouted. "And I don't like coming here every other weekend."

When my eight-year-old stepson directed those words at me, a wave of anguish swept over me. "It's okay to call me by my first name," I said as I fought back the tears. "Your dad and I love you and the time you spend with us."

"I still don't like you," he scoffed while playing with two favorite *Star Wars* action figures. "And I'm not making my bed or doing any chores, because I don't live here."

I ignored his rants and was determined to make it a pleasant weekend. "I know how much you love *Star Wars*. Would you like to go shopping for *Star Wars* posters and a bedspread for your room?" I asked.

"Okay, let's go!" he yelled, a grin on his face. I felt a tug on my heartstrings—he looked just like his dad—the same mischievous grin, thick red hair and freckles scattered across his nose.

While we shopped, he talked about his mom, dad and school friends, and confided how every other weekend visitations disrupted his life. He'd never opened up to me like that before. I admit it was a form of bribery, but I took advantage of the opportunity and gave in when he asked for duplicate *Star Wars* posters and bedspreads for both households.

On the ride back to his mom's house that evening, he chose the passenger seat to be near his dad. From the back seat, I listened to them discuss the statistics of football legends, players, coaches and managers. Excitement ensued, because they had tickets for an Oakland Raiders and San Francisco 49ers exhibition game. I marveled at their bonding over football.

When we reached our destination, I was pleased my stepson smiled and thanked me for the *Star Wars* gifts. But my moment of bliss was short-lived when he hugged his dad goodbye. "Please come back home and live with Mom and me," he begged, and then raced to join his mom, who was waving to us from the front porch.

On the drive home, my husband pondered what to do to make his son feel welcome in our home. It'd been five years since the divorce and we'd been married for a little over a year. "We have to be patient," I offered. "Every book I've read on step-parenting states it takes time to have a harmonious household and become a blended family.

My husband had a heart-to-heart talk with his son during the Raiders and 49ers game. After the football weekend, I asked about the father-son conversation. My husband spared the details and my feelings. "I told him he'll love you as much as I do once he gets to know you." I smiled, choked back the tears and pretended my feelings weren't hurt.

As I drove the ten miles to work that morning, I couldn't control the tears streaming down my face. When I reached the office, I touched up my make-up and whispered to myself in the mirror, "Be patient. Don't give up hope."

Visitation weekends improved when we let my stepson choose what he wanted to do. Saturday breakfasts at his favorite diner, movies, baseball and bowling made him happy.

But as he grew older, the more homework he was assigned. Weekly spelling words and multiplication tables had to be scheduled in between weekend activities. Suddenly, weekends entailed angry outbursts aimed at me. I was the villain — my husband's attempts to smooth the relationship failed.

When I heard Spider-Man was my stepson's latest phase, I made him an elaborate red and blue Spider-Man costume for Halloween, embellished with black fishnet and rubber spiders. "I think I'll win first prize at the school parade," he said when he tried on the costume. Since there was no animosity between my husband's ex-wife and me, I was invited to the Halloween parade. We were all elated when Spider-Man took first place.

That evening my husband gave me a high five. "Today, you sure scored stepmom points."

After that, weekend visits were amiable. My stepson joined a little league team and we attended the games. Occasionally, weekends included birthday parties or sleepovers with friends. He was growing up.

The seventh grade proved to be a challenge for my stepson. Since our school district provided tutoring and special classes for students working below grade level in reading and math, it was agreed he'd move into our home and visit his mom every other weekend.

Seventh grade at the new school wasn't easy. He detested the special classes and extra homework. It was a battle I wasn't winning, but I didn't give up. Almost daily he shouted, "I hate you and the stupid school!" Eventually, he made new friends, his grades improved, the school year was bearable and he tolerated me. High hopes prevailed.

However, during summer vacation he had a change of heart and pleaded to return to his mom's house and attend eighth grade at his former school. The eighth grade was a bumpy ride for him.

That fall, he returned to our house and entered ninth grade at the neighborhood high school. He made the football team and was positive it'd be a good year. But before the end of the season his grades plummeted, making him ineligible to play. He packed his bags and insisted on going back to live and attend high school in the old neighborhood.

After that move, he chose to meet only his dad for breakfast at a diner near his home. No explanation was given for excluding me, not even to his dad or mom. My heart ached, but I refused to believe he wanted to banish me from his life forever.

Regretfully, yo-yo schooling and living took their toll. After my stepson and his parents met with a school counselor, it was agreed he should obtain a GED and enter junior college.

He studied hard and earned his GED. But he quickly lost interest in junior college and all part-time jobs, informing us he was moving to Hilo, Hawaii to find himself. We tried to discourage the move, to no avail. "Don't worry, I'm going with a couple who know the island," he said. "We'll find jobs, sleep on the beach and rough it."

It was a worrisome two months before postcards and photos arrived in our mailbox. We breathed a sigh of relief when we knew he had a job, a roof over his head and was learning to surf.

Three years later he returned to the States. When we picked him up at the airport, it was obvious he'd become an independent, confident young man.

He greeted us with a smile and a group hug. "I'm so happy to see you guys!" he shouted, then turned to me. "Mom, your brat's home. Can you ever forgive me for how badly I treated you?"

Tears welled in my eyes and I returned the hug. "Son, all's forgiven. I always had high hopes you wanted me in your life."

Indeed, patience and time healed all wounds.

~Georgia A. Hubley

The Axe

Unconditional forgiveness is the path to your own inner peace.
~Jonathan Lockwood Huie

M y husband Dave and I returned from town one afternoon to find Dave's best Fiskars axe, broken in half, lying on the kitchen counter. Beside it was a note from my fourteen-year-old son: "I'm sorry Dave, I'll buy you a new one from Canadian Tire."

I remembered the last time he'd borrowed an axe from his father. He'd forgotten it in the back yard, where it had rusted. He'd quietly endured ongoing vicious verbal assaults for months after that incident—an opportunity too good to miss for a father who pushed the well-behaved, timid boy further into his introverted shell every chance he got.

Dave had no knowledge of the past incident, but a lump formed in my throat as I watched him read Ed's note. I knew exactly why my son had made himself scarce that afternoon: His stepfather was too new of an addition in my children's lives for them to be sure he wouldn't react in the same manner they'd come to expect of a father.

"Poor kid. Must be a big adjustment for him, making the move here and leaving his friends. I thought maybe he'd work off some of that pent up anger chopping wood. You think the Fiskars company would believe their 'unbreakable axe' was no match for a frustrated boy?"

Then he sat down and wrote at the bottom of the note: "It's okay,

Ed. Things happen, especially when you're carrying a heavy load and won't ask for help, or just talk. I forgive you. Love you, Dave."

The forgiveness he extended that day marked the beginning of healing in Ed's life and the start of many father/son evening chats by our living room fireplace. Even though Ed is twenty-two and setting up his own home, those chats still occur today. And they still warm my heart.

~Beverly Fox-Jourdain

These Things Take Time

In some families, please *is described as the magic word.*
In our house, however, it was sorry.
~Margaret Laurence

I came to motherhood late in life and all at once. One moment I was thirty-six and single, and the next I was married with three stepchildren, ages thirteen, seven, and five. For many reasons, this was destined to be a somewhat fractious situation because the kids lived predominately with their mother 3,000 miles away. Except for two separate yearlong interludes, we saw them only during summers and the rare Christmas holiday. Even so, and despite my gross lack of experience as a parent, the kids and I managed to forge a mostly amicable relationship.

My stepson Anthony was an affectionate child who delighted in art, reading, and superheroes. We became particularly close, but this began to change as he grew from an endearing five-year-old into a truculent teenager. Hindsight, of course, is 20-20, but at the time neither my husband nor I realized the many issues that plagued him. All we knew was that our immensely likeable son had seemingly turned overnight into the Terminator—difficult to talk to, impossible to reach, and combative over the least little issue. Our relationship degenerated into a tense, battle-ridden landscape of sullen silence broken by argument and confrontation.

Everything came to a head one Christmas. Anthony was living with us at the time, but according to the terms of the parenting agreement, he flew to be with his mother for the holiday. No sooner did he get there than he called to say he wasn't coming back. We were stunned. My husband talked with him at length, but he was adamant. I also spoke with him, apologizing for my behavior and lack of patience, acknowledging my part in our difficulties and asking him to come home so we could work together to find a way back to where we'd been. He refused. At that point, I'm afraid I did one of the worst things a parent can do—I gave up on him. Although Anthony and his father stayed in guarded contact, he and I didn't speak again for six years.

Then one night my husband came to me and said, "Anthony's on the phone and wants to talk to you." Cautiously, I took the receiver and said hello. "I just want you to know I'm sending you a letter," was all he said before hanging up. I wondered what hate-filled message I was about to receive, but when it arrived, the opening words read: "First of all, I want to say I'm sorry." By the end of the letter, I was crying. When I got myself under control, I picked up the phone.

It took enormous courage and a willingness to risk rejection for Anthony to reach out to me after so long. It took immense trust in our past relationship and the belief that we could reconnect for the two of us to begin again. Slowly, we worked through our issues, coming to a clearer understanding of not only each other, but of ourselves.

Over the past ten years, our relationship has grown into something wondrous. Not only are we mother and son, but we're good friends as well—maybe even best friends—calling to share details of our day, a joke, or to offer support during difficult times. In a way, those years of silence worked to our advantage. But we would never have reached where we are today if it hadn't been for Anthony's bravery and desire to begin again and regain what we had lost.

~Melissa Crandall

26

Moms Are Like That

Life becomes easier when you learn to accept an apology you never got.
~Robert Brault

My sweetheart Paul and I had eloped to Yuma on a whim. It was the most romantic and thrilling weekend of my life. Leaving town was easy but coming back on Sunday night to face our parents was hard. We had a huge wedding planned for the following September—but this was May, and Paul was home on his first leave from the Marine Reserves boot camp.

Paul's parents joined us at my parents' house the evening we returned. We hoped this would be a happy meeting of our newly merged families.

Seated around the living room, Paul's mother was the first to speak.

"I don't think Paul and Sallie should stay married! They are too young. How will he support a wife? Where will they live? We need to get this marriage annulled!" my new mother-in-law shouted to the family members assembled at my parents' house.

BAM! My father had let her rant for several minutes before his fist hit the coffee table with a loud slap. "If these kids want to stay married, then by God they're gonna stay married," he yelled back.

He turned to Paul. "Do you want to stay married?" Turning to me, he said, "Sallie do you want to stay married?" We both nodded yes, our eyes wide at all this drama.

"Then they can live with us until Paul gets home permanently," my dad said in a calmer tone. Case closed!

Mrs. Rodman had been thwarting me at every turn, trying to postpone the wedding plans. She even went so far as to tell Paul we were too young and we were from two different classes and he needed to marry a college graduate. On and on the objections went.

Sure, I was only nineteen and had one year of college. But we were both from middle-class families, although I admit I probably had a few more material advantages since Paul came from a family of eleven.

We did stay married, but to appease his mother we lived apart one week until we could be married in our church. The next week Paul went back to the marines. I moved in with my mom and dad and got an apartment nearby for the weekends. It was like playing house... work all week, pick up Paul at Camp Pendleton on Friday, spend the weekend at our "hideaway," then take him back to camp on Sunday night.

After Paul's basic training as a reservist was over, he went back to his job. He served one weekend a month and two weeks in summer training camp while we anxiously waited to hear if he would be called up for Vietnam.

My new mother-in-law didn't come around much since Paul's father was ill. They had a family tragedy and their house burned down. She was working and running in so many directions.

Meanwhile our family had grown, with a son and then a daughter, one year apart. I hoped when things got back to normal we could talk. Perhaps I could win my mother-in-law over since I loved her son so much and she adored him too. But that was not to be.

The entire chain of events came crashing down early one cold February morning three years into our marriage. I wrote a poem about it:

The Final Revenge

A phone ringing, ringing, breaking the 5 o'clock morning.
My husband plunging through the door where the white
    wall phone stubbornly commands.

From the bedroom, my curiosity arousing itself from a
    long night's sleep.
The words ambulance and hospital send me reeling
    through the door.
Thoughts flashing through my brain like summer
    lightning.
But no, it's not my mother, older and graying.
The younger woman has been chosen instead.
My husband replaces the phone into its slot, tears running
    down his face.
"She is dead; my mom is dead."
We are rocking back and forth in each other's arms.
He cries for her, I cry for him.
Her words echo in my mind,
"You stole my favorite son!"
A sudden thought.
What's today?
Monday, February 20th.
Recognition.
My birthday.
I whisper to myself, "Happy birthday, kiddo."
Forever on this day he will remember
who was born and who died.

And so I never got to know this woman, my husband's mother. I soon forgot her slights and unkind words since she was absent from our lives and I was busy with two toddlers. I did vow that when my children grew up and married, I would welcome their choices with warm hugs and loving words no matter what.

Now here I am forty-seven years later. My husband Paul died a little over three years ago. It recently dawned on me while lying in bed one morning and thinking about him that, since I believe he is in heaven, his mom is probably with him. I found myself overcome with anger and jealousy.

I wanted to yell out, "You can't have him. He is mine! I loved him to the moon and back. We were happily married for so many years. Wasn't that enough for you?"

Then I realized I still haven't forgiven her for those long ago hurts. What good is hanging onto such old wounds? I want and need to forgive this woman. I am dealing with a tremendous loss in my life. I don't need to add anger on top of that.

In my quest to understand and forgive her, I recently spoke to my husband's sister Joan. I confided my feelings about their mom, hoping she could help me. She counseled me. "Oh Sallie, Mom was like that with every date we brought home. She just loved her kids so much she was afraid of them being hurt. It wasn't personal."

Acceptance is replacing the anger as I realize that is what I had in common with my mother-in-law—we both loved our children, and moms only want the very best for their kids. Sometimes we overstep, but our hearts are in the right place. That is something I do understand and can certainly forgive her for.

My only hope is that when Paul talks to her in heaven he tells her, "See Mom, she was a keeper! Forty-six years—and you thought it would never last."

~Sallie A. Rodman

27

As She Prayed

You don't need strength to let go of something.
What you really need is understanding.
~Guy Finley

Even though my ex-husband and I had recently divorced, his family and I enjoyed a pleasant relationship. Throughout the divorce, my sister-in-law and I had remained friends. She lived around the corner from me, so we often socialized. Unfortunately my niece—her older daughter—had experienced painful headaches for several months. As the headaches increased in intensity, the family traveled out of state to consult with a specialist.

When my sister-in-law called to give me an update, I immediately sensed something was wrong. "They discovered a brain tumor," she murmured. Several minutes passed before her words sunk in. "The operation's been scheduled for tomorrow, but they won't know if they can remove it all or if it is malignant until they reach it. Please keep us in your prayers."

"How is your mom handling this news?" I asked, for I knew my mother-in-law had offered to stay at their home and watch their other two children. "Do you think she'd like company while the operation is taking place?"

"Would you mind?" she asked with a relieved tone.

"Not at all," I replied, and hung up the phone.

Everyone knew I had a turbulent relationship with my mother-in-law. Before the wedding, our relationship seemed amicable. Yet after the marriage, it became volatile. Of course, I respected my elders, but the wicked mother-in-law characters portrayed on TV portrayed my mother-in-law perfectly.

Nothing I did satisfied her. As a result, she never hesitated to publicly voice her distaste. She stuck her nose where it didn't belong while she endlessly doted on her son. Whenever she disagreed with my actions, she would become verbally abusive. In truth, I felt intimidated, so I kept my distance.

However, at this moment, I envisioned her with her grandkids, feeling distraught and alone. As a mother, I could not imagine how anxious she felt. Officially, she was not my mother-in-law, but I felt a deepening urge to reach out and protect her from all of this.

That afternoon, my children stayed at the neighbor's house while I walked to my sister-in-law's home. My mother-in-law stood waiting at the door.

"Thank you so much for coming," she said, in her thick Dutch accent. "I'm so worried about her." Both of us had received news that they shaved my niece's head and presented her beautiful auburn locks to her mother.

"Would you like tea?" she asked. But before I could answer, she poured me a cup. "Would you like to pray?" I asked, and then glanced at the clock. "It's almost time."

"Oh yes, please," she replied. Her hands trembled as she pulled out her delicate handkerchief and dabbed the tears from her eyes. Without hesitation, I clasped her hands tightly in mine.

As she prayed, I opened my eyes and searched this woman's face for answers. Where had we gone wrong? When had I passed judgment and decided she was cold and callous? At this moment she seemed anything but intimidating. In fact, she appeared vulnerable and terrified.

Suddenly, the years of built-up baggage released and a channel opened. It felt as if a vacuum cleaner had sucked away my grudges. By the time she had finished her prayer, the bottled-up anger and hatred ceased to exist. At the same time, I felt relieved and refreshed.

For the first time in eight years, she was simply a woman. I harbored no animosity, no defensive walls, and no hostility. As a result, I listened to her words with an earnest and unprejudiced heart. She spoke frankly about her life in Holland, the death of her first husband, and her marital problems.

Even though she never apologized for her behavior, I felt as if she had. While it was too late for us as mother-in-law and daughter-in-law, suddenly I had nothing but compassion for this woman, and an immense sense of freedom. Through the power of forgiveness, I had obtained complete liberation.

Eventually my children and I relocated to another state. Several years later, my mother-in-law passed away. At that time, I heard that even after my ex-husband remarried, she had kept my photograph on her wall—in its place—with the family photos. When I heard about the photograph, I smiled. It appeared that not only had I forgiven her, but perhaps the photograph symbolized that I too had finally received her forgiveness.

~Jill Burns

A Gift I Gave Myself

You will know that forgiveness has begun when you recall those who hurt you
and feel the power to wish them well.
~Lewis B. Smedes

I sat alone in the guest bedroom of my in-laws' house. I use the word "house" deliberately because it would never be a "home" to me. Tears streamed down my face, the result of yet another insult from my father-in-law, Bob.

"Why?" I asked the empty room. "Why does he dislike me so much?"

Since Robert and I had married several years earlier, his father had sent a constant barrage of criticism and snide remarks my way. He demeaned me in every way possible, including telling Robert and his three sisters that I didn't take proper care of the children or keep the house the way their mother did.

To understand the depth of my despair, you have to understand our background. Family closeness is a tenet of our church. That I had failed in achieving that with my father-in-law made me feel like a failure on the most basic of levels.

When Robert came searching for me, he took one look at my face and knew what had happened.

"Your father strikes again," I said, wiping away tears.

"He doesn't mean it that way," Robert said.

"Oh, and what way does he mean it?" I retorted.

"It's just his way."

"His way stinks."

Robert sighed. "I know. And I'm sorry. I can't do anything to change it, though."

"Why can't you stand up for me just once?" I asked, crying again. "Why do you let him get away with it?"

"I'm not letting him get away with anything," my husband said. "But I don't know how to make him change."

I turned away. The argument wouldn't be solved today. A family wedding had brought our little family from our home in Colorado to Utah. I needed to get our two small children and myself ready.

As if on cue, our four-year-old daughter and two-year-old son burst into the room.

I gave my husband one last look before beginning the process of dressing two squirming, uncooperative children.

A tense silence remained between Robert and me for the rest of the weekend. With strained feelings, we returned to our home two days later. Bob's treatment of me and my husband's refusal to come to my defense were a source of constant arguments and fights.

Years passed and still Bob was unkind. He now included the children in his criticisms, those comments stinging far more than anything he could say about me.

When his wife passed away, I thought he might mellow. Instead, his barbs and nasty comments only grew more pointed and mean-spirited.

After years of hurt feelings and tears, I decided that if I were to make any headway in my relationship with my father-in-law, I needed to forgive him. The irony was that he would have been surprised at my decision. He never saw that he had done anything that required forgiveness.

I started with making an inventory of Bob's good qualities. He had been a devoted husband and continued to be a stalwart member of his church. An avid genealogist, he had traced his family's line back many generations.

As I honestly acknowledged his attributes, something occurred that further softened my heart toward him. Complications with a knee replacement had sent him to a rehabilitation center for a month.

Through the family grapevine, I learned that Bob was deeply lonely and depressed. I resolved to try to cheer him up during this difficult time and wrote him faithfully every week, even asking my children to do the same. I called him and told him that the family was praying for his swift recovery.

My decision to forgive my father-in-law has not changed him. To this day, he continues to criticize me and to remind me that I will never measure up to his standards. To be honest, it still occasionally bothers me, but I've learned to accept that and to accept him. Though we will never be close, I have come to respect him and appreciate his strengths.

An added benefit of my decision to forgive my father-in-law was that my relationship with my husband grew stronger.

"Thank you for being willing to get along with my father," Robert said one night. "I know he doesn't make it easy."

A new air of peace and love filled our home.

Forgiveness did not come in a day. Nor did it come without much prayer and help from the Lord. The other ingredient was my recognition that the only person I could change was myself. Accepting Bob as he was, flawed and imperfect, made it easier for me to accept myself, complete with my own set of flaws and imperfections.

In the end, forgiveness was a gift I gave myself.

~Jane McBride Choate

29

The Tide-Turning Whisper

Forgiveness is the fragrance that the violet sheds
on the heel that has crushed it.
~Mark Twain

From day one, I made my ill feelings toward my mother-in-law crystal clear to my new husband. "Joe, why does the photographer keep inviting your mother into every photo?"

"What? He's not."

"Sure he is. All I keep hearing is, Mrs. Beck, we need you for a photo."

"Annie, he's talking to you. YOU are the Mrs. Beck he wants in the photos."

"Oh," I said, a bit chagrined. I was so certain that the photographer had her in mind as the star of the day instead of me, the bride. And thus it started. My silent declaration of war against my mother-in-law.

Oh Mary Beck was pleasant enough, but she had ulterior motives. I'd been observing her and Joe's relationship for three years. Her slightest whim, once stated, became Joe's main mission. Whatever we had planned always took a back seat to Mary's wants and needs. Or so it seemed to me.

She also incessantly dropped little innuendoes about "her Joe" and always within earshot of me. She knew it got on my nerves. Well, we were married now. Clearly Joe belonged to me and I had the paperwork to prove it.

After our wedding in January of 1984, Joe flew back to Centerville Beach Naval Facility in California. I was not expected to join him until June, after which we would be mother-in-law-free for two whole years. Yay!

About mid-February, Mary invited me to lunch. She wanted to share some wedding photos. Ha! Did she expect me to sit there and act interested in photos she took of "her Joe"? Forget it.

I could have called her to say "no thank you" with a suitable excuse. Instead, I had the audacity to write a letter and explain that I simply wasn't a social person, which shouldn't upset her. In other words, "don't expect to see too much of me, lady."

In June, Joe came home to Philadelphia to collect me and say goodbye to his family. Then we would be off to California. When the day came to say goodbye to his mom, I declined the opportunity. After all, she wasn't my mother. Joe could just go over and say goodbye himself. And so he did, without ever being cross or asking why.

Paradise waited on the other side of the map, where Joe would be mine—all mine. Once settled, Joe called his mom once a week and every time I discretely made my way to the front door and slipped out for a nice long walk.

Two years went by, and before long, we were packing to go home. My sulking started right at the Pennsylvania border. I'd just spent two years avoiding all contact with Mary Beck and now I'd have to face her again.

Joe's mom lived in the city, and as soon as we arrived home, I insisted we get an apartment in the suburbs. When holidays came along, I dutifully purchased a gift and handed it over with a forced smile. Of course I never missed an opportunity to grumble a snarky remark or two, especially if she invited us to come for dinner or worse, suggest that we all go to the movies or a show.

As the months passed and I made no attempt to improve my attitude toward Mary Beck, my relationship with Joe spiraled downward. I repeatedly made mountains out of molehills where she was concerned. Though Joe said nothing about that issue, we grumbled at each other about everything else. As time went on, Joe and I stopped communicating all together and he began sleeping on the couch. That went on for months.

One Saturday I decided I'd had it with him too. I wanted him and everything he owned out the door and out of my life. I was tired of him lying on the couch and ignoring me, and saw no way out other than to split. I told him to pack his things and leave. He changed position on the couch and ignored me some more.

I'll fix him, I thought. So I called his mother and told her flat out that I was through with her son and she'd better get his brothers over to our apartment to collect him and his belongings. She didn't agree to it. She just asked me to give the phone to Joe. When he hung up he said his mother wanted to see us right away.

"Good," I snapped back. "Let's go over and get this move organized. The sooner you're gone the happier I'll be."

Mary opened the door and let us in. Joe headed toward the couch, but before he had a chance to flop down, Mary barked at him in a tone I'd never heard before.

"Oh no, mister, you get right back over here. I want to talk to you."

Joe sheepishly turned and stood beside me.

"Joe, I don't care one bit what this is about. I'm telling you right now, Annie is right and you are wrong. She is the woman who is going to take care of you for the rest of your life. You'll never find anyone who loves you more. Now, listen to me—stop being an idiot and make up."

Then she hugged me and whispered in my ear, "Annie, I learned a long time ago a man will never treat his wife any better than he treats his mother. That's a good thing to remember. Joe will behave himself now he knows I mean business."

And there you have it—the tide-turning, life-changing moment.

Snippets of my past outrageous behavior flashed in my mind as I looked at Joe and saw him smile, and I started to cry.

After years of pushing nothing but snide remarks and selfish behavior in Mary's face, she instantly forgave every transgression and stood up for me. Never was a person less deserving of forgiveness or more grateful for it than I.

Unfortunately we only had about fifteen years to share before Mary passed away, but she and I made the most of it. She loved me as strong and true as any mother could love a daughter, and I returned that love with the same sincerity.

At the very end as Joe and I were at her bedside, I held her hand as she tried to sing something in a whisper, but I couldn't make it out.

Later that evening I asked Joe if he knew what she was trying to sing.

"She was singing, 'So Long, It's Been Good to Know You.'"

What an understatement.

~Annmarie B. Tait

Chapter
4

The Power *of* Forgiveness

Patching Up Rifts with Siblings

I learned a long time ago that some people would rather die than forgive. It's a strange truth, but forgiveness is a painful and difficult process. It's not something that happens overnight. It's an evolution of the heart.

~Sue Monk Kidd

30

The Gift of a Rose

There's no other love like the love for a brother.
There's no other love like the love from a brother.
~Terri Guillemets

It was Thanksgiving Day. My sister Sandy arrived with a plate in her hand. "I brought you Thanksgiving dinner. I did not know what else to do." On the table before me was a blank birth certificate the nurse had given to me that morning. I put off completing it. As I pondered my daughter's name, I just could not print the name my husband and I had chosen for her: Amber Rose. I suppose it was hope that made me want to reserve the name Amber for the future, just in case. With tears in my eyes, I discussed my dilemma with my sister. I decided to just name her Rose. I filled out the form and Sandy took it to the nurse's station as she left the hospital.

This was not supposed to happen. I expected my heart to fill with joy when my daughter was born. I had expected her to be born healthy and breathing, just like my two sons. Instead, I had given birth to a full-term stillborn infant. The placenta had separated when I had gone into labor, and my daughter did not have the environment or oxygen needed to survive. I gave birth to her the night before Thanksgiving.

As if naming my daughter was not bad enough, on her next visit to my room the nurse asked if my daughter was going to be buried or cremated. I just looked at her, bewildered. I suppose, still in shock, I assumed the hospital took care of the body. It didn't seem right to have to have a funeral for a baby who was only alive to me. No one else had seen her but my doctor and the attending nurses. My husband was just as unprepared to deal with the circumstances or make funeral arrangements. The only thing I knew was that cremating her was not an option for us. My father-in-law and my mother stepped in and explored options for funeral services, caskets and cemeteries.

I was discharged from the hospital on Friday. Raymond picked me up, and we retrieved our sons from my mother's house on the way home. As my father-in-law arranged everything with the funeral home, and my mother dealt with the cemetery, we finalized funeral arrangements for Rose by phone, from the privacy and comfort of our home. All the arrangements were finalized by Friday evening.

Rose would be buried on Monday, three feet below the ground and three feet above where my father's body was laid to rest at Mountain Grove Cemetery. She would be placed in a small white casket. Family and friends would be able to gather at the gravesite that morning. The funeral director would carry her little white silk-lined casket to her grave and perform the benediction. We were informed there was no charge to the family. The only fee we had to pay was to open her grave.

Flower arrangements and messages began to arrive on Friday. By Sunday afternoon, we had nearly forty flower arrangements in the house. Flowers were everywhere — on the tables, the mantle, the floor, even atop the wood stove. A message came that my brother Dan was thinking about going to the funeral. We had not spoken in some time, because of something I had said or done. Though I had begged for his forgiveness many times, he refused to talk to me. Most of my thoughts were about my mother; I was worried about how she was going to feel seeing my father's grave opened. My thoughts then wandered to the following weekend when we planned to host a gathering at our home in honor of my in-laws' fortieth wedding anniversary. I cried quietly at night after my sons and husband went to sleep. I showed few tears in front of anyone; I was more comfortable grieving alone.

Before heading to the cemetery Monday morning, I wandered around the house looking at the flowers and reading the condolences written on each little card. When I entered the living room, I saw a dozen red roses sitting by themselves on the coffee table. I bent down and read the card. It simply said, "Love Dan." As I smelled the roses, I fought back my tears. I knew at that moment that my brother loved me. Even though we didn't always see eye to eye, we would always be able to see heart to heart. I knew even if he was not at the funeral service, his heart was with me. As I stood, one rose seemed to stick up a little higher than the other. As I looked at it, I wondered if Dan knew I named my daughter Rose. As I reached out to gently touch the petals, I noticed a drop of water, just like a morning dewdrop. It appeared to be a tear. I started crying and sensed my brother was crying too. I took the rose from the vase and carried it with me to Rose's graveside service. I placed it on top of her casket as I left the cemetery that morning.

This past year, during a visit to my brother Dan's house, I shared with him how special those roses were to me at that time. I told him I did not remember a lot of details about that day or even if he was there. He said he was, and he described details that I did not recall as it was mostly a haze to me.

As I pondered writing this story, my brother came to mind for another reason. He is not talking to me again; the disagreement between us has bothered me greatly over the last few months. But I think I have found away to resolve the issue between us. I am going to send him a red rose with a simple card that reads: "Please forgive me. Praying this rose cries too. Love, Deb."

With that, I am praying he remembers; we do not have to always see eye to eye, but we will always see heart to heart.

~Deborah Lienemann

Rest in Peace

A sister is a little bit of childhood that can never be lost.
~Marion C. Garretty

"Practice what you preach," I muttered to myself shortly after I'd learned of the death of my sister. "Forgive and forget. Let bygones be bygones."

In childhood and early adolescence, I'd always looked up to my big sister. Her beauty and talent were an important part of my early years. I'd even published a story once about how she won a WWII War Bond in a talent contest when she was only six years old, belting out a bluesy version of "Don't Sweetheart Me."

Something happened, though, as we grew up. She never became the role model I'd hoped for; instead she became an embarrassment. She insulted our parents, their friends, and her teachers. She got expelled from junior high and, before abandoning her education, two high schools. Eventually, after an epic disagreement with our parents, she moved in with another relative. She found a job in a bakery. I wished her luck… and hoped she'd stay miles away.

Maybe that was a harbinger. Within a few years she severed her connections with our family entirely, disappearing one spring, abandoning her two small children with an ex-husband's sister.

"Be careful what you wish for," I reminded myself as the decades passed. I often thought of how I'd wished earlier that she would quietly disappear. I never suspected she really would. In the beginning, our family waited for a phone call or a letter. We figured she'd be in touch as soon as she needed money or a place to crash.

"It's not as if she can cope on her own," we'd reassure one another.

But years passed and we heard nothing. We worried if perhaps she'd died. Before the Internet, it was far more difficult to track people down. We tried, but finally gave up.

Three decades later she resurfaced, with another life and children and grandchildren. Unbeknown to any of us, she'd settled in a seaside community five hundred miles to the north.

Although I lived in another country at the time, one of her children finally contacted our little brother. When I visited California, I welcomed a chance to catch up on our lives. We visited for a few hours one evening, and I met two of her grown children who our family had never known existed.

Eager to learn what she'd been doing all those years, and why she'd never tried to contact us, I confessed that our mother worried about her throughout her remaining years. My sister just shrugged. She had no kind words to say about either of our parents.

I left the States again for another overseas job. I'd expected we'd keep in touch. Though I wrote long detailed letters about what I'd been doing, where I'd traveled, what I'd read, how I'd lived, my sister rarely responded. She'd send a greeting card on my birthday, with news of her grandchildren.

I longed for her to fill in the gaps. I'd pepper my letters with questions. Why had she fled to the north? Who was the man she'd married? What were their children's early lives like? Didn't she ever think about the two she'd left behind? All my concerns went unanswered.

When I returned to this country, we made plans for a Thanksgiving reunion. I drove hundreds of miles to meet her, but at the last minute she cancelled the date. She wasn't well that day, she claimed. I remember trembling with disappointment.

Though we spoke on the phone from time to time, I kept hoping for a face-to-face visit.

Then I got the phone call with the news she'd died.

All evening I simmered. Instead of grief, I wallowed in unhappy memories. How had my sister wronged me? I counted the ways. My resentment grew with each unpleasant incident that I recalled. I couldn't even cry, knowing that any tears would be shed more from self-pity than grief.

I know that clinging to grudges diminishes a person's ability to function in a healthy way. Life, unlike a computer keyboard, doesn't come with an "undo" button. Why just recently I'd helped a friend forgive a husband who had a fling with another woman on a sales trip. She'd finally realized that it would be better to accept his abject apology than to continue to seethe with resentment.

But for me, "forgive and forget" didn't seem to be working. I'd had big expectations of my big sister, ever since she had steadied me when we were toddlers riding tricycles together in Grandma's orchard. None of those dreams I'd had of us sharing an ideal lifetime of sisterhood had come true. Now they never would.

Then one afternoon I turned on my car radio and heard the old B.J. Thomas tune, "Another Somebody Done Somebody Wrong Song." I began to giggle. Good grief, I'd fallen into the trap of thinking of myself as The Injured Party.

I turned off the radio. Suddenly another phrase popped into my head: rest in peace.

Why not? If I could concentrate on invoking peace for my sister's soul, maybe I could find peace within myself, the kind that comes with letting go.

Right then I took a deep breath. I repeated to myself, "rest in peace, rest in peace, rest in peace."

Peace came. I remembered my sister when we were children again, pushing our twin baby dolls around Grandma's orchard in their tiny buggies. We'd been close for those first few years. I have chosen to remember her that way. So rest in peace, my sister. Rest in peace, and I will too.

I can practice what I preach.

~Terri Elders

I Make Up

Having a sister is like having a best friend you can't get rid of.
You know whatever you do, they'll still be there.

~Amy Li

I n the best of times, we were a unit: close, connected, loving, and always there for each other. My relationship with "Big," the silly name I called my tiny older sister Ruthie, has been a constant in my life, a steady anchor, and fixed point in a whirling universe.

Sure, we had our battles growing up in bedrooms next to one another. There was plenty of sound and fury over who owned which sweater and who had neglected the daily job of washing and drying the dinner dishes.

But those scuffles ended quickly because we had a mother who didn't tolerate the foolishness of embattled daughters. When the going got rough, she would have us face each other, noting that she didn't care who was presumably wrong and who was presumably right. She had us hold out our hands and say the simple words "I make up!"

And as soon as we did, the magic worked. We were back in each other's rooms—and lives.

We even went to the same college, with me trailing two years behind her. We took courses together, studied for finals together, and ultimately married in the same synagogue, sure our unions would be forever.

Mine has been, if fifty-three years counts as "forever."

Ruthie's lasted only four.

Our lives, once so similar, began to diverge. But nothing, we resolved, would damage what we had.

We had sister spa weekends, mutual friends that made sisterhood even more special, and then our "twin" careers as writers.

I generally wrote about hearth and home; Ruthie traveled the world and shared her adventures in faraway places.

When our father died suddenly, we mourned together. Ruthie, the "rational" sister, and I, the "emotional" sister, had different ways to mourn, but thankfully, we could still share loss and grief.

Then along came our most monumental challenge. Our mother — our remarkable mother who had survived two husbands, a challenging career and reasonably good health and independence for nearly ninety-four years — had a recurrence of the lymphoma that she had fought off a decade before. This time it was back with a vengeance.

Mom had already had the mild antibody treatments that had carried her through several months. But now they were no longer an option. Now, it was a matter of choosing heavy-duty chemo or rejecting it and saying, "Enough!" At ninety-four, she finally began to lean on us, her daughters, for help in decision-making.

I will never forget the phone call that began a siege unprecedented in our sibling history.

It came after a particularly sensitive office visit with Mom's oncologist. This dear man, who had come to love Mom had told her that she needed to decide soon. My sister wanted her to opt for chemotherapy. She strongly believed that where there's life, there's hope. On the other hand, I was increasingly making peace with the concept of having Mom enter hospice care for palliative help so she could go in peace.

My sister and I fought through that terrible time. We had faced so many other rocky times together, but this time we became unglued, undone and ultimately torn asunder.

There was no banging of doors like those that echoed through our teen years. There was, instead, a terrible week that felt like a year of tangled feelings.

We became intransigent in our positions. And on one terrible afternoon, we faced each other across coffee cups and then stalked away, each of us retreating to her corner.

And my mother, bless her, sensed what was going on and announced that she was making her own decision. And it was to cease treatment.

Was it a victory for me? Maybe. Maybe not.

Was it a defeat for my sister? Maybe. Maybe not.

How would we ever forgive and forget this war with such high sister stakes?

Mom died peacefully just a few weeks after the hospice angels saw to her last days. My sister struggled with the what-ifs as we planned her simple graveside funeral.

We spoke civilly, calmly, but Ruthie and I both knew that the stakes were even higher now. Without Mom, we might drift into a new and potentially permanent coolness.

On the unseasonably warm December day of Mom's graveside funeral, we stood by our mother's grave, two sisters who had loved a mother—and each other—dearly and deeply.

We stood apart as the mourners gathered around the simple pine coffin that would be lowered into the ground.

Neither of us could possibly pinpoint who made the first gesture. It seemed to come spontaneously at the same instant.

In the noonday sun of that winter day, we approached one another, arms outstretched, and just stood, holding one another for dear life. "I make up," we said through sobs.

Forgiveness had come in a great gulp of pain and hope. It had come just as the woman who had given us life was about to be lowered into the earth.

We both like to believe that Mom left us knowing that her daughters said those childhood words, simple—and profound—as they were: "I make up!"

~Sally Friedman

Heavenly Forgiveness

You know you really love someone,
when you can't hate them for breaking your heart...
~Author Unknown

My older brother, Paul, had a very troubled life. We moved around a lot as children, partly because my parents were always trying to get him away from what they called a "bad element." After moving fifteen times, they reluctantly admitted that he was the bad element. When he couldn't find trouble in a new location he created it.

There were some whoppers. Like the day he came home with soot on his hands and told my parents it was only dirt. Later they saw an article in the local paper about a mysterious fire in the back yard of an abandoned house down the street. There were constant reports of school fights and disruptive behavior in class. Paul's black eyes actually overlapped. He always had a fresh one while the last one was yellowing.

I was shy and grew accustomed to my parents giving more attention to Paul because of his bad behavior.

My brother and I played together a lot as young children, but around the time that he became a teenager, he started using alcohol and marijuana and changed drastically. The brother I knew, who had always protected me from bullies, began to bully me severely. I didn't understand what was happening to him.

Many people scoff at the idea that marijuana is a gateway drug, but in my brother's case it was absolutely true. When he was sixteen, I was skateboarding with friends when one said to me, "Isn't that your brother?" I saw Paul across the street, skipping along the sidewalk and singing, clearly high as a kite. He saw me and came over. Nothing he said made any sense. He was like a different person. I was terrified. He was my brother but not my brother.

Eventually, he started using heroin and spent a total of eight years in jail for drug-related offenses, including burglary of a pharmacy. He was shot in the ankle during that arrest. The officer was either a bad shot or merciful.

I wasn't perfect but I avoided drugs, mainly as a result of seeing Paul's life deteriorate. I also didn't want to add to our parents' pain.

One night in a supermarket parking lot I heard a familiar voice behind me and turned to see Paul shaking down an elderly man for change. As drug addicts often do, he had become a panhandler, struggling to get enough money for a fix. The only thing that saved him then was my parents' support. They let him live with them, fearing he would die on the street if they didn't. When he finally moved out, they paid his rent for many more years. It was all for naught, however, because he died of a heroin overdose at the age of thirty-seven. It was the grand finale of a lifetime of mayhem and misery.

I had grown increasingly resentful of him over the years. It started with the bullying as children and grew as a teenager when my parents and I visited him in prison. I couldn't believe he was dragging us through that dark world with him. With every tear my mother shed, my resentment and anger grew. The only thing that kept our bond from breaking completely was my memory of the brother who played with me in the sun as kids, who consoled me when I cried, and with whom I shared an identical sense of humor. In fact, our ability to laugh together was the last connection we had in his most troubled years. There were moments between bullying sessions when he was a lot of fun to be with and we laughed ourselves sick. He was the only sibling I had, so I was always eager to connect with him.

When we got older, I spent countless hours talking with him, struggling to find the right words to divert him from the destructive path he was on. He always hugged and thanked me, but he never changed. During the last year of his life, I stopped talking to him completely. It hurt me to abandon him, but I was desperate and thought I would try "tough love" for a change. I had already tried everything else.

When he died, I felt guilty for two reasons—I never forgave him for the pain he caused my parents and me, and I couldn't forgive myself for not being there for him at the end. I couldn't stop thinking that abandoning him added to his pain and made him more careless, or that I might have been able to save him somehow if I had been accessible to him. For months after he died, I buried my grief under anger. When it finally subsided, I prayed for his soul and asked him to forgive me, hoping he could hear me somehow.

He never talked about it, but he had become a Christian in prison. I only knew this because of a journal I found in his apartment after he died in which he had written, "I can't win this fight. I'm laying it all down at the foot of the old rugged cross," referencing an old hymn. On another page, he had written about feeling guilty for not being a better brother to me. He ended this passage with, "Despite it all, I love Mark and I know he loves me, too." I tore that page out and carry it in my wallet to this day, fifteen years later. There were also many rambling entries about his past and present problems.

A month or so after he died, I took the journal to his grave and burned it page by page, hoping the smoke would reach him in heaven, and praying to him to let go of all the pain and confusion those pages represented.

I have always imagined heaven as a place where our pain-filled bodies fall away like worn-out clothes, where sadness is washed away, and where we forgive others and ourselves for our mistakes in life. I can't imagine we bring all our mortal pettiness with us or heaven would be as full of misery as earth is. As Colossians 1:13-14 says, "For he has rescued us from the dominion of darkness and brought us into the kingdom of the Son he loves, in whom we have redemption, the forgiveness of sins."

One night, I had a dream that Paul and I were on a beach where we had spent many happy days as children. In life, he was heavily tattooed from his time in prison and had lost most of his teeth from drug use, but in my dream he looked pristine and healthy. He said, "Mark, stop torturing yourself. Of course I forgive you. You didn't do anything wrong. I made the mistakes, not you. You were just trying to save me."

I hugged him and cried. I told him I forgave him too, and begged him to let me take him to my parents because they needed him back so desperately. He said, "I can't. I have a new home now." I asked where. He smiled and looked up. It was a smile filled with the peace he was never able to find in mortal life. I just kept hugging him and crying, afraid if I let him go he would be gone again. I woke up heartbroken that it was only a dream, but with a heart lighter than it had been since he died. I felt like I had just seen him again.

The psychologist Sigmund Freud said one of the main purposes of dreams is wish fulfillment. Since there is no greater wish than to see our lost loved ones just one more time and make peace with them, I know there may be no supernatural reason for this dream. Nevertheless, I choose to believe that my brother came to me that night to ease my pain, and perhaps his own.

In the years since, as I have meditated about that dream, I have often thought about the many times he and I argued, and how we had always forgiven each other afterward no matter how upset we had become. Why wouldn't he forgive me from his "new home" as I had forgiven him? As his journal entry said, despite it all, he always knew I loved him. No matter how messy life gets, in the end, love is all that matters, and all we take with us. There is no need to beg those we have lost for forgiveness. It comes naturally in heaven.

~Mark Rickerby

Moving Past the Past

Forgiveness means letting go of the past.
~Gerald Jampolsky

"I gave you one with Melvin's signature on it. You remember don't you? The oil painting with a goat in it."

"Sorry, Nita, but you never gave me such a painting or any painting for that matter." I looked at my wife and she nodded in agreement. "And we don't have any with goats on them." Uncle Melvin was an accomplished artist, especially with oils, and Laura and I had always wanted one of his fabulous landscapes. That's why I commissioned him to paint one, a western scene with relatives around a campfire.

"Well, you probably lost it then," Nita replied, "or gave it away to someone."

"No, we never lost it or gave it away because we never had it in the first place." The bickering with my sister escalated tensions in the room and pushed my patience to the limit.

"Well, all I know is that you had one."

"That's it, Nita! I'm done!" There was no reasoning with her. My stomach hurt and I had a headache. Disagreeing with each other had become part of every family holiday gathering since Mom died. I stormed out of Nita's front door on Thanksgiving Day. Arguing over whether I ever owned a certain painting from my uncle had turned from ridiculous to impossible, dredging up past hurts. "I'm out of here, and I'm not coming back."

As I drove home that afternoon, my mind played back the unresolved issues from our childhood. There were many of them: some silly, others serious. Fighting over seating positions in our car was a little of both. Thinking they could settle the problem, our parents assigned us to opposite sides in the back seat. Beads of vinyl divided the sections. My section was on the right, hers on the left. The middle area served as a demilitarized zone to separate enemy combatants. We were not allowed to cross it.

Nita would sit as close as possible to her boundary and then move her little finger across the forbidden zone. When I yelled that Nita had crossed the line, Mom and Dad would turn around to catch the culprit. However, just before they did, my sister would move her finger back as if nothing had happened. She would look at them with those innocent eyes, and swear, "I've been on my side the whole time." That was a lie, of course, or at least a half truth. All I knew was that I needed to even the score. Our foolish confrontations escalated year after year—and so did my resentment.

I suppose one should be thankful on Thanksgiving, but I didn't feel that way. After the big upset with my sister, I just wanted to get home, fast. Fortunately, I only encountered one stoplight—at the light rail crossing on SE Burnside Avenue. While waiting for the MAX train to clear the station, I turned on the radio, trying to drown out my thoughts. Maybe it was the music or seeing the train, but something jogged my memory, taking me back to the week our sibling rivalry had turned ugly.

Nita had received a gift that week, a new GE clock radio. From then on, she played her obnoxious rock music constantly. It bugged me and she knew it. According to the house rules, she needed to shut down her music at bedtime—but that seldom happened. If I yelled for the parental police, she would turn the radio off before they entered the playroom, adjacent to our Jack and Jill bedrooms.

One night, I heard static on her radio when I switched off my desk lamp. Then I tried it again—more crackling. I soon realized that if I turned the lamp switch halfway on, the flickering light bulb would create static on her radio. The tables had turned now and Nita became the victim, complaining that I had somehow jammed her radio. I guess I'm not a good liar, because I was deemed guilty and grounded for two weeks. Nita, of course, received no punishment at all. No matter, a payback plan was in the works.

Two nights later, I lay awake in bed, waiting for Nita to finally turn off her radio and fall asleep. Slowly, I slipped out of bed and tiptoed to my closet. Underneath the laundry box was my Lionel train set. Working quietly, I opened the box and pieced the O gauge track together, section by section, and eased it out my door into the playroom. I had just enough track to reach my sister's room on the other side.

Leaving the other freight cars in the box, I placed my Steam Locomotive #2018 on the track and attached the coal car, my whistling tender. I plugged in the transformer and made sure the wires were connected correctly. With everything set, my engine left the station in my room and slowly moved down the line to Nita's room. Then, with the electrical power at full throttle, I hit the whistle lever on the transformer. The sound pierced the silence. I heard Nita scream and jump out of bed. I tried to reverse the engine and bring it back before she knew what had happened. However, the extra power derailed my engine in the middle of the playroom. My train, of course, was confiscated and given to charity.

The retribution was sweet, but I had allowed something much worse to take root. As the years passed, our sibling relationship grew cold. Resentment and animosity lay just below the surface. I became offended at almost everything she said or did. Our once loving relationship became one of contention and ill will. The root of the problem was lack of forgiveness. Although neither of us would admit it, we were both infected with it.

I avoided family gatherings after the Thanksgiving Day fiasco. I made up excuses, but everyone knew the real reason. I had grown frustrated with all the bickering, fabricated stories, and endless conflicts. Trying to deal with the issues just brought old wounds to the surface again. I needed a solution that would help restore our relationship.

After some serious prayer and contemplation, I suggested a new strategy—that we take each other out to dinner on our birthdays—no gifts, no rehashing past issues, no teasing, just a pleasant dinner and some friendly conversation. The first time was a little awkward for both of us, but each year it became a little easier. Now we look forward to it.

I think forgiveness is a commitment to move beyond the past and start fresh. By establishing our new tradition, my sister and I made a similar commitment. It helped us reconnect, experience forgiveness, and find healing for our relationship. Forgiveness is a powerful force. It can release people from a prison of bitterness, resentment, or whatever else that holds them captive. And it doesn't take two to forgive. One is enough to begin the process. I never asked my sister to reciprocate. I simply forgave her and offered a long overdue apology.

My lack of forgiveness is gone now. Knowing the damage it can cause, I will never give it a foothold again.

~Charles Earl Harrel

He's My Brother

Life is too short to hold a grudge, also too long.
~Robert Brault

Like the Christmas before, we didn't send Christmas cards; we called my family in Canada. Ginny and I talked to my mom. We spoke to my uncles and aunts. I hadn't seen any of them in seven years and Ginny hadn't met them yet, but she hoped to one day.

Those calls were completed, but I couldn't relax. I still had one more call to make, and I was afraid. I paced the house. I wasted time at my computer. I needed to call but I couldn't.

Five years before, I had received an e-mail from my brother. At the time, I had been out of work for several months. My life was very stressful. My brother's e-mail was nothing terrible but it made me angry.

I wrote back. As I typed, my anger grew. Months of frustration flowed into my nasty response. I said things that were not nice, but I hit send anyway. More thoughts occurred to me. I wrote a second nasty e-mail.

I basically told my brother to go to hell. I didn't care if I ever heard from him again.

The next day I received another e-mail from him. I didn't read it. I just deleted it, and then I blocked his e-mail address.

For five years, he tried to get through to me but I ignored him. I had lived with this terrible guilt. I thought about contacting him, but was ashamed of myself for what I'd said.

It was time to fix it. I picked up the phone and stepped outside. I wanted privacy. Ginny didn't know I was calling my brother. I took a deep breath, blew out a cloud of my breath into the cold December air, and dialed his number. Even after five years, I still knew it by heart. A phone rang 3,700 miles away in Nova Scotia.

There was no answer. I left a message. "Bob, it's Mike." I paused to take another breath. My hand holding the phone shook. "Bob, I guess I'll start by saying I'm sorry. I said some things I regret. I want to wish you and Delores a Merry Christmas and hope all is well with you. I realize you may not want to talk to me, but I thought I would try. I want to make it right again. If you want to talk…" I left my number.

I walked back into the house and looked at Ginny. "I did it."

She looked puzzled. "You did what?"

"I called Bob."

"Oh, honey!" She walked up to me and put her arms around my neck. "I'm glad. You needed to do it. It's family Mike and it's been too long." She kissed me. "You did right, hun."

Christmas came and went. I waited for the call that never came. I prayed for his forgiveness. The phone didn't ring. Then a week after I called, I received an e-mail. My brother left me a message on my Facebook page. He said he listened to my voice message over and over and knew I was sincere. In the weeks to follow, we e-mailed back and forth. The healing began.

Why had I let five years of my brother's life slip through my fingers? Why was I too proud to call and say I was sorry?

If I had the answers, it would never have happened in the first place, but I knew I don't want it to happen again. I had wrecked my relationship with my brother. Like a jigsaw puzzle that has been dropped, the pieces had scattered everywhere. It was time to gather them up and try to put them back together.

Since then, we have grown close again. Even though I haven't been able to afford the trip home, we are still family.

I swallowed my pride. I did it. Five years was too long. After all, he's my brother.

~Michael T. Smith

I Did Not Understand

The knowledge of the past stays with us. To let go is to release the images and emotions, the grudges and fears, the clingings and disappointments of the past that bind our spirit.
~Jack Kornfield

Dear Rona,

I wish I knew your address in heaven, so I could send this letter of apology directly to you.

I apologize. I apologize for the years I did not understand. I apologize for the years I did not hug you and say, "How can I help you?" or "I'm sorry for what has happened to you," or "I love you."

I did not understand. Please forgive me.

You see, growing up when we did, there was a stigma about mental illness. It wasn't something that happened in a happy functional family. It was the era of institutions, not rehabilitation. Mom and Dad were embarrassed, frightened, and unenlightened. None of us understood what was happening or suspected anything serious. We thought it was a phase, an association with incompatible friends, or the need for a job suitable to your talents. How could we know? Even when we dared to seek counseling, the experts focused on how the family dealt with anger. Why didn't they suspect schizophrenia? It would have saved us from a great deal of agony.

I did not understand. Please forgive me.

I was furious with you. Why did I have to work two jobs when you didn't maintain one job for more than a few weeks? I was told, "There are problems." What problems? There was no diagnosis.

Forgive me if I was impatient when you stole and misused my credit card, or ate dinners I purchased for myself. Forgive me if I screamed, "Get your own life!" after you pleaded with me to take you wherever I went. I didn't know you feared being alone with your voices.

I did not understand. Please forgive me.

When you were finally diagnosed, it explained your behavior but did not make it easier. I lived five hours from you. It was the first year of my marriage, and I was pregnant and a full-time teacher. Mom and Dad protected me. They kept me uninformed. They reassured me they had everything under control and you were being treated by an expert in the field of mental illnesses. When I saw you after your first shock treatment, your robotic movements terrified me. Please forgive me for not hugging you. I thought you might push me to the floor as you had your elderly neighbor.

How could I imagine what it was like to be inside your head and hear voices? How could I understand that it was beyond your control when you threatened people with knives? How could I forgive you when Dad died at age sixty-six from a massive coronary? I blamed you for being a burden on him and Mom. How could I understand that you did not take your medication because you disliked the side effects? How could I understand that I should listen rather than reason with you when you called to tell me you were pregnant by a movie celebrity? What was I to make of your visions of hair clips dancing on the bureau, the Lone Ranger chasing you, or the refusal to eat my cooking when I knew you loved food? It was hard to comprehend your world of shattered reality and paranoia.

I did not understand. Please forgive me.

Forgive me if my conversations were short and focused on the weather when I visited you. I was afraid I might say something that would trigger a flare up, and I didn't want to be a victim of your venom. I walked on eggs. I feared that if I stepped too heavily, the shell might crack and the yolk break.

A few years ago, Mom made a collage that hangs on her bedroom wall. I stare at it when I visit her. I study each photo. I search for clues. Which photo is you? Is it the three-year-old clutching a toy doggie while a photographer wipes away your tears? Is it the five-year-old with blond pigtails poised on the seesaw opposite me? We are frozen in a moment of equilibrium before we teeter on the fulcrum. Is it the teenager with a well-proportioned figure, playful smile and twinkle in her eyes, posed in front of the lifeguard stand? Is it the performer who, à la Ethel Merman, belted out songs that reached the rear row of an auditorium and brought audiences to their feet with applause? Is it the last photo of you as a young professional, with white cotton gloves, bouffant hairdo, and a pastel blue linen suit, preened and ready for Daddy to drive you to your first job at an insurance company?

There are no signs in these photos of demons or of a body and mind ravaged by a disease. The photo of you as a 180-pound woman with a forced smile, stringy grayish blond hair, and a face distorted from medication is hidden in a desk drawer. I often look at that photo, because it reminds me of the cruelty of mental illness. Forgive me for storing that image in my internal camera. Forgive me for not hugging that body. I forget that you were once well groomed and beautiful.

I did not understand. Please forgive me.

I asked you to forgive me when you were dying, but you were in a coma, so I don't know if you heard me. Maybe you did hear me but were unable to forgive me because I allowed Mom to halt an inquiry into the cause of your cardiac arrest. I wanted to pursue it. There was a rumor that the nursing home was negligent. Maybe you did hear me, but could not forgive me because I agreed with Mom to remove the life support equipment. Did you think we were doing it for selfish motives so we wouldn't have to tend to you any longer? We wouldn't have to deal with your phone calls on nights with full moons, or seek a new residence for you after each release from a hospital? The doctors declared you brain dead. No recovery. No reversal. Besides, you looked so peaceful in the bed. No twitches. No outward indication of inner turmoil or voices. Peaceful with hazel eyes staring straight ahead. I assumed you'd be happier. But who was I to decide whether you would be happier dead or alive? Maybe you had the right to live and be happy, even if you were a menace to people and your day focused on food and sleep. Who was I to define happiness for someone who is a schizophrenic?

I did not understand. Please forgive me.

I hope you are well in heaven. I hope you are singing in harmony with the angels. I hope they are keeping the demons away from you and that you rest peacefully.

Love,
Lois

~Lois Kipnis

Chapter
5

The Power *of* Forgiveness

When Bad Things Happen in Love and Marriage

Lord, make me an instrument of your peace,
where there is hatred, let me sow love;
where there is injury, pardon; ...
For it is in giving that we receive;
it is in pardoning that we are pardoned.

~attributed to St. Francis of Assisi

Forgiveness Is Possible

Do all things with love... keep your love in your heart. Being deeply loved by someone gives you strength, while loving someone deeply gives you courage.
~Jackielou Camacho

I t was November 2011 and I was driving home from a very long day at the office. When a call from my ex-husband interrupted the blissful silence of my drive, I wondered if I was ready for one of his raging phone calls. We had divorced six years earlier, and unfortunately his anger toward me for the divorce had not softened. We only spoke to each other if absolutely necessary. I hesitantly answered the phone. I hoped my chipper attitude would help set the tone for our exchange.

His words took my breath away. He had stage IV esophageal and stomach cancer.

All I was able to whisper was, "I am sorry, so sorry."

Tears stung my eyes as I thought of our children who were seventeen and fifteen, too young to lose a father. My head swam with questions as I pulled into my driveway. How would the children handle the loss of their father? Who would take care of him? I ran into the house as I retched up my lunch. My head hung over the toilet bowel as tears streamed down my face.

My phone rang again; it was my real estate agent. I was numb from my ex-husband's news when she excitedly told me there was an offer on my home.

"That's great," I mumbled.

As I hung up the phone, I wondered about the statistical probability that I would receive an offer on my home the same night that my ex-husband was diagnosed with terminal cancer? My house had been on the market for three years. Clearly the universe had spoken to me. In that moment I knew what I needed to do.

I resolved to move the children and myself in with him. I had faith that this would be a turning point for my ex-husband, and he would embrace spending quality time with our children. They would have the opportunity to know their father. I worried the caretaker role would fall on my daughter otherwise. If we moved in together, I could assume this role so my children would not be burdened with the responsibility.

Despite my resolve, I was concerned. I had worked so hard to divorce my husband and the process had been scary. How could I live with him again? Everyone thought my idea was crazy, even our children.

We moved in just before Christmas and began a sophisticated dance of living as a family unit once again. The children had spent very little time with their father in the years since our divorce, with infrequent visitation. My hope was that they would have the opportunity to get to know their father and reconnect. We would live together for the next ten months. It was not easy. We had our share of tender moments and we had our share of meltdowns.

A few months into living together, the stress began to take a toll on me. Each day his actions and behavior brought up old hurts and wounds from the past. The anxiety-related anger and hostility created irregular heart rhythms. I was reliving our history each day. I knew I must do something to break the cycle. I had to find forgiveness.

Over the next few weeks, I searched for answers on the Internet and in bookstores, but nothing resonated with me. I was desperate to block the pain of the past. I wanted to stop replaying the old movies from years ago that were triggering my emotions. While I could not control his actions, I could control my emotions. I could chose to feel like a victim or embrace happiness and separate myself from his behavior.

We are a product of our lifetime of experiences, and his shaped his choices. He grew up angry, defensive and afraid. Every bad choice he made was driven by his fear. The minute I stopped judging my ex-husband's actions, I broke the link between his behaviors and my emotions. When I could view his actions without judging them, I no longer felt any emotion toward his conduct. By separating his actions from my emotions, I created space in my heart where I planted the seeds of empathy and compassion, and forgiveness began to grow.

My days became happier and calmer. Peace filled the house as forgiveness took root. I often felt as though my energy was reverberating at a higher, more harmonious level, which gave me strength.

It is easy to say the words, "I forgive," but they have no impact if your actions are not aligned with your thoughts. So I began to place the intention of forgiveness into every daily chore and interaction. Cooking has always been the way I demonstrated love for my family and friends. As the end approached, I hosted many lunches and dinners for friends and family in our home so they could say their goodbyes.

The payoff came one bright sunny morning just a few weeks before he passed. We were preparing for the last set of guests to arrive. Only family would be allowed to visit after this day. He thanked me for entertaining the multitude of friends over the last week. As he left the room, he turned and said he loved me and without thinking I responded, "I love you too."

I was stunned as the reality of my words sunk in. It was an honest moment, and I did love him. Not as my husband, but as the father of our children. I loved him for just being a human being, a child of God. Forgiveness had given me the ability to stop judging him and accept him for who he was. I was finally at peace with our past. It was time to let go of our history, so we could both move on. A warm glow washed over me, filled with the power of grace and forgiveness.

Just three weeks later, he passed peacefully at home early one morning in his bedroom with our family dog by his side.

Today both our children are in college and embracing life without their father. The time we spent together building positive memories as a family has helped to soften the grief process for them. Most importantly, we have experienced the power of forgiveness.

~Karen Todd Scarpulla

A Family Serving Time

Forgive, not because they deserve forgiveness,
but because you deserve peace.
~Author Unknown

"I'm having an affair with your husband." I clenched the phone as my stomach churned. Her voice was childlike, teasing, taunting. In the silence I could hear her breathing on the other end of the line.

"That's impossible," I uttered, glancing at my two children playing in the next room. "John would never do that. Why are you saying this to me?"

I heard her laugh as I swallowed back something sour. After so many hang-up calls over the last several months, I went numb simply hearing a voice. It was a sick joke. I should have slammed the receiver down, but something told me this was more than a prank. Why would she have targeted me for so long?

"I can tell you where you can find us together," she continued. "We're always at my apartment or in the park during his lunch break. I can show you cards he's given me and I have his blue jacket. I've got all the proof you need."

Tears blurred my vision as I began to believe her. There seemed to be no air to breathe. "Do you have sex with my husband? He works sixty hours a week. He always comes right home to me, so I don't see how..."

"Oh, yes." She laughed again. "We have lots and lots of sex."

I could barely respond. Only one more question came to mind. "Does he love you?"

For some reason, that must have been her weak spot. She didn't respond at first, just peppered the silence with her breathing. I heard a shuffle, as if she changed the phone from one hand to another.

"Does he love you?" I shouted, aware of both of my children standing in the doorway staring at Mommy as tears of bewilderment ran down my cheeks.

She paused again as if her answer actually pained her. "No," she stated matter-of-factly. "He doesn't love me... he loves you."

I couldn't take any more. It felt like a cruel game of cat and mouse. I hung up on her and brushed my tears away. Thirteen years of marriage were crumbling around me. Our little girls, Mariah who was two years old, and Vanessa who was ten, came up to hug me and ask what was wrong. I pasted on a smile and told them Mommy was fine and to please go back to playing in the other room. Once they did as they were told, I dialed my husband at work and exploded in a way I didn't recognize. I shouted that I knew his secrets. I sobbed and asked how he could do this to his family. I expected him to say it was all some mistake, but instead he sounded defeated.

"I'm coming home," he said in a tone that ran chills up my spine. "Just try to stay calm. I'm leaving now, so we'll talk when I get there."

But, my husband never did come home. Not hours later when I put the girls to bed, not in the dark hours of the night as I waited by the window, and not in the early morning hours when something told me to call 911. I had a cold feeling that my husband had taken his own life instead of mustering the courage to tell me his soiled truths.

It took hours, but the Mansfield, Ohio police detectives finally came to my house and told me what they learned. John had gone to this young girl's college where she was on break between classes, argued with her as she sat in her car, then shot her multiple times in front of everyone. My best friend, my soul mate, the father of my children, was in the county jail charged with murdering his mistress. When his trial came up nearly a year later, his sentence was eighteen years to life. I remember leaving the courtroom on rubbery legs, choking back sobs as they led John off in shackles. His attorney came up and patted me on the back.

"He won't serve that long," he said, as if this was a football game his team had just lost. "With good behavior, he'll be out in eight to ten."

The pain went so deep that even after the girls and I moved from Ohio to Florida to be near to my parents for moral support, only alcohol and sleeping pills got me through each day. I was a single mother with a shattered heart and more questions than answers. I had two beautiful girls who were hurting right along with me. Mariah clung to me every day, afraid I'd disappear just like Daddy if she let me out of her sight. Vanessa was mostly angry, needing to take a break from school due to stomach issues. Counseling was merely a Band-Aid over a wound that went too deep to heal.

After months and months of falling deeper into depression, I decided to take my own life. I couldn't stand another day of this horrific pain. I could no longer be a good mother. The girls would go to my sister if I died. She was married and had a lovely home an hour away in Orlando. The girls would have a better chance that way.

On the last night of my life, I placed my hands together and prayed that God would give me the strength for what I was about to do. I prayed my daughters would one day understand. I didn't want to feel anymore.

That morning I awoke to a peculiar sensation. I felt light, calm. I soaked in the sunshine spilling through the curtains. Something that felt like hope had sprung up, despite my confusion. Then a whisper spoke to my heart as if it were the response to my prayer the night before. It told me that suicide isn't the way to stop the hurting. The way to stop the pain was to forgive.

It was in that moment that I realized the true meaning of the word. To forgive wasn't a gift to John, but a miracle I could give to the girls and myself. It would free us of the past, release all the pain and open the door to a brand new future.

Forgiving isn't easy. It isn't something you decide to do and every-thing magically goes away. It takes work and you have to fight for it. But if you hold onto it with both hands, you can free yourself from the prison you were locked in. The key is in your hand and once you make the choice to use it, you've done the most important thing of all. A new life awaits, no matter what you've been through, as long as you give yourself the gift of forgiving.

~Diane Nichols

How to Heal a Family

...and forgive us our trespasses as we forgive those who trespass against us,...
~Gospel of Matthew

Once upon a time I was married and everything seemed wonderful. Until it wasn't. My husband and I went from love to separation. It was a difficult time.

Our custody agreement allowed me to move back to my hometown with our son. My ex-husband would get holiday and summer visits. Years passed and my ex and I never talked. He'd call and ask for our son. I'd pass the phone over and that was it.

As time went on, our son told me that his dad had suggested living with him for a year. I wasn't thrilled about the idea and resisted. However, our son mentioned it several more times until it hit me that maybe he hoped I'd say yes. I thought about what it would be like as the parent with only occasional access, and I realized I could do this difficult thing for our son's sake. Hiding my heartache, I told him he could live with his dad if that's what he really wanted. He looked at me like I'd suggested he live on the moon, firmly replying: "No Mom, I want to live with you." I felt something rush out of me, a fear I'd held for far too long, and realized something had to change in this broken family.

I wrote a letter to his dad, forgiving him both a monetary debt and past hurts, adding that I hoped he'd forgive me too. I wrote that I wished to be at our son's graduation, marriage and special occasions, asking if he wanted that, and noted that it wasn't likely if the cold war continued. I acknowledged that he might not be ready to forgive but that my door would remain open. As that letter dropped into the mailbox, so did my feelings against my ex. I knew then that it didn't matter if he forgave me; that was his choice. But I had freed myself by forgiving him.

I wish I could say the situation resolved within the month. However, years passed with no response to the letter. Other challenging events occurred that indicated my ex wasn't yet on the reconciliation path. But those issues didn't bother me as they once would have.

Then one day he called, and I heard him say my name for the first time in years. I offered to get our son, but he stopped me, saying he had called for me. I was shocked yet thrilled. I'd waited so long for this and it felt like the next step toward fixing what we'd broken. We chatted about our child for a half hour and I thanked him for calling, recognizing that he cared as much about our son as I did.

As the call ended, the office door swung open. In rushed our son, who'd overheard my side of the conversation. With an incredulous look on his face, he asked, "Was that Dad?" I nodded and he threw himself into my arms, hugging me for all he was worth. I realized then just how hard our delay in forgiveness had been on our young son, who'd shown such a happy face to the world. I spent the next few years apologizing to him (until he begged me to stop).

Now, long before our son's graduation, something so serious happened that it brought my ex across the country to where we lived. Our son needed open-heart surgery. Family members from both sides joined us and we met at Children's Hospital at dawn on the day of his surgery. It was our first time together since our son entered primary school. The meeting was cordial, with our son's huge courage and excellent sense of humour helping everyone through the next hour. When it was time for him to go into pre-op, the surgeon asked if he was ready. "Cut me, Doc," was his response. He'd already asked for the Harry Potter cut.

Despite this, it wasn't easy saying goodbye to our son, not knowing if we'd see him again. He was wheeled away while the hospital staff escorted us to separate waiting rooms—one for his dad's side of the family, one for mine.

The procedure was to take eight hours. After a few hours, I went to a nearby church, inviting my ex's family to come along. They did, and though we sat in separate pews praying for the success of this dangerous surgery, it still felt like we were getting closer.

We happened to be in the same waiting room when the door opened and the surgeon walked in several hours later. The moment seemed suspended in time while we waited for him to speak. With a brisk nod, he said: "He made it through surgery—it went well." My heart could have exploded with joy at this news and I fervently thanked God.

My ex and I were allowed into post-op where we learned that the next twenty-four hours were critical. If our son made it through that time, his chances of living would improve exponentially each day. It was difficult to see him lying there with a tube down his throat and several intravenous drips and high-tech monitoring gadgets attached to him in various places. The data from these flashed onto machines and computer screens behind his bed. Suddenly something went wrong. An alarm sounded, and my ex and I were pulled out of the way as the doctor and nurses rushed to our son's bedside. I felt numb with fear, my throat closing up and my body tightening into a knot.

"How much blood did he get?" the surgeon snapped, his face registering deep concern. Someone yelled, "Two pints!"

"Give him the third!" came the command. Instantly another bag filled with blood, one of three I'd donated over the course of several weeks, was inserted into the intravenous line. The surgeon carefully watched the screen that had first raised the alarm. He finally relaxed as it began to register that the most precious heart in the world to me was beating more steadily. He turned to us, explaining that usually only two of the three pints kept ready for this type of surgery were necessary. Our son's case was the exception.

I suddenly become conscious that my ex and I had been clinging to each other throughout this crisis. In that moment it didn't matter who had failed whom, but only that our son's parents were there for him. We looked at each other and hugged, a genuine hug of caring and joy that our son was alive. In those brief, terrifying moments, our broken family was finally healed.

~Cecilia Heather MacDonald

True Forgiveness

Prayer requires more of the heart than of the tongue.
~Adam Clarke

"I forgive you." I said it long before I meant it.

The claim confused my estranged husband. "How? Why?" he asked.

"Because I'm supposed to. But I do—I forgive you."

After finding that my husband of twenty-eight years had strayed into the arms of another, my emotions were all over the place: fear, hate, heartbreak and bitterness.

I had read and studied enough to know forgiveness was always the right thing to do. I knew I had to forgive; I just didn't know how. Still, I repeated it to him often, "I forgive you," hoping it would stick and become true at some point.

I didn't convince him. Mainly because I hadn't yet convinced myself.

For the longest time I satisfied my conscience by pretending to forgive. My hurt still felt too deep and fresh to absolve him. Besides, his choices had disrupted my life so much that I had no desire to forget any time soon.

Many months later, as I drove to town flipping through radio stations I stumbled upon a teaching already in progress.

"Not forgiving gives the bad guy control over you, your feelings, and your actions…" The unidentified speaker offered examples and his message intrigued me, so I pulled into a parking lot to hear more.

"Holding a grudge never affects the offender in any way. It's us, the hurt ones, who stand to forfeit the most."

I searched for a pen and wrote furiously, trying to capture the message on the back of a grocery receipt. The pastor's list continued.

"Number five. Forgiveness has nothing to do with who was right or wrong, who did what, or who started it. Forgiveness is a choice you make, allowing God to handle it. Six. Forgiveness frees the one who forgives."

Hmm… that was interesting.

As the speaker pointed to scripture, I stopped listening to think. Had I given control of my life to my soon-to-be-ex-husband simply by not forgiving him completely?

Just a week prior, my friend and I had driven around the parking lot of an Olive Garden three times, making sure my husband's car wasn't there. And when he hinted he might stop by one night I didn't want the drama, so I turned off all the lights and faked sleep. Yep, he had control of my life!

"Eight." The pastor captured my attention again. "Forgiveness does not mean you forget—there are lessons to be learned and kept. Nine, forgiveness does not mean you have to maintain a relationship with that person, but rather, you trust God to make the relationship what He desires."

I reached over to turn down the volume. I had heard enough. I leaned my head into the steering wheel. "Father, how many times have you forgiven me? Your forgiveness is continual and without exception. I never deserve to be forgiven, yet you do so freely and often. I want to forgive him, but I need your help. I do not want to carry vengeance in my heart a second longer. Please don't let me default into a negative spin of disobedience after you have brought me this far in the healing process. Help me to forgive him. And her. I forgive them both. I forgive."

I leaned back in my seat and took a deep breath. The radio pastor's voice droned on and I caught his concluding words: "There is a test for forgiveness…" I turned up the volume again, and grabbed the paper receipt and pen. "If you can pray God's blessings on the person who offended or hurt you, only then have you adequately forgiven him."

I bowed my head once more. Every good and perfect thing—all the blessings—I usually prayed for those I loved, I now prayed for those who had hurt me most. It was a practice I would continue for years.

True forgiveness completed.

~Cynthia Mendenhall

The Path to Wholeness

I wanted revenge. I needed vindication. While the real estate agents at work hurried around me to meet clients and show houses I daydreamed about ramming my car into the front steps of the house where my husband and his male lover lived. I wanted to show how angry I was. For a couple of months, I fought the urge to call and scream at him. Resentment was clinging to me like a leech.

Then one night I woke around 3 a.m., shaking in the darkness. Beads of perspiration formed on my forehead and my heart raced as I sat up in bed. I took short, forced breaths and braced myself, palms down on the mattress. It took a moment for my mind to be clear enough to recall the dream I'd just had. I shuddered as the images replayed in my mind.

In my dream, I'd walked through our home looking into every room. I peered around door jams, walked into the bedrooms, climbed up and down the stairs repeatedly. Slowly, I made my way around, trying to find my husband. I was frustrated. Where was he hiding? Why couldn't I find him?

As I remembered the dream, my heart raced faster. Scenes flashed before me and I winced as I saw myself clutching the handle of a large silver knife. I was hunting my husband to kill him. My fury had grown to the point of wanting to murder the man who had deserted my children and me and had hurt us so deeply. The dream frightened me enough that I called my counselor the next morning and made an appointment.

"I'm capable of murder!" I cried, as I sat in the armchair in her office and shared the dream with her.

"You're capable of dreaming about murder," she replied.

"But I wanted to kill him!" I said. "And I don't know what to do with what I'm feeling."

"What are you feeling?"

I hesitated and stuttered as I attempted to speak.

"I h-hate him." I paused at the sound of my voice uttering those words. They sent chills down my spine as I continued. "I'm not supposed to hate."

In her usual calm, unruffled, and reassuring tone, she said, "Don't you think God knows how you feel, Annalee? Confess it to Him and ask for help so you can come to forgiveness."

"I don't know how to get to forgiveness," I said. "But I don't want hatred in my heart either. I don't like how this feels!"

"Are you willing to forgive?" my counselor asked.

"I don't know. Not yet."

"Let me ask you this. Are you willing to be willing to forgive?"

I put my head down and thought for a moment. I could handle that much.

"Yes, I'm willing to be willing."

"Then give your anger to God," she said.

"But how do I give up the anger I feel? I have a right to be angry."

"Yes," my counselor replied. "You have a right to be angry, but do you want the consequences of allowing it to consume you? Perhaps if you give up the anger, there'll be nothing left of the relationship. Could that be why you're holding onto it?"

Tears flowed as I reached for a tissue on the end table next to my chair. I looked up at her and knew she'd touched on something deep in my heart. I wasn't willing to give up what I felt because it was all I had left of the marriage. If I let go of the anger and resentment, there would be nothing left. And I needed something to keep me connected, even if it was a life-controlling negative emotion. I had spent twenty years being one with my husband. Part of my identity was being his wife. Who would I be if he were no longer in my life?

I went home and lay face down on the living room floor. Confessing my hatred and lack of forgiveness, I asked God to remove it from my heart and help me to forgive.

I sobbed. I groaned. I felt like I was wrestling with an unseen demon. The muscles in my arms and legs ached as if I'd been running up hill while carrying a cinder block.

I waited for a few minutes before getting up. I expected an immediate feeling of relief but it didn't come. However, in the days that followed, as I continued to repeat that mind and heart commitment to forgive, the anger and bitterness diminished.

It took a few months, but eventually, the feeling of forgiveness came. I was free from the burden of anger that had felt like a rock tied around my neck for so long. I accepted the reality that there was no longer anything to connect me to my husband—and it was okay.

Before long, I understood that forgiveness wasn't for my husband, but for me. It freed me to become all that I could be and to go on in spite of the pain and uncertainty I faced each day. As I let go of the past, the future unfolded before me, surprising me at every turn. I flourished. I went back to college after twenty-three years and finished my bachelor's degree. After a short break, I went on to complete a Master of Divinity degree at seminary on a full scholarship, became ordained and entered church ministry.

Now, when I counsel others who are going through circumstances where they feel they can't forgive, I share my own experience with them. Letting go of unforgiveness and bitterness may feel like death to our souls because it's all we have left to hold onto in a relationship.

But when we find the courage to take the higher road and forgive, we free ourselves to nourish bigger and fuller souls that can guide others to the place of wholeness that we've found.

~Annalee Davis

Roses Don't Bloom Better on the Other Side of the Fence

He who cannot forgive breaks the bridge over which he himself must pass.
~George Herbert

My husband had broken my heart. He and a female coworker had been spending too much time working together, and work time had gradually become play time. I'd had my suspicions that they seemed to enjoy each other's company a little too much. Rick insisted they were just friends. I finally discovered how truly close they were when I had to borrow his cell phone to make a call and found several flirtatious texts.

"She means nothing to me, but I'm so sorry," Rick replied, devastated, when confronted. "It started out harmless, got carried away a little, it was wrong... really I'm so, so sorry... I'll stay away from her... I love you...."

How could he have allowed himself to play with fire, getting that close to another woman instead of valuing what he had with me, and worst of all lying about it? What else didn't I know after sticking beside him for twenty years? Was our relationship worth saving when I could barely stand to look at him for betraying my trust?

With my four children in school, I had just started volunteering with the true love of my life, horses. There was a Christian youth camp with sixty horses nearby that needed all the help it could get, so I began showing up twice a week to help with chores to earn riding privileges. Now that the rug had been pulled out from under me in my personal life, it was a welcome escape to leave a home that didn't feel like a home anymore and spend the day surrounded by animals that provided me with unlimited, unconditional love. On top of that, one of my coworkers provided me with encouragement and lots of laughs to replace the insecurity and tears.

I worked with him side by side, feeding, grooming, and cleaning. He was always patient, always appreciative, always finding the funny side of things at a time when that was exactly what I needed.

When I'd return home in the evening, Rick and I would tiptoe around each other, he embarrassed at what he had done and me seething about it. When we'd try to talk about what went wrong, what exactly happened, what we were going to do about it, it always ended either in shouting matches, tears, or cold shoulders on both sides.

The ranch was my escape. When at the ranch, Coworker and I had coffee breaks together, ran errands, and fixed fences.

"Here's a flower for you," he said, smiling at me as I left the barn one day. He had beautiful, knockout red rose bushes growing in front of his office door, and while picking off dead blooms he had plucked off a perfect one for me. His smile was innocent enough, but something in me flickered as I accepted it. It had been quite a while since Rick had given me anything but grief. I dug out my rose bowl when I got home and placed the flower inside. Every time I looked at it I thought of Coworker and looked forward to seeing him and his horses again.

Once a week I would cut a rose or two from the barn's bushes to replace the first one. It helped me hang on to my utopia from one volunteer day to the next. For his part, Coworker treated me like a sister, close but not too close. He was happily married, twenty years and counting, just like I thought I was until I wasn't. But brotherly love was better than nothing at all.

I finally abandoned this slippery slope one morning when Coworker and I loaded the hay wagon from the loft. The hay barn was deserted. He was on top of the wagon where he placed the last hay bale, then went to climb down but missed a step and landed awkwardly beside me. I reached out to help him balance and he grabbed onto my arm to keep from falling. For just a second, we were suspended in time. In that instant I knew how Rick had felt when he got too close to his coworker and how easy it was to get swept up in the moment. We're all just one decision away from disaster. I could either decide to make Rick suffer or I could learn from his mistakes, forgive him and decide this would go no further.

"Whew, I could have hurt myself!" Like a good husband should, Coworker laughed off whatever had just happened and jumped on the tractor. I climbed onto the back.

"With all your ministry work, do you do marriage counseling?" I asked suddenly, staring off into the field.

"I have in the past," he answered slowly, choosing his words carefully. "Not with friends though. I recommend it, because if someone needs help they should get it."

Rick and I did start counseling sessions with our pastor, started studying marriage manuals together, started sincerely and humbly praying together. We both learned to forgive, to leave the past in the past and go on to a new beginning with renewed respect for each other.

And totally without my prompting, Rick did something unexpected: he planted knockout red rose bushes all along the front of our house. Now once a week I cut off a rose from those bushes and put it in my rose bowl. A bright red rose from my husband to me. Love can bloom forever if we weather the storms.

~Jane Smith

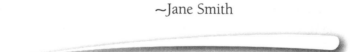

No Apology Necessary

Freedom is the oxygen of the soul.
~Moshe Dayan

"How can I forgive someone who refuses to apologize for what he did?" The woman looked around the room as many of us nodded in agreement. One of those bobbing heads belonged to me.

I was sitting in a church basement in a class called Divorce Care. The class was designed to help people get over one of the most hurtful experiences a person can go through, but so far it hadn't helped me all that much.

A few months before, my ten-year marriage had ended with the stereotypical "I love you, but I'm not in love with you." This bombshell was dropped in a telephone call on a Tuesday morning, four days before Christmas.

It was positively brutal. And when friends began telling me they'd seen my husband out to dinner with another woman, my pain turned into anger.

I'd tried to force him to admit he'd cheated on me, but he insisted he'd met her a few weeks after our split. I didn't believe him. "Don't you even feel bad for what you did to me?" I'd ask. "Don't you think you owe me an apology?"

"You want an apology?" he'd answered. "Okay, here goes: I'm really sorry that you failed to make me happy in our marriage. I'm sorry that your constant concern for our children and negligence toward me made me feel like a fifth wheel in my own home. I'm sorry that you are a poor excuse for a wife and you left me no choice but to leave you."

"Just because a sentence begins with the words 'I'm sorry' does not make it an apology," I said, barely hanging onto my composure.

"Well, I'm sorry that you aren't willing to take responsibility for the failure of our marriage," he said. "Because it is your fault."

I hung up and dissolved into tears.

To this day, those words are the only "apology" I've ever been given for ending a ten-year marriage that produced two children. My fatal mistake, it seemed, had been loving my children too much.

And now I sat in a church basement listening to Matt, the leader of the Divorce Care class, tell the wounded souls that they needed to forgive the person who'd hurt them the most.

How? How was I supposed to forgive someone who refused to apologize?

"Forgiveness isn't about the other person," Matt said. "It's about you."

"But he's never apologized for what he did to me," Kim, the lady with the original question, said.

"Does your ex-husband care if you're angry with him?" Matt asked her.

Kim folded her arms across her chest. "No, he's too busy taking his new girlfriend out on the town."

I could relate to that.

"How long have you been divorced?"

"Five years."

"And how long after your divorce did your ex-husband move on with his life?"

Kim snorted. "About seven minutes."

"And how long did it take you to move on?"

"I still haven't," Kim answered quietly. "That's why I'm here."

"What steps have you taken to get past your divorce and move on with your life?"

Kim shrugged. "I can't move on because I'm still so angry at my ex-husband. He has never apologized for what he did."

"We've already established that your ex doesn't care that you're mad at him. So, Kim, who is your anger hurting?"

We all knew the answer to Matt's question. Hating our ex-spouses had very little impact, if any, on their lives. We were the ones affected.

I looked at Kim and could easily imagine myself in her shoes. Our stories were similar. We'd both been completely crushed by what had happened to us. But five years later, she was still angry and hurting. I didn't want to end up like that.

"Matt, we all see your point," I said. "We realize that our anger is hurting us and holding us back. We want to let go of it, but we don't know how. We are taught as children that when someone says, 'I'm sorry,' the proper response is 'I forgive you.' But how do we forgive when we've never received an apology?"

Matt thought for a minute. "The answer is as simple and as complicated as this: You've got to decide that an apology is not necessary. You may never get one, and if you keep waiting for something that never comes, you'll never be able to move on."

"But he doesn't deserve my forgiveness," Kim said tearfully.

"He might not deserve it, but you do, Kim, and so do I," I said, also fighting tears. "We deserve to move on with our lives and be happy again. We deserve to let go of the anger and pain."

"But he didn't apologize…." she said.

I shrugged. "Mine didn't either. But Matt is right. Forgiveness isn't about the other person. Forgiveness is about us. It's a way to free ourselves from the past."

"I don't want to talk to him," Kim said.

"You don't have to," Matt said. "You don't have to tell him you've forgiven him because you aren't doing it for him. You're doing it for you."

Kim thought for a minute and then nodded. "I've hated him for so long, and it's taken so much emotional energy to feel this way. I think it's time to let go of it."

Matt nodded. "Good for you." He smiled at me and added, "Good for both of you."

And while forgiving my ex-husband didn't happen overnight, it did happen. Over time, I was able to let go of my anger toward him and even remember the good times we'd shared.

He still hasn't apologized for his part in what happened, but I no longer need him to. I didn't forgive him so he'd feel better. I did it so I'd feel better.

I let go of the past and moved on toward a happier future.

And I'll never be sorry for that.

~Anne Jones

44

Finding Support and Finding Myself

The first step to getting anywhere is deciding you're no longer willing to stay where you are.
~Author Unknown

"Ouch!" Pain shot through my little toe after I tripped on my husband's suitcase. Hobbling across the dark bedroom, I wished again that my husband, who worked a thousand miles away, were home more than one weekend a month. I would be able to join him once our house sold. Unfortunately, months turned into more than a year with no serious bites on our spacious country home.

I slid between the sheets beside my husband. His breath caught in mid-snore before he rolled over to snuggle. I felt secure in his muscular arms. His sleepy voice croaked, "You okay, Sally?"

Staring into the blackness, my body stiffened. I hissed, "No. And who is Sally?"

The silence went on too long before he groaned. My world tilted. Struggling for air, I grasped the betrayal of the man to whom I had pledged my life.

This was the start of six painful months of accusations and discussions that fed my rage, insecurity, and desire for revenge. I could not forgive the betrayal and reconciliation was not possible. My sixteen-year marriage was over.

My husband had been the center of my world and my introverted personality had kept me from developing close friends. Once divorced, I longed for close family or women friends to scheme with. I was sure revenge against my ex and Sally would give me peace.

Then one day I suffered the consequences of my obsession. "Panic attack?" I said to the young man in the white lab coat. "I've never had one. I was Christmas shopping, got short of breath and dizzy. I saw sparks of light and it sounded like a train running through my head, then everything went black."

He nodded and flipped through the chart. "Your blood pressure is high and triglycerides and cholesterol are at dangerous levels. You say you take no prescriptions?"

"I don't like pills."

The doctor's lips tightened. "You told the nurse you have a lot of stress—don't sleep through the night. Do you take anything over the counter for anxiety?"

I shook my head, aware that he was watching my hands twisting one corner of the top sheet around my fingers. Sympathy seeped into his voice. "Do you have someone to talk to?"

"You mean a psychiatrist?" My chin lifted. "I went through a divorce over a year ago and still struggle a little, but I'll be fine. Really."

"Even so, make an appointment with your regular doctor. I'll give you a prescription to help you sleep. Only a few days' worth."

He left for a few minutes and returned with the prescription and a brochure. "This is about a local divorce support group with a good reputation."

"Oh, no. I can take care of myself." I shivered at the thought of talking to a group of strangers.

He smiled. "We all need someone to talk to once in a while." Pointing at the brochure, he said, "You know, I think divorce is one of the worst things a person can go through. My sister said that the support group at that church was the best thing she ever did. You might think about it."

"I will," I responded automatically. Yeah, right. A church. God deserted me years ago.

My mother and father didn't go to church but their marriage survived more than fifty years. What was their secret? It was too late to ask them, and I wasn't comfortable discussing it with my grown daughter from a previous marriage or my three older siblings.

The church on the brochure had four thousand members. I figured I could blend into the background and avoid an inquisition about my nonbelief in God. Instead of the divorce group, I chose a Sunday morning class for single people that sounded beneficial. I sat next to Brenda, a widow, and during the six-week class she taught me what being a real friend meant. With a non-judgmental manner, she encouraged me to attend an upcoming Christian weekend retreat for the widowed and divorced at Camp Beckwith on Weeks Bay.

For a while at the retreat I kept my car keys in my pocket, prepared for a quick escape. Finally, I realized that all thirty people attending were just like me, trying to find answers to the unfairness of life. In a large group, we listened to team members talk about different topics like anger and trust in God. After listening, each of us found an isolated spot to write answers to a list of questions in our journals. Later we discussed our thoughts in our small group.

Since Friday night, I had written little and shared nothing with the group. Saturday evening, after a team member presented her story on how she dealt with her guilt and shame, I went to an isolated bench overlooking the bay. My shoulders and head ached as I related to the similarity between the presenter's life and mine. Answers about my guilt and shame flowed onto my journal pages. I sobbed as I accepted my part in the death of my marriage. Self-centeredness, inability to communicate and passive-aggressive behavior topped the list of my own faults.

Back in the group, hands trembling, I read my list. Judy, the leader, said, "Did you divide your guilt into realistic and unrealistic, what's based in reality and what isn't? What you could and couldn't control?"

"I ran out of time before we had to be here, but I'm guilty for blaming my ex for everything."

"Yeah, but you can't control what another person does," one man said.

I stared at the floor. "I'm so confused. Now I have to forgive him and me."

The woman next to me said, "I wrote that forgiving frees me, my thoughts and actions." She patted my shoulder. "Honey, how many minutes, hours, and days have you wasted thinking about 'what ifs' and 'should haves'? Do you enjoy giving up your time to think about your ex?"

I gasped. "Of course not. Am I crazy, or what?"

Chuckling, Judy shook her head. "You didn't get to the final scripture verses and questions?"

When I shook my head, she had me read aloud 2 Corinthians 2:5-11 and Colossians 3:12-17 and answer the final questions: Since God forgave your sins, how are you to handle forgiveness of others who sin? What should you do if you are not strong enough to forgive? Do you know God's love for you is unconditional?

The last question made me cry. I realized that I was worthy of love and that I could forgive. I felt a heavy weight lift and I felt the wall around my heart starting to crumble. I was filled with hope and excitement. I knew that I faced a new future and each new day would offer new chances to grow.

~M.M. Jarrell

Free Wedding Gown — Never Worn

The truth will set you free, but first it will make you miserable.
~James A. Garfield

The man I was going to marry had just told me he was breaking up with me and marrying someone younger. Bill didn't want me. He asked for his engagement ring back and I gave it to him.

No drama, no anger, no tears. It was a quiet, civilized, dignified, mature breakup. I was so stunned I felt like I was sleepwalking.

I had a wedding gown, I had invitations, I had a church reserved — I had everything for a wedding except a groom.

I felt sad and empty. I was also embarrassed. I'd been dumped. I wondered if other people knew it was coming before I did. Why didn't my friends say something? I guess they didn't want to hurt me, but I don't know how anything could hurt more than being left at the altar. Well, I wasn't exactly left at the altar — I was given two months notice.

I'd spent months sewing pearls and sequins on the train of my gown. I had a hundred printed invitations; I had two hundred napkins with our names and our wedding date printed on them; I had paper plates and cups decorated with wedding bells. Some things could be cancelled, like the photographer, church, minister, reception and flowers. I was just stuck with the other things.

I felt ashamed, like I should apologize to everyone that I'd been jilted and the wedding was off. I felt like I'd disappointed people. Mostly I just wanted to hide, I wanted to run away. If I hadn't spent all my money on the wedding, I'd have gone to Hawaii or someplace to escape all of the "I'm so sorry" conversations ahead of me. How many times would I have to say, "Oh, I'm fine. No, I don't have any hard feelings. It's for the best."

We lived in a small town; it would only take a day or two for everyone to hear the news. Thank goodness I hadn't had any bridal showers yet, so I didn't have to return gifts to people.

I was still in love with Bill. I knew Jessica, the woman he'd chosen over me. I didn't know her well enough to even speak if we passed each other on the street, but I knew who she was.

To make matters worse, my cousin was getting married in two weeks and I was her bridesmaid. I'd have to walk down the aisle at my cousin's wedding, smiling and looking happy. I knew she'd understand if I cancelled but I couldn't let her down. She was counting on me. I'd hold my head up and be happy for her.

I knew someday I'd get married, but I knew I couldn't wear the wedding gown I'd made for my wedding with Bill. I put an ad in the paper and said I'd donate a new, never worn, size twelve wedding gown to any woman who was marrying a man in the military. Four days later a nice girl named Tammy and her fiancé Jack, who was in the army, left my house with the gown, veil, and plates and paper cups with bells printed on them. I gave them everything that didn't have my name and Bill's printed on them. All the hours of sewing sequins and pearls on the gown weren't wasted; Tammy would look beautiful at her wedding.

My pride was hurt. I felt like people were gossiping about me, wondering what I'd done wrong to drive Bill to another woman. I cried. I couldn't sleep. A dull pain throbbed inside of me.

I hoped I would find someone fabulous and get married before Bill and Jessica to show him I was over him and had moved on. But I wasn't even dating anyone and Bill and Jessica got married a month after our breakup.

I tried to keep busy. I tried new hobbies. I started going to a different church because I just couldn't keep going to the same church where I had planned to get married. I wondered if I'd ever stop hurting, stop feeling the pain of rejection, stop feeling humiliated.

Six months later I saw Bill and Jessica together. They didn't see me. I was sitting in my car looking at my shopping list when I saw them walking down the sidewalk. There were holding hands and laughing. They looked happy. They were having fun.

They weren't thinking about me at all. They weren't wallowing in guilt or shame or embarrassment. They were enjoying their lives.

I watched them go into a restaurant. He held the door open for her and she looked up at him and smiled.

I wondered if Bill and I had laughed and smiled at each other when we were together. Had we held hands when we walked down the street? I couldn't remember. Our relationship had seemed more serious, more sensible. It wasn't fun. He didn't make me laugh and I don't think I made him laugh.

I suddenly realized he was with the right person now. It showed on his face. They were happy. He'd done the right thing for both of us when he broke our engagement. And I also realized that after we broke up, my thoughts were mostly focused on the wedding itself, not on our future together. The wedding had become more important than the marriage.

I was shocked. All this time I'd made Bill the villain but maybe he'd been the hero. Okay, he wasn't the hero but he'd done the right thing. He'd saved us from making a mistake. We wouldn't have been happy together, the marriage wouldn't have survived.

I laughed for the first time in months. I was over it! I didn't hurt anymore. I was okay with Bill being happy with Jessica, and I was so relieved I wasn't married to him.

It's funny. I thought I'd never recover, never get over it, and then suddenly it was like the sun coming out after a storm. Everything seemed bright and fresh and new.

I felt good. I felt free. I was okay!

~Holly English

Canvas of Forgiveness

Every portrait that is painted with feeling is a portrait of the artist,
not of the sitter.
~Oscar Wilde

I remembered being a kind person, generous in spirit, and naive about the evils of betrayal. That woman seemed to disappear with the judge's decree: "Divorce granted."

At first, like a victim of an earthquake, I just dealt with daily survival. Slowly my new life became familiar — the lesser home, the smaller circle of friends, and the emptiness. I became cynical and bitter.

I was fortunate that not all my friends deserted me. I was part of a book group and a Bible study, I met with several close friends for lunch once a week, and I had breakfast with one very special friend every Monday.

It was during the small Bible study that my new attitude surprised my friends. One of the women brought a quote about love and interwoven hearts nurturing each other. In the silence that often follows something beautiful, as everyone soaked in its deeper meaning, I said, "That is so sick."

There was an audible gasp. The one who had read it to the group asked, "What did you hear?"

With a shaky voice and tears I couldn't hold back, I said, "Obviously, something very different than the rest of you."

Thank God for their tenderness. That was a turning point for me.

I knew I couldn't continue living with the anger. The bitterness didn't just wrap around my own heart, but wounded others.

Night after night I took long walks after work. I cried out to God: "I don't know what to do. Help me."

Weeks passed and I asked, "What are you going to do with me, God?" As I became hopeless, my entreaty became simply, "Fix me."

Searching for some release, I decided it would be good to reconnect with the artist in me. I painted portraits, although I hadn't for quite some time. Actually, I had not painted since I had begun a portrait of Jimmy, my now ex-husband, and his dad. I would never paint over that canvas. I planned to burn it and dump the ashes in the trash. For now, it was in the farthest corner of a packed storage unit. It was beyond the reach of Betty, my ex-mother-in-law, who had demanded it so she could have someone else finish my work.

I began to attend art shows and browse the galleries in our town. I enjoyed the oils, acrylics, watercolors, and pastels. Photography and collages caught my attention.

One afternoon, as I returned to my little home, I noticed how bare my hallway walls were. I had paintings throughout the house, but nothing in my hallway. Why should I waste that space? I could create a family gallery made not from my art but from photographs stored in boxes in my closet.

I immediately began sorting through my collection, choosing my favorites. Some of them showed Jimmy standing next to other family and friends. Scissors would take care of that. I gleefully cut out the image of my betrayer and separated him from those I loved.

By the next week I had the hallway walls filled with framed pictures of the people who meant the most to me. As I stood surveying my work with great satisfaction, I heard a voice say, "It's time to finish the painting for Betty."

I turned around looking for the source of the voice. No one was there. Out loud I said, "And how am I going to do that?"

No answer came.

It is not a normal occurrence in my life to hear the voice of God.

Several days passed before I dug through my possessions to retrieve the almost finished canvas. I stiffly carried it to the trunk of my car. My stomach churned. My throat constricted. I drove home, parked the car in the garage and went for a walk. I did not talk to God that night.

The next day, after work, I opened the trunk and lifted out the offensive thing. Even unfinished it looked just like them. I put it on my easel and stared at it. Then, I went for a silent walk. Bedtime came very early that night.

On the third day, I squeezed paint onto my palette and began mixing the colors. What was the minimum I could do until I could call the painting "done"?

An incredible thing happened as I began adding tints that brought life to the cheeks and sparkle to the eyes. I thought about how surprised Betty would be when she received the finished work. I smiled. An unexpected joy washed away the anger I felt toward Jimmy, Betty, and his dad. Bitterness and cynicism could not survive the joy I felt in performing the loving act of finishing the painting for my ex-mother-in-law.

Even now, twenty years later, a song of praise and awe for the God who rescued me accompanies the memories. Never could I have imagined the path to freedom was completing a portrait of the man who had hurt me so deeply and giving it to the woman who gave him birth.

For months I had begged God to give me back the woman I had been. He had a far superior plan. He gave me the woman He designed me to become. I am a woman who looks at life with open eyes, nestled in peace and confident in God's faithfulness and love.

My struggles—my ugly thoughts—metamorphosed into beauty. I was planning a bonfire but God was planning a piece of art.

~Sheila Kale

The Gift I Needed

Forgiveness is the giving, and so the receiving, of life.
~George MacDonald

I swallowed hard, willing away nausea. Did I misunderstand the words of this young man who now held my grocery bags hostage? Leaning forward, I listened for an explanation. He said it again. "Ma'am, there's a problem with your check. I suggest you speak to a manager at the service counter."

I had been shopping at this particular supermarket for more than five years and had never heard those words. My cheeks flushed with embarrassment as I imagined the eyes of the other customers watching me walk toward the manager.

Nervously, I bit my lip as he reviewed the register's printout pertaining to the check. "You need to contact your bank," he said, looking me in the eye. "There's a problem."

I hurried to the nearest exit and marched across the parking lot to where there happened to be a branch of my bank. After explaining the dilemma to the manager, she entered my account number and searched the computer file. Immediately, she spotted the problem. "Your account is overdrawn," she calmly stated.

"How could that be?" I argued. "My paycheck was transmitted by direct deposit this morning. Surely there is money in this account. There must be a mistake."

The branch manager searched further and identified the problem. "Take a look at this," she said, turning her computer monitor toward me. "Your employer deposited the paycheck, but apparently someone withdrew all but twelve dollars."

I worked hard to blink back tears. I knew who "the someone" was, and this time he had gone too far. How could he? My husband had taken my entire paycheck to support his drug habit.

I knew that I should have seen this coming. For the last few months, he had been abusing drugs and money had started to disappear. However, I never expected that he would go this far, would take the money that I needed to buy food for our children.

I rushed home, determined that he make it right. My husband needed to put the money back in the account. Secondly, he owed the children and me an apology. But I soon discovered that the money had already been spent and he felt no remorse for his actions.

Nothing was going to change, so I packed up our two young children and left our home behind. I was bitter for years after that. My joy was gone.

Ultimately, I sought the help of a therapist. I wanted to change and I was prepared to do just about anything to feel better. Dr. Wade looked at me and said, "You will never get beyond this unless you forgive your husband."

They must have heard me in the reception area when I shouted, "That's not possible!"

Dr. Wade, who apparently was accustomed to this type of response, sat still and waited for me to calm down.

I didn't. "Because of him, we lost our home, furnishings, bank accounts, and cars. I can barely face the children or myself. He's destroyed us."

I continued ranting; and when I was finally exhausted from shouting and crying, Dr. Wade spoke: "There is a gift you need."

I took a tissue from the box next to the sofa and dabbed my eyes as I absorbed what she had said. "The gift you need is not something that anyone can give you. It is a gift you must give yourself. It is the gift of forgiveness. The forgiveness of your husband's actions," Dr. Wade paused, "and forgiveness of yourself."

I buried my face in my hands—too absorbed in my own anger and grief. Days turned into weeks and weeks into months before I began to comprehend. Almost a year to the day of that session, I awoke one morning from a dream. In the dream, a large package was before me. It was wrapped in the most unique paper I had ever seen—like that of a rainbow. I marveled at its brightness and was grateful that it was mine. I began to untie the white satin bow around the box. I loved its feel against my fingers. This had to be a really good gift, I thought.

But when I pulled the top off the box, the phone rang, awakening me. As much as I wanted to see what was in that box, I couldn't. The dream was gone. I never saw the gift inside.

Rattled from the experience, I thought through all the unnecessary bitterness that I had harbored over the years. My children deserved better, and today was the day I would begin to offer it to them. Still in my pajamas, I reached for my journal and wrote. I didn't stop until five pages later, where I laid out my complete forgiveness to my husband. And when I saw him again a month later the words, "I forgive you," came right after my greeting. He followed up with a smile and shared his surprise that I had come to this point. Of course, he too profusely apologized for his actions—something he'd done many times before. We never got back together but for both us this was a turning point.

But there was one more thing needed in my life. The gift remained incomplete. I needed to forgive myself. I had wasted so much time being angry. When I accepted what awaited me in that gift box, I realized that nothing is more liberating than when one decides to forgive. Had I understood this all-important gift, I would have acted sooner. From that day forward, I committed to never hold myself hostage in this way again. By God's grace, I have stuck to that promise.

Forgiveness. What a wonderful gift!

~Yvonne Curry Smallwood

Guess Who Came
for Dinner?

A loving heart is the truest wisdom.
~Charles Dickens

I still couldn't believe I'd invited him for dinner and that he accepted, especially after all that had happened between us. We'd had a fiery divorce, so getting together for dinner at my house some twenty-seven years later was something I never thought would happen. But here I was preparing meatloaf, Bob's favorite meal, and he was due at my door shortly. While setting the table, I reflected again upon this spontaneous invitation to my former husband. It was completely unfiltered. It had just popped out of my mouth. Actually it caught us both off guard, and if the truth were known, he probably accepted due to pure shock.

Several weeks earlier, my former husband Bob and I had come face to face at the funeral of a mutual friend. It had been years since we'd had any contact, but I'd recently been informed of Bob's heart surgery and other complications. Although I knew he wasn't doing well, absolutely nothing prepared me for the decline I saw. This once vibrant, high-powered businessman was now painfully thin, stooped and frail. While it was true we'd both aged, at least I had my health. Perhaps that's what caused me to blurt out the "surprise" dinner invitation, maybe out of gratitude for my own good fortune.

Stuffing a few of my garden's blooms into a beautiful antique vase, I gave the table a once-over. "Not bad," I mumbled, and adding my usual touch of sarcasm, "I hope he realizes what he walked away from and regrets it all." Oddly enough, a spirited conversation I'd had with my sister several years ago came to mind.

"Don't you think it's time you started forgiving, Sis?"

"Let me tell you, getting over hurts and betrayals is easier said than done," I snapped. "Besides, you're married to a great guy so what could you possibly know about hurt and betrayal?"

"You're right, but you still love him. Love never goes away. It just takes on a different form."

Angry now, I set her straight. "Really? Well believe me, you have no idea what you're talking about."

"Maybe, but I read a quote once that said, 'regardless of circumstances, love never dies, it just sleeps until forgiveness wakes it up.'"

"Drop it, will you?" was my reply, and she never mentioned it again. But somehow I never forgot it.

"Anybody home?" It was Bob. "I knocked but no answer, so thought maybe you changed your mind." Always a charmer, he continued, "Sure smells good in here. Of course, you always did make the world's best meatloaf. Did I ever tell you that?" Then laughing, he added, "Obviously if I did, it wasn't often enough. Right?"

We spent the next hour or so chatting over a bottle of Chablis. It had been decades since we'd sat together. It was nice and it felt good. In fact I was surprised at the ease we both seemed to feel. He filled me in on his declining health, but was quick to remind me that he'd had a great life. We laughed at old times and when he asked how I was doing, I felt he sincerely meant it. I even gave him a tour of my modest home, and he appeared impressed. "You've done well, kid," was all he said, but to me that was praise from Caesar.

By now it was time to eat, and we continued our pleasant conversation throughout dinner. It was comfortable. Actually, we lingered, and it was nice. Maybe it was the ease I felt, or maybe it was the two glasses of Chablis, but suddenly I decided to tell him how I felt.

"I know I've been more than angry with you over the years, but what happened between us was my fault too and I'm so sorry," I began, "and I want you to know, I love you, Bob, and always will. You taught me so much, and I will forever be grateful for the time we had together and for the time we had apart. Maybe it was all necessary. I forgive you and I just hope you can forgive me." By now I was crying but somehow it all seemed good. In the dim light of the little chandelier over the kitchen table I noticed tears coming down his cheeks too and there was a silence between us that on some level said it all.

It was getting late and our bittersweet evening had finally caught up with us. Strange, but I sensed that neither of us were quite ready for it to end. We kissed goodbye and I mentioned again that I loved him and hoped he could forgive me. He just smiled and simply said, "There's nothing to forgive. Tonight proved that." I watched him shuffle slowly down the front porch steps to his car while carrying a Macy's shopping bag filled with leftover meatloaf and apple cobbler. Even the streetlight swathed our evening in a soft reassuring glow. We waved goodbye and with tears streaming down my face, I watched him pull away. Every angry thought I'd ever had about him was gone. That was the last time we saw one another. He passed away eight months later.

Since then, I've thought a lot about Bob, our time together, myself, and my sister's quote. Maybe she was onto something. Maybe love does sleep until forgiveness wakes it up. In fact, I wonder if that's what happened to me that night. When I found myself forgiving, surprisingly, I found myself loving. And for the first time in years, the stone in my own heart was gone.

~Linda LaRocque

Forgiving Truth

The real things haven't changed. It is still best to be honest and truthful; to make the most of what we have; to be happy with simple pleasures; and have courage when things go wrong.
~Laura Ingalls Wilder

"Jenny, I think I am gay." There aren't even words to describe that moment. My eyes filled with tears and I pulled away from my husband, quickly moving down the hall of the home we had bought together a few years before.

"Gay!" I screamed. "What does that mean?" I was balled up on the floor crying. He tried to comfort me; he reached for me as he had all the years of our marriage. This was different. As he reached for me, I had suddenly forgotten how to let him hold me, love me. It felt like I was dying inside.

Weeks passed. We talked endlessly, stayed up all night, yelled and cried. We numbly tried to pass the days and care adequately for our three children. Would I throw him out? Did I love him? Should we divorce? We kept it all secret as we celebrated holidays, watched fireworks, buried the ones we loved, waiting for peace and clarity to come.

After months of talking, we decided that we had to try, that maybe being honest about who he was would be enough, that we could continue as we were. We moved, got our kids settled, focused on everyday life and spent the next year and a half fairly happy. From the outside, no one knew. From the inside, it only seemed slightly different. We loved hanging out, fought about very little, and our routine worked We made a great team, but we both knew our marriage had changed in ways sometimes unrecognizable. I loved my husband. I always have and I always will; he is my best friend. He has seen me through the birth of our children and been a wonderful father to them. He is the rock in my little world.

I realized I wasn't angry with him because I understood what he was going through and could relate to his emotional struggle. Then one night in our new home, where our kids were doing well, where we were settled and happy, he said, "Jen, I've been talking to a man and I would like to meet him."

This time there was no anger. I was just confused. Why had he not told me? Why had he pretended everything was fine? Why had he not trusted me or our friendship? I knew then our marriage was unraveling, and I was afraid. Who was I without him? Could I start over?

I had no answers. All I felt was fear and confusion. That night he held me on the couch. Tears ran down his face, something rarely seen since we had met in the sixth grade.

"My god, I never meant to hurt you Jenny. You're the one person in my life that has been through all of it with me, and look at you, I've hurt you."

I realized that I was more worried about being alone than about our marriage. I didn't want my kids to have a part-time dad, and I didn't want to lose my best friend. With a lot of anxiety, I agreed it was time for him to meet this new person. We loved each other and we both wanted to be happy, together or apart.

Our story is difficult, unusual and scary, but our love is made of something stronger. I forgave my husband and I set him free. I made peace with my husband's truth, and I stopped blaming myself. It was only in forgiving him that I was able to move forward and find a new kind of happiness for myself. I did not lose my best friend—in fact I gained the friendship of the man he fell in love with.

~Jennifer Hunt

The One Truly Freed

It takes a huge effort to free yourself from a memory.
~Author Unknown

"You got a few minutes?" If my friend's tone of voice was anything other than normal, I didn't notice.

"Sure." We walked to the resort's pool, empty at this time of the evening. "The lecture was good, wasn't it?" I sat down and dipped my feet in the water.

"It was," she said. "It affected me deeply. That's why I wanted to talk with you."

Rosie had bounced plenty of things off me over the past few years. She faced difficulties working in the private school she and her husband founded. Raising their children when she wanted to continue her education had been a frequent struggle. I assumed she might ask me to pray for her to be a more supportive wife or devoted mom.

"What's up?" I asked when she remained quiet.

"The speaker talked about how important honesty is for a good relationship. Your husband and I..." She stopped long enough for a feeling of foreboding to wash over me. "We've been pretty close."

"I know. You work well together." He had been teaching at their school for two years now and was great with the children.

"It isn't that." Was she going to confess that she was attracted to him?

"Earlier this year, we stepped beyond the boundaries of... you know, marriage."

I didn't want to know any more, but I had to know. I forced myself to speak in a low tone of voice. "How far beyond?"

"Pretty much all the way."

My mind raced back in time. She said earlier this year. I'd had a baby in April. He was now seven months old. Rosie and my husband worked together, but they didn't have private time, did they?

"When was it?" I asked.

"Valentine's Day."

Tears clouded my vision. "When I was visiting my parents?"

"Yes. Diane, I'm sorry. We never should have. We've been close since then, but we've never gone that far again."

"What do you mean by close?" I swallowed hard. It wasn't the time to cry.

"You know, just kissing and stuff."

Just kissing.

"I knew it was wrong. Going behind your back."

I couldn't speak. I wiped my face quickly, not wanting Rosie to see my tears.

"He really loves you, you know. It's just been a difficult time."

I wanted to scream at her. He loves me enough to have an affair when I was seven months pregnant? Enough to pursue a relationship that breaks every rule of love and trust?

"I'm sorry." She spoke as if her apology made everything okay. In her mind, maybe it was because she stood to go. She never mentioned it again.

When we got back from the women's retreat, I asked my husband about it. He apologized and said it never should have happened. He opted to quit the job that brought him into contact with Rosie every day.

She phoned me the following week, angry that they no longer had a teacher and she had to take up the slack while they looked for another one.

I couldn't respond to her over the phone, shocked that she didn't seem to understand why he quit.

Over the next weeks, I plunged into depression. I considered leaving my husband. It made sense to me. He could pursue whatever relationships he wanted. I could take the baby and move in with my parents until I found a job.

Didn't I have the right to do that? But a phrase kept running through my mind, words I spoke in my vow when we got married. "What God has put together, let no one put asunder."

I knew my husband and I were meant to be together. So I stayed with him. I didn't move out, but my heart was far away. I simply blocked out the brokenness and the wounding emotions that came with it.

Three years passed. My husband found a new job. I had a second child, then a third. I went back to school. I heard that Rosie and her husband had moved to another state. Life continued normally on the outside. But when I took time to think about it, I was going through life's motions without joy. And I didn't know how to find it. Whenever I thought of Rosie, my heart burned almost physically.

One day in January, my husband struck up a conversation. "I heard from Adrian."

Rosie's husband. I nodded. My heart raced.

"Rosie left him and the kids. She moved in with some guy."

"Couldn't have seen that one coming," I blurted without thinking. "It was just a matter of time. That horrid woman has no heart for anyone but herself."

"Why are you so bitter?" my husband asked.

I glared at him and stomped off. Why was I bitter? Hadn't he cheated on me with that very woman? Hadn't he broken my heart when he vowed to protect me and love me?

I got in my car and drove, not knowing where I was going. When I began to cry, I pulled into an alley behind the local library because I could no longer see the road. There, I cried. They were not tears of sorrow, but rage. Not at Rosie though. Beneath my animosity toward her, my heart seethed with anger at my husband. It was him that I was bitter toward, him that I would not forgive.

But I couldn't. I didn't know how. I couldn't tell him, "I forgive you." It wasn't that simple. It wouldn't work anyway. I had to do something, though. And it came to me.

Valentine's Day.

We hadn't celebrated it for three years. Of all days, he had chosen that one to be unfaithful. He didn't deserve anything for Valentine's Day.

"Do it anyway," a voice seemed to tell me. Even though part of my heart was against it, another part convinced me to go through with it.

I planned a perfect morning. Made sure the kids would be out. Made the menu for a great lunch. Picked up a romantic movie. Decorated the house that morning while he ran errands. He came home, unsuspecting and pleasantly surprised. I played the part of a loving wife.

It's just a role, I thought. But something inside me loved those moments. The morning had been perfect.

I told myself to keep playing the part. Pretend I was enjoying married life. For my children's sake, if nothing else. I kept at it. A small deed here. A kind word there. A loving glance.

Weeks passed. And I found my role had changed. I was no longer playing a part. That faithful, loving wife was me. Really me. Joy that had evaded me for so long finally filled my heart. I had forgiven my husband. And I discovered that the one truly freed was the only one who had been bound all along.

Me.

~Willow Swift

Forgiveness
After Forty Years

When you hold resentment towards another, you are bound to that person or
condition by an emotional link that is stronger than steel. Forgiveness is the
only way to dissolve that link and get free.
~Catherine Ponder

In the winter of 1967 I met Marina, the girl of my dreams. We
began dating, and before long we were inseparable. Our relationship typified the classic teenage romance — spending hours
on the phone, writing letters, going out on weekend dates and long
Sunday afternoon drives. We had fallen in love and our dating rituals
continued uninterrupted until the spring of 1968 when I was drafted
into the U.S. Army.

I spent the first half of my two-year enlistment stateside, so Marina
and I were still able to see each other but with far less frequency. We
missed each other terribly, writing letters almost daily. During my off-
duty time, I would go to the nearest payphone with a fistful of change
and spend every last cent listening to her sweet voice.

Then in the spring of 1969 I was sent to Vietnam for a yearlong
tour of duty. Marina's frequent letters were just what I needed, for a
soldier had no greater morale booster than knowing he had someone
at home waiting for him. I loved Marina and I thought about her
every day.

Initially, Marina's letters were filled with passion and she always wrote about the day we would be married. Then, around the midway point of my tour, her letters abruptly stopped for nearly a month. There was no problem with the mail delivery because I was still receiving correspondence from my family, so something else had to be wrong. Finally, a letter from Marina arrived, but it read like someone else wrote it. The familiar passion was gone and the words were mechanical and held little meaning. Although Marina continued to write, the frequency was sporadic and at times the content was not worth reading. She was slipping away and I was helpless to fix the situation because I was so far away.

I knew that if I were able to see Marina, then I could get our relationship back on track. But the only way to make that happen was to send for her. After six months of duty, Vietnam servicemen earned a full week of vacation known as R&R, Rest and Relaxation. The only stateside location soldiers were allowed to visit was Honolulu, Hawaii, where spouses, sweethearts and family members separated by the war could be reunited.

The trip was arranged, and one month later I was at the Hawaii R&R center anxiously waiting for Marina to rush into my arms. Instead, my sister stepped off the plane in her place. To make matters worse, when I phoned Marina from my hotel, she thought that I was the guy she had been secretly dating while I was in Vietnam. I nearly died when she mentioned how much fun she had had the previous week. When Marina realized it was me on the phone, the long uncomfortable silence confirmed my every fear. I had lost her months ago and never knew it.

We slowly resumed our conversation but it was muddled. Even though I did not want to know any details, Marina confessed that she had been intimate with the other guy. I was crushed. We said goodbye on somewhat friendly terms and she promised to write more often. Big deal—any future letters would be from someone who used to love me.

I finished my Vietnam tour and returned home. The first person I went to see was Marina. If she still had a tiny spark of love for me, then perhaps we could renew our relationship. Although she tried,

Marina's heart was elsewhere and we parted ways less than two months after I came home. I was devastated. Marina was the only girl I had ever truly loved and she no longer wanted me.

After our breakup, I drifted in and out of lousy relationships. I was unable to trust or love anyone, and I cursed Marina for what she did and for having such a hold on me. My heart hardened. For several years I hated her even though I still loved her. I became lonely, depressed and drank heavily, which caused me to fall into poor health. However, my illness turned out to be a blessing because it forced me to get sober. That was when I realized that if I were ever going to find love again, I would have to forget about Marina. So I locked her painful memory away and although she occasionally rattled around in my head, I managed to no longer allow her to have influence over me. Eventually, I met my wife and we have been happily married ever since.

Then in 2010, almost forty years after I last saw her, Marina contacted me after a member of her immediate family had died. The tragic event caused Marina to reflect on her life and try to undue any harm she had done to others. I was the first person that she thought of. She admitted to having made some terrible choices regarding our relationship, which unknown to me, made her life just as miserable as mine was so long ago.

Initially, I was angry that Marina awakened my dormant memories because I was soon reliving the heartache all over again. I even thought about ways to strike back at her for contacting me. However, nothing would be gained from revenge, especially since Marina's plea for forgiveness was genuine.

The passage of time certainly helped to soften me. But more important was the realization that Marina played a significant role in my life during a period that helped define who I am today. Now, whenever I am reminded of those days, I can do it with a smile.

~Arthur Wiknik, Jr.

Chapter
6

The Power *of* Forgiveness

Forgiving Friends and Colleagues

Holding on to anger, resentment and hurt only gives you tense muscles, a headache and a sore jaw from clenching your teeth. Forgiveness gives you back the laughter and the lightness in your life.

~Joan Lunden

Golden Glitter

Her absence is like the sky, spread over everything.
~C.S. Lewis, A Grief Observed

Sweet potatoes boiled on the stove. With my right hand, I switched the range fan to high while, with my left, I gripped the mixer that smashed the baked pumpkin for pie. Tomorrow was Thanksgiving and, as usual, my family would host the holiday meal. Following tradition, I had set aside Wednesday evening to prep the do-ahead food.

This year, however, my beautiful, intelligent, and energetic fourteen-year-old daughter wouldn't be home to help. The constant chatter and laughter she brought to last year's feast preparations were replaced by the silence of her absence.

I took a few steps across the kitchen to my iPod anchored in the speaker dock and skipped the playing song. I had thought Pandora would be safe. It wasn't. Although I had only been cooking for an hour, the radio had somehow selected two of the songs sung at my daughter's funeral.

Then the doorbell rang. I glanced at my watch. Eight o'clock. I wasn't expecting anyone. My husband was working late; my young son and daughter were home with me.

Crossing the living room, I approached the front door and stood on my tiptoes to peer out the top window. The entryway was shrouded in darkness. Flipping on the porch light, I recognized a classmate from my daughter's first semester of high school and unlocked the door.

I had seen her a few times before. Once I had spoken with her. Opening the door, I invited her in. Shaking her head, she held out her hands.

"This is for Jenna's tree," she said. Her palms cradled a flat wooden star that she had painted yellow and coated with five spokes of golden glitter.

"How did you know?" I asked. Then, before she could answer, I recalled the Facebook status I had posted two weeks earlier, announcing that my family would decorate a Christmas tree in memory of Jenna and inviting those who knew her to design heart ornaments to adorn it. Though many friends had responded, none from Jenna's distant high school had participated. Until now.

"Thank you," I said, as she handed the sparkling star to me. I wanted to say more but I was caught off guard and didn't know what else to say.

"I have to go now. My dad is waiting in the car," she blurted out. I was surprised to see the normally confident queen-of-her-class trembling. Tears streamed down her cheeks. She spun on her heels and ran to the car. Standing in the doorway, I watched her leave.

Stunned, I wandered back to the kitchen and turned off the stove. Without realizing what I was doing, I walked down the short hall to my bedroom, opened my closet door, and withdrew a manila folder. Sitting down in a wooden rocking chair in the corner of the room, I pulled out the printed copy of my daughter's computer journal. Flipping to the next-to-last page, I found what I was looking for.

I had remembered correctly; her name was there. My eyes scanned Jenna's words:

Your social infrastructure, your bullying, is the most hurtful thing anyone could ever come up with. I wanted to be friends with you, but you and your group completely excluded me. Words are painful. People's feelings are not something to be played with. Even though it's not exactly your fault that I'm gone now, being kind could have saved my life.

Leaning back in the chair, I forced myself to breathe deeply. My hurting heart thumped. I closed my eyes, and the tears fell.

A few minutes passed before I opened my eyes. Something lower on the journal page caught my attention — a prayer Jenna had penned only days before her death that I had forgotten was there:

Mom. That is probably the biggest thing I ask for. Please, God, you know how tired she is. I ask you, partly for my sake but mostly for hers, to give her a long break without any repercussions. Please send people to take some of this burden off of her shoulders. And, most importantly, bring her irrational joy.

With the reading of those words, tears cascaded down my face. Maybe the girl who gave the star was guilty of failing to include Jenna, of failing to be a friend. But I, too, was guilty. Guilty of being too busy working — too busy with the stuff of life that no longer seemed so important — to recognize the pain growing inside Jenna's heart. Like every mom, I could replay a thousand memories, wishing I had done things differently. The survivor's guilt pressed on me like a heavy weight. As I closed the journal, though, I saw the final words left by Jenna in her parting letter:

My family, I love you all so much, and I'm so sorry. Please forgive me. I would hate to die knowing that you never forgave me for what I did.

Forgive her? I already had, even though, in a moment of despair, she had made a devastating choice that no one had seen coming — a choice that had shattered the hearts of her family and friends and sent aftershocks into the lives of hundreds of others who knew and loved her.

In that moment, I decided that I could — I would — forgive those who had intentionally or unintentionally hurt my daughter, just as I wanted them to forgive me and forgive Jenna, just as I had been forgiven by my God who loved me and gave His life for me. Because of this, I would even forgive... myself.

With the reading of Jenna's words, forgiveness happened that evening in the rocking chair. But I didn't know how real it was until six weeks later.

January 2nd marked the one-year anniversary of my daughter's death. Gray clouds gloomed in the sky. A cold rain sprinkled down. I had just returned from my first trip to the distant gravesite and was expecting friends to come by in an hour to remember with my family when the doorbell rang.

Thinking some family friends had arrived early, I swung open the door. Instead, the girl who had given the star stood there, her long hair swooped over to one side.

"Please come in," I said, and this time she did, extending hands that held a dozen yellow roses.

"These are for Jenna," she whispered.

She looked into my eyes, and I looked into hers. With each of us fighting back tears, we talked. She told me about school. Then, after ten minutes, I wrapped my arms around her in an understanding hug.

"If you ever want to talk, I'll listen," I said as we embraced one another.

She nodded as she gave a slight smile. Without dismissing the need for change, we were acknowledging that the forgiveness was real and the healing of two broken, remorseful hearts had begun.

~Beth Saadati

My Fifth Grade Bully

Throughout life people will make you mad, disrespect you and
treat you bad. Let God deal with the things they do, cause hate
in your heart will consume you too.
~Will Smith

When I was in the fifth grade, there was a boy in my class named Kyle. At the time, he was the meanest person I had ever met. For the first couple days of school, Kyle and I sat across from each other. He would stealthily reach his legs across the table and slam his shoe down on mine, causing a rapid rush of pain. Eventually, I told a teacher, and my seat was moved. But Kyle's abuse didn't stop. He continued to call me names, such as "stupid" and "freak." His words were quite distressing to an eleven-year-old girl. He also continued to physically hurt me. In "morning meeting" he once stepped on my foot so hard that I burst into tears. This continued for most of the school year.

Kyle also bullied my friend Megan. At one point she ran out of the classroom because he mimicked her nonstop. Both of us were absolutely miserable. And despite meetings with teachers and guidance counselors, nothing changed. We had a large class of rowdy boys, and the teacher had a hard time keeping order.

The climax of the Kyle saga occurred in mid-May. Kyle had elbowed me into a wall and insulted my brother (who has special needs), calling him a "retarded freak." I lost it. With my teacher standing behind me, I told Kyle exactly how much he had hurt Megan and me—both physically and emotionally. I had tears streaming down my face and probably looked ridiculous, but I didn't care. I had been waiting for the opportunity to tell Kyle how much I hated him for months. At the end of our confrontation, I glowed inside as Kyle quietly apologized. I felt as if I had conquered Mt. Everest, I was that happy.

Kyle's teasing didn't completely end, but it definitely subsided. He never physically hurt me again, and the final month of school went by fairly smoothly. Kyle was going to a private school the next year; I wouldn't have to worry about him. Summer came and went, as did sixth grade, and seventh grade. I had only seen Kyle once, at a movie theater. We did not speak, instead preferring to look at the floor and pretend we didn't see each other.

It was only in eighth grade that I really thought about fifth grade again. It was late at night as I remembered the abuse Kyle had put me through. I waited for the pang of anger I'd always felt when thinking or talking about Kyle. But no anger came. I tried again, thinking about the marks he'd left so many times on the tops of my feet, the words, the pain… but I felt no hate for him. Instead, I felt a small beating of pity inside my heart. This boy, who had ruined a great portion of my fifth grade experience, had probably been going through his own issues back then. He was obviously mad at the world and maybe, I reasoned, he was simply taking that anger out on my friend and me. It was no excuse for what he did, but it was a reason.

I felt as if I'd had an epiphany. Being angry with Kyle for what he had done was—as Buddha puts it—like drinking poison and expecting him to die. By holding my hatred for Kyle inside of me, I was only hurting myself. That night, I chose to let old wounds heal, and I forgave my fifth grade bully.

In letting go of that pain, I felt free. I wasn't letting a three-year-old incident bother me. In that way, I guess forgiveness is the most important tool humans have been blessed with. Because, with it, we can let go of unnecessary burdens and truly own our lives.

Who knew an eleven-year-old boy could teach me that?

~Kathryn Malnight

Don't You Remember?

A childhood is what anyone wants to remember of it.
It leaves behind no fossils, except perhaps in fiction.
~Carol Shields

For almost twenty years, I avoided June Johnson. It wasn't easy in the small town where we both lived, but I managed. If I discovered June and I were in the grocery store at the same time, I'd feign interest in the magazine rack until she was safely out of sight. When I learned she frequented the early morning aerobics class at the YMCA, I became a regular at the afternoon class. I made it a point to ask if June would be attending a party before I'd accept an invitation.

Why? Because for some reason I couldn't understand, June had made it her hobby to emotionally attack my son Andy when he was a little boy.

It started in preschool, where June's son Ted was in the same class as Andy. Ted had a birthday party. June prepared elaborate personalized goody bags for the children who attended. When the party was over, she was one bag short. Andy's. He left the party with tears rolling down his cheeks. As the years went by, Andy's name was frequently left off Ted's party list, even when every other child in the class was invited.

June's husband was the coach during the only year Andy played soccer. At the end of the season, every player on the team got a trophy—a big shiny trophy with the child's name engraved on it—for participating. Except one. "I don't know what happened," June told me with a shrug as she handed all the kids except Andy their trophies. "Maybe the engraver still has it." My five-year-old son barely made it to the car before he started sobbing.

When the boys were in fourth grade, June discovered that Andy hadn't yet finished a hot-off-the-press Harry Potter book that both he and Ted had been reading. "Go ahead, Ted," she urged, "tell Andy how it ends so he won't have to waste time reading it." June never failed to remind me — always within earshot of Andy — that Ted was in the "gifted class" at school. Andy wasn't. She even liked to point out that her son was taller than mine.

By the time the boys reached middle school, I'd had enough. I encouraged Andy to find a new circle of friends. And I perfected my June-avoidance techniques. I won't pretend it was easy. Being constantly on the lookout was exhausting. But I feared that if I didn't stay away from June, I'd be forced to give her a piece of my mind. The ugly, hurting piece. It was better to simply keep my distance.

Years passed and Ted and Andy grew up. On the rare occasions when June and I encountered each other, we'd nod politely and quickly move on.

Andy got a job in a different town and bought a house. One with plenty of storage space for his childhood memorabilia. As I sat on his bed one Saturday morning helping him load comic books and merit badges and countless other keepsakes into plastic containers, I picked up a couple of his baseball trophies.

"Want to take these with you?"

He nodded.

"Remember playing soccer when you were in kindergarten?"

"Sort of," he answered.

"Mrs. Johnson never did get your trophy to you," I said smugly.

Andy frowned and shook his head. "I don't know what you're talking about."

Sitting there surrounded by a lifetime of memories, I let my pain and anger spill out. "Don't you remember," I asked, "how awfully she treated you? How she snubbed you at Ted's birthday parties? How she ruined Harry Potter? Don't you remember how she was always bragging about how much smarter and taller Ted was? Don't you remember that you didn't get a big shiny soccer trophy with your name on it when you were five?"

His eyes grew wide. "Mom," he said. "Get a grip. No... I don't remember any of that stuff."

"Are you serious?" I was practically trembling with rage. "How could you forget all that?"

Andy shrugged and gave me a crooked grin. "I don't know. I guess it just wasn't important."

I felt a lump rising in my throat and worked hard to blink back tears. Two decades of resenting and avoiding June, all for nothing! She hadn't hurt Andy. And my anger hadn't hurt her, not one little bit. It had only hurt me. Sitting cross-legged on my son's sagging bunk bed, I realized it was time to let it all go, to dump my anger in the big black trash bag with all the stuff Andy had decided not to keep. In that moment, I forgave June for trying to hurt my son, even though she hadn't succeeded. And it felt wonderful.

Does that mean June and I suddenly became best friends?

No. But it does mean I no longer waste precious time or energy avoiding her at the grocery store. I attend whichever aerobics class I want. And if I'm ever seated near June at a dinner party? I'll just smile with as much enthusiasm as I can muster and ask her what's going on in her life. And in Ted's.

~Jean Morris

The Slow Learner

Forgiving what we cannot forget creates a new way to remember.
We change the memory of our past into a hope for our future.
~Lewis B. Smedes

I never really knew why Jane Anderson resented me so much. To be honest, I never really paid much attention to her at all. I realize now that much of the blame over what she did to me was my fault.

When I got the job in the same office as Jane and four others, she had already worked there for over five years. I was five years younger, full of confidence and bright ideas and not shy about sharing them. Our boss liked my positive approach and soon promoted me. I moved to an office adjacent to Jane, and within a year I had moved further up the ladder.

I found Jane very quiet. I chatted away to her, but as time went by, got less and less response. I never gave her a second thought.

After two years, a fairly senior post arose; it offered more responsibility and a much higher salary. My husband Eric and I were hoping to move to a better house and a job like this would really make that possible. My boss told me that although the decision was not solely his, the job was more or less mine.

I went through a couple of interviews, and then was called in to hear the decision. I nearly fell through the floor when they very nicely told me that I had not gotten the promotion.

It wasn't just disappointment over not getting the job, but how it affected our ability to move as well. Then my boss made a mistake. He told me the reason I did not get the job was that Jane had told them she was there for the long term. "I know you must be considering Joyce, because she is very good, but she told me she is only going to be here for another year and then she and her husband are moving abroad. I really feel that it's not fair to the rest of us or to you, not to mention this."

My mind drifted back to a couple of odd questions at the second interview—would I ever consider moving abroad, for instance. I had honestly answered that yes, I probably would, never thinking it as a real possibility.

My anger at Jane knew no bounds. She had lost me my promotion and my new home. I waited until the others had gone before I barged in on her. "You liar, you cheat. You lost me the job and my new home. I hope you rot in hell!" I marched out, and I resigned from the company, unable to face the thought of looking at her every day.

I soon found another job, but we lived in a small town. If I saw her coming, rather than cross the street, I would march toward her, and look her straight in the eye with all the hate I felt. Another year went by, and my husband and I moved away when he received a promotion. I saw her occasionally when I was home visiting my parents and she could never look me in the eye.

After fifteen years, I was visiting my mum when I bumped into Karen, a woman who had worked with Jane and me. I mentioned Jane and said that I had never forgiven her for what she had done. She nodded and said, "I can understand what you must have felt, but she did have her reasons. Jane had a sister, a lot like you, who was so much her parents' favourite that it must have really hurt. Jane was quiet and worked hard for the five years before you arrived and suddenly you were there and everyone liked you and you got promoted quickly. I suppose she saw the situation with her sister happening to her all over again.

"The day she was told about that promotion, I came back to the office from somewhere and she was sitting crying at her desk. I knew she'd gotten the job and I couldn't understand why she was unhappy. Then she confessed to me: 'I did something wicked, I have to go and tell them what I did. She should have gotten the job.' She poured it all out to me and I'm sorry Joyce, but I told her to say nothing. You were young and it was obvious you would find something else, but this was her only chance.

"Jane died of cancer about nine months ago, I had kept up with her and I went to see her. She always associated me with you because you and I were quite friendly. She never forgave herself for what she did because she asked me, 'If you ever see Joyce, ask her to forgive me.'"

As Karen fell silent, I was stunned and felt a lump in my throat. "I wish I had known that. I wish I had taken the time to know her better."

For many weeks after, I went over and over the situation. I began to see that I'd only thought of myself and how easy it would have been for Jane to resent me. It weighed on my mind. Finally I went back to town, to the cemetery where Jane was buried. I stood at her grave and with tears in my eyes I said, "I forgive you, Jane. Now I need you to forgive me. I was self-centered and uncaring, and although what you did was not right, it was little more than I deserved. I'm sorry and I wish we could have been friends." I put flowers on her grave and suddenly felt as if something like a cord that had been tied around me had burst open. I felt free of not just resentment but anger too. I wiped away the tears. I had come to tell Jane I forgave her, but I left much happier because I felt she had forgiven me too.

I know it was fifteen years too late for both of us. Sometimes I still wish I could hug her and we could both say, "Sorry." It would have been a much better solution. I learned so much from that visit to Jane's grave.

That was many years ago now. Since then I have always tried to see someone else's point of view and not bear any resentment. Life has been so much easier and happier for me as a result. I hope Jane knows that she has helped me become a better person. I might have been the go-getter in those days, but I have to admit I was a slow learner when it came to something more important, like forgiveness.

~Joyce Stark

56

The Magic of Forgiveness

Forgiving is rediscovering the shining path of peace that
at first you thought others took away when they betrayed you.
~Dodinsky

The day began crisp and cool. It was autumn and early in the first semester of high school. I returned to school after a two-day teacher conference, assured that my substitute had maintained the same order and expectations I had for my classes. However, later that day, as the sky clouded and rain threatened, several students reported to me that although the substitute teacher had followed my lesson plan, some students had not. Specifically, one student—a beautiful girl of some talent and "smarts"—had spent the two class periods texting on her phone.

Because using a phone is forbidden in my Advanced Placement Literature class, I was somewhat indignant. Furthermore, I was surprised that these students had the initiative, temerity, and courage to come forth and inform me. Generally, high school students tend to be metaphorical lemmings that mindlessly follow and condone the actions of their peers. Clearly, these particular students were different. They had decided to enlighten me as to what had transpired while I was absent. And they did so, I believe, because I had trusted them to be responsible.

All in all, the offense did not matter. What mattered was what followed. One of the girls who reported to me about what transpired was Kimberly, who was then singled out by the misbehaving girl. That girl and her "minions" taunted, threatened, and bullied Kim. These girls walked the halls as if they owned them. They were the proverbial mean girls.

Why they singled out Kim is unknown to me. Perhaps it was a "pack" reaction to isolate one victim and go in for the "kill." Perhaps it was because she was a high-achieving, ebullient spirit with an inner light who seemed unworried about her image. Her self-possession may have intimidated them. Whatever the reason, they set about trying to destroy her.

Kimberly was hounded in the halls. The girls dogged her as she arrived at school, when she had lunch with friends, and when she walked home, staring her down, whispering insults, and calling her humiliating names. They even threatened her with bodily harm. She remained silent and stoic for a while, but they upped their threats and she finally broke down. There was a discussion with me. She cried—admitting that they were tearing apart her resolve to be strong. I was incensed. There was a discussion with her counselor. The counselor also was infuriated. Then, all the students were called in. Parents shouted. One girl dissolved into sobs. The "mean girls" were warned.

There were other repercussions. The girls were stripped of their offices in the Associated Student Body. This was a mere wrist slapping on a high school level but it was something. And Kim felt vindicated—to a point. She had fought the good fight and won—or so she thought. As it turned out, the rest of the year was difficult for her. Camps were formed, as only they can be formed in high school. Kim felt ostracized and alone. She began to have stress-related symptoms. She cried after school. She felt depressed and demoralized. The charming, intelligent student that had so animated class discussions was transformed into a panicked, defeated girl.

Then, she forgave them. She had the courage to let go—of all of it. She and I discussed how sometimes it is supremely more difficult to let go than to hold onto anger—especially, as in this case, righteous anger. She turned to me and said: "Holding onto fear and anger destroys the inner life." I was transfixed and amazed. This seventeen-year-old student had stumbled onto a deep truth. "I forgive them, of course," she said with purpose.

And the world began to shift. Its axis tilted. Karma reared its mystical head.

Several of the "mean girls" competed with Kim for the Gates Millennium Scholars Program. This is an incredible opportunity based on applicant grades, need, and numerous essays. For its recipients, the scholarship provides for full college tuition through graduate school. Kim won. She was awarded a full ride to a prestigious college. And the "mean girls"? Not a one who applied was awarded. And the main "mean girl"? That smart and talented girl was not accepted to any college of her choice.

Whoa? What does one say? The power of forgiveness may transform the universe.

This story does not necessarily illustrate that forgiveness creates justice. That is for the universe or Providence to decide. But it does raise the question: Just how powerful is forgiveness for all involved? For my student, forgiveness was the key for her to move on, to integrate and make sense of the "meanness" of the world, and to recognize that standing up against the crowd can be a valid and marvelous choice. Although she suffered greatly, she attained victory in the end. This does not mean one should forgive to gain something—it may just mean that in many ways, forgiveness is magical.

As I finished out the school year, I thought of Kim often and the lessons she taught me. Forgiveness may not only bring inner peace, it may also allow the universe to right itself. Forgiveness is not about vengeance, or even justice, but sometimes it facilitates the latter. Forgiveness can transform both the forgiver and the forgiven. I do not know if those "mean girls" ever came to a personal reckoning with themselves. I certainly hope they did. And both Kim and I hope that they have had the insight to forgive themselves.

I have pondered why I was witness to this forgiveness and to Kim's spirit. And I think I know. I must forgive someone very dear to me. I must forgive myself for failing certain people in my life. Finally,

I must forgive all who, intentionally or not, have hurt me or maimed my spirit. I am working on it. I am praying for it. Forgiveness is what knits up the troubled soul and makes it whole again. My wise and compassionate student taught me this.

~Sherry Morton-Mollo

57

When Forgiveness Seems Impossible

We must be willing to let go of the life we've planned,
so as to have the life that is waiting for us.
~Joseph Campbell

I stared at the e-mail in disbelief. Tears surfaced as I read, "I am so very sorry for all the hurts that we have caused you.... To this day I have no idea how we could have made such a mess of things. I ask your forgiveness, even though I would never expect to get it...."

I didn't think I would ever be able to forgive Debbie for the part she played in destroying my marriage. The memories of those hell-on-earth months remained open wounds for many years. For some reason, it was far more difficult for me to forgive Debbie than my ex-husband, Peter. How could I forget that ominous phone call on my forty-first birthday?

"I don't know how to tell you this, Barb, but something is going on between Peter and Debbie. I'm not sure it's sexual, but I have good reason to believe they're having an emotional affair."

My heart raced. Nancy, a friend and former member of my church, wouldn't be calling me long distance with this sort of news unless she had strong evidence.

I already knew my nineteen-year marriage was in trouble. Big trouble. The past year had been like a bad dream. Although my pastor husband proclaimed from his pulpit that I was his best friend, we weren't communicating at home. His aloofness and anger baffled me.

I reasoned that at forty-two years old, he could be having a mid-life crisis. Or pastoral burnout. He had worked hard mentally and physically on a church building project, and the lack of acknowledgment hurt him deeply. He only seemed happy when we were with our friends Debbie and Troy. Peter insisted they join us in almost everything. We skied, fished, roasted hot dogs, and ate every Sunday lunch together.

If Troy had to work, Debbie was still invited to tag along. Although she was my friend, her constant presence became a sore spot between Peter and me. He accused me of being jealous and overreacting.

That past week had been a nightmare. One morning while cleaning the house I received an inner warning that Peter was on his way home with bad news. We lived a distance from the church, and he seldom came home for lunch.

I soon heard our car in the driveway. A few moments later Peter solemnly walked through the front door.

"I need to talk with you, Barb," he almost whispered.

We sat down at the dining room table. I could feel my chest tighten, so I took a deep breath. What could be so horrible that he couldn't tell me on the phone?

"You know we've had problems in our marriage for a long time," he began. "Well, I think we should get a divorce."

I couldn't digest his words. Our marriage wasn't perfect, but divorce? What about the kids? What about his ministry? What about us?

"Is there another woman?" I looked straight into the dark eyes that had made me fall in love with him. I couldn't bring myself to ask if it was Debbie.

"No, there isn't," he assured me.

I never felt so alone in all my life. Who does a pastor's wife confide in when her husband asks her for a divorce? My best friend was out of the country. And I didn't want church members or relatives to know in case Peter changed his mind.

I decided to tell only my sister. We cried together over the phone and made plans for me to stay with her for a while. I would tell our teenagers their mother needed a break.

Now Nancy's call confirmed my deepest fears. I'd been suspicious of Peter and Debbie's "friendship" for some time. To make matters worse, the church women's executive committee was treating me to lunch—and the "other woman" would be celebrating my birthday with me!

The Royal Regency could have been a hot dog stand for all I cared that afternoon. I can't even recall eating or opening my gifts. But I do vividly remember the look of dismay on Debbie's face when I confronted her after the luncheon.

She flatly denied the accusations. Embarrassed, and feeling a strange mixture of defeat and relief, I apologized and retreated back into my confused state of mind.

A couple of days later I was on my way to my sister's home. Peter and I planned to meet at a ministers' conference at the end of our separation, but that never happened. He phoned to inform me that Debbie had asked Troy for a divorce. He also told me he had resigned from the church. I knew at that point that our marriage was over.

The next few weeks were painful beyond words. I wasn't the only one who was hurting. Our three teenagers. The church members. Our parents, friends and relatives. It was incomprehensible the damage one decision could make.

Since I knew my kids desperately needed their friends, I decided we would remain in the same town, house and even church. It was the best decision I could have made. The love and warmth I felt from my church family were the beginning of my inner healing.

For the next few years I tried to put my life back together. I got a job working in a medical clinic. My kids finished high school and moved on to jobs or college. I eventually married a wonderful man and moved to a bigger city. I followed my dream to become a writer and speaker.

But one issue remained unresolved through all the changes. I had never forgiven Debbie. Peter, yes. How could I not forgive him when I was also at fault for our failed marriage? But Debbie was a different matter. Unlike Peter, she had no reason to hurt me. Not only had she taken my husband, she had robbed me of my self-worth for a long time. Those wounds still festered.

As the years passed, I convinced myself that everything was okay. Since I never had contact with Debbie, I seldom thought about her. Occasionally she popped up in a conversation or dream. As my children's stepmother, she was still in my life but at a distance. That was until I encountered the "Forgiveness Prayer."

My husband and I were helping with an evangelism program in our church. At the end of the sessions, when the participants were challenged to accept Jesus Christ, the leader asked everyone to bow their heads while he read this long prayer asking forgiveness from almost every person they knew (I forgive my mother for... I forgive my father for... I forgive my neighbor for... etc.).

I was praying along fine until he came to the part that read, "I forgive the one person who has hurt me the most..." My mind instantly went to Debbie. I could see her standing there. Young. Long hair. Classy clothes. Smart. And the old wound began to hurt.

Tears streamed down my face. "I can't forgive her, God," I prayed silently. "You know I can't do this."

Somewhere during those few moments of honesty, God let me know that I would never be able to forgive Debbie without the power of His Spirit. It was simply impossible. And the only way I would have peace was to give it all to Him.

"Okay, Lord," I finally prayed. "I'm giving this to you, but you are going to have to give me the ability to forgive her."

When I opened my eyes, I felt at peace. I knew a weight had been lifted. But was it for real? How would I ever know if I never encountered her?

The opportunity came when my oldest child married. For the first time since the divorce, Debbie would be attending a family function. Although I felt I had forgiven her, I really wouldn't know until we met face to face. And we did. Right between the ceremony and the reception. I turned around from talking to someone, and there she was. What happened next was truly a miracle—especially since she still looked the same fifteen years later!

Without thinking, I hugged "the other woman" and told her it was good to see her after such a long time. And I meant it. You see, when I looked at my old friend, it was like nothing had ever happened. What I didn't know was that she had sent me an e-mail before the wedding asking for my forgiveness!

Forgiving Debbie changed me—and our family—forever. Since then, we have had many family gatherings with everyone present. My children are pleased that there is no longer tension between their parents. Some scars from the divorce will always be there, but forgiveness healed the one that seemed impossible.

~Barbara Kruger

58

Rank and File

Forgiveness is the key that unlocks the door of resentment
and the handcuffs of hatred. It is a power that breaks the
chains of bitterness and the shackles of selfishness.
~Corrie ten Boom

After following leads on a break-and-enter suspect (I was a police officer for over twenty years), I came across information that could lead to an arrest. I knew our district detectives were getting desperate, hoping to put an end to the local crime spree. So, I passed on some vital information to a colleague, a detective. He thanked me and said he'd look into it. He promptly obtained a search warrant and made the arrest without me.

The inspector glowingly praised his work and dedication to duty, not mentioning my crucial lead, or my partner's contribution. But how could he have? My detective friend had purposely left out our involvement in the report. I thought a little recognition would have been nice and bolstered the relationship between us "uniforms" and the esteemed detectives.

My partner responded with a shrug and muttered under his breath, "defectives..." Not wanting to follow suit, I realized I had two choices: I could vent my disappointment and anger—likely on the next speeder—or give it to a higher power, knowing that He has already blessed me and thought no less of my abilities.

Why is it so difficult for us men to initiate forgiveness? I pondered that question as I sat in my patrol car. My wife, even when wronged by a close friend, finds it easy to forgive. For me, I know it's an issue of pride, based on performance. Whenever I've been offended, there's always that part of me that wanted to hang onto the hurt to show I've been wounded.

Does it help to harbour resentment for a past transgression? Truthfully, it only works against us, delaying forgiveness. So how did I respond the next time I ran into that detective in the police station hallway? First, I resisted the urge to look the other way, or turn around, effectively ignoring him. Second, I made eye contact, greeted him by his first name, and walked on without making a snide comment. Not an easy thing to do.

In the long run, not a whole lot had changed, but I knew he knew I wasn't harbouring resentment toward a fellow officer. It wasn't my place to challenge him, to persuade him that he had blown it. It was something he had to figure out on his own. The last thing I wanted was for the issue to linger. After all, we may end up working together some day.

The Good Book tells us to deal quickly with a transgressor, even when that person has no intention of righting the wrong. We need not, nor should we, expect the offender to apologize. Our part is clear: forgive the offender and move on. After all, God doesn't ignore our prayer of forgiveness or put off His mercy. And for that I'm truly grateful.

~Robert J. Stermscheg

The Reconnection

A friend is someone who knows all about you and still loves you.
~Elbert Hubbard

My heart pounded as I made the long distance call, the telephone receiver gripped tightly in my hand. Maybe it's the wrong number, I thought. Maybe she won't even remember me, or she'll hang up at the sound of my voice, or... A female voice answered on the fourth ring. "Hello?"

"Hi, Pat, it's me," I said.

"Oh my god," she whispered. "It's been so long. I thought I'd never hear from you again. I don't even remember how we came to lose touch with each other."

Her voice, low pitched and gravelly from years of cigarette smoking, sounded achingly familiar. I'd heard it for years back in upstate New York when we were across-the-street neighbors and the best of friends. It was hard to believe we hadn't spoken in almost twenty years.

•••

Pat Kelly and I were friends from the first. We met in the summer of 1970, near Syracuse, New York, when I knocked on her door to welcome her to the neighborhood. We were young married women, each twenty-six, and each with two sons born four years apart.

Pat towered over me, a full-bodied, six-foot-tall earth mother, with long black hair and a hearty laugh. She was the worldly one, having traveled and held a variety of jobs before starting a family, while I'd married young and never worked outside my home. I was the artistic one, the painter, working my way toward a degree at the local university, juggling academic and family responsibilities, trying to have it all. I warmed to her quick sense of humor and confident manner, and she to my talent and determination. We bonded immediately and over time became close as sisters—sharing thoughts and feelings about daily life as well as deeper issues, and providing each other with unwavering loyalty and emotional support.

I earned my BFA in 1973—a year before my marriage unraveled and my former husband relocated, becoming a long distance dad, and leaving me to raise our sons pretty much on my own. My mom's financial help kept us going until I found a job. But I doubt I could have survived that first, terrifying year as a single parent without Pat's practical advice on just about everything—from dealing with my new boss to my first date as a single woman.

"Trust me, you're going to get through this," she reassured me. "You're getting stronger and more capable every day."

She was right; I was gaining strength and confidence. Still, I was stuck in a dead-end job, without time or opportunity to use my artistic talents. I felt my life in our small town was going nowhere. Then, in late 1975, an opportunity came up to manage an art gallery/coffeehouse in San Francisco. It was an adventure and a chance to make a fresh start. Hard as it was to leave Pat behind, I couldn't turn it down.

"What will I do without you?" she asked when we said our goodbyes.

"We'll keep in touch," I promised, hugging her. "We'll telephone, write, and visit when we can."

"Friends to the end," we assured each other, and felt certain, despite the physical distance between us, that would never change.

• • •

Never say never, as the saying goes. West Coast life was good to me. The job at the coffeehouse didn't work out, but I began selling my artwork at Bay Area street fairs, and provided well for my family. I made new interesting friends, dated, and enjoyed the multicultural offerings of city life. I was becoming the strong, confident woman I wanted to be.

A year later, I took my family back to upstate New York for a visit. While our sons were delighted to see each other again, my relationship with Pat simply wasn't the same. What I'd once seen as strength and confidence seemed bossy and controlling—and when I challenged her right to advise and instruct, as she always had, we clashed. Words were said. She called me a college-educated idiot, and I called her an overbearing know-it-all. Feelings were hurt. Trust was shaken. Neither of us would back down.

We communicated less frequently after my return to San Francisco and I began to feel we had outgrown the friendship. When I moved in with my new husband, in 1986, somehow I forgot to send Pat my new address and phone number. When I finally called her, months later, the number was out of service and my Christmas card came back stamped, "No longer at this address." Pat had disappeared from my life.

I never felt right about the loss of that friendship and thought of her many times, recalling the closeness we'd shared. In 2009, my urge to reconnect with her intensified, until it led to an Internet search, yielding a phone number in a small town near Syracuse.

The joy in Pat's voice when I called was heartfelt. I felt the prickle of tears in my eyes.

"I'm sorry for whatever it was we fought about," I told her.

"I can't remember either," Pat chuckled, softly. "So what have you been up to for the last twenty years?"

We talked ourselves hoarse that evening, filling in each other on the details of our lives. And just like that, all was forgiven and the friendship renewed.

I visited her that summer. We were two white-haired women who cried in each other's arms when we met—and when we parted. She was still bossy and overbearing, in my opinion, but what mattered to me now was that we were still friends. After that we stayed in touch by phone and e-mail and talked about her coming out west to visit me the following summer. But that never happened. By then, Pat had learned she had lung cancer and began a long, futile course of treatment.

I called while she was in hospice care. She said I made her laugh in spite of everything. We talked every day until the day she said, "I love you, but I just can't talk anymore." She died the next day. Friends to the end.

~Lynn Sunday

When Old Friends Become New Friends

Two persons cannot long be friends if they cannot
forgive each other's little failings.
~Jean de la Bruyere

The friend request appeared on Facebook as I was trying to figure out how to upload a picture to my newly created account. One glance at the name and my body stiffened.

Memories washed over me — trips to her cabin in the summer, lazy days on the porch swing and school dances. No one knew me better than she had. Every dream, great and small, had been shared. She knew secrets no one else knew. Yet it had been twelve years since we last spoke.

My finger hovered over the mouse as I debated clicking accept. On one hand, I felt a stir of excitement in reconnecting with someone who had been like a sister to me growing up. On the other hand, I wasn't sure I wanted that sister-friend back. Old scars of betrayal still remained.

We were in high school. Silly girls crushing on every cute guy that walked by. Teachers frowned upon passing notes, so instead we passed a notebook back and forth in the hallway between classes, filling its pages with snippets about our crushes. She had a boyfriend that she met in 4-H, but they were breaking up. I was spying on the cute boy in my neighborhood.

We attracted very different guys. An extrovert, she was tall with long brown hair and easily became friends with everyone, including the hot guys. I, on the other hand, was short, shy and attracted the dorky guys with whom I'd rather just be friends.

So I was super-psyched when I met my step-cousin's cute friend at an end-of-summer family picnic and found out he was interested in me. We spent that day horsing around, and when dusk came we disappeared into the quiet house where we could talk. Before he left he gave me his phone number.

I tossed and turned all night, waiting for morning so I could call my friend and share my exciting news. She was delighted, and when school started she encouraged me to ask him to the Sadie Hawkins dance so we could double date. Sadie Hawkins was a fall dance where the girls asked the boys. My friend was going "just as friends" with the brother of one of the girls she knew from band.

It took a few days of encouragement, but I worked up the nerve to call my step-cousin's friend and ask him to the dance. To my astonishment, he said yes!

My friend and I planned a shopping trip. Sadie Hawkins has a silly tradition where the couples wear matching shirts. It was hard to find matching shirts in extra-large and small in the young men's section. We shopped for hours, finally settling on un-sexy flannel shirts. I was swimming in mine. She looked cute in hers.

The four of us met at a restaurant before the dance, squeezing into a booth. My friend indicated I did well by winking at me, then nodding in the direction of my date, who was busy looking at the menu. I smiled. This was going to be a great night!

While we waited for food, my friend started talking to my date, asking where he was from and about his interests. They were in the middle of a conversation when I realized things were going south for me. I could see it in his eyes, the way he looked at her, the way he lit up every time he caught her looking at him. Halfway through the dance she traded her date for mine.

My heart sunk as they slow danced just feet away from me. My best friend had hit it off with my date! I felt the knife twist when they officially started dating. I couldn't understand the betrayal or how she could call herself my best friend and then steal the guy I liked.

Their relationship only lasted a few months. By the time they broke up I had moved on to my stepbrother's cute friend.

She and I started talking again. Although the wound was still raw, I took her back as my "best friend." She started hanging out at my house again, and lo and behold, my stepbrother's cute friend fell for her after I decided I liked him.

Fool me once, shame on you. Fool me twice, shame on me. So we went our separate ways.

I stared at the friend request, faced with a serious decision—did I want her back as a friend? Could we even be friends again? In the twelve years that had passed we'd both surely grown up. I clicked "accept." In a private message, she asked for my phone number.

When the phone rang, I stared at her name on the caller ID, letting it ring again and again. Curiosity won and I answered before the answering machine came on.

We talked forever that first night about the past and present. We caught up on all that we had missed through the years—college, jobs, weddings, children and illnesses. She filled me in on how her parents were doing and I filled her in on my dad and stepmother. She had stayed in touch with my stepbrother's friends through the years and updated me on their lives. I had abandoned everyone when I left for college. The pain had been too much.

She told me all about how she had dated my stepbrother's cute friend for a few years until she found out he was cheating on her. I guess the universe has its own way of working things out. Ironically, he was the second person to send me a friend request. It turned out the cute guy wasn't so cute anymore. He was overweight and balding, not at all like the young college guy I remembered.

I hung up realizing we could be friends again—maybe not best friends, or good friends, but friends. Forgiving her for the hurt she caused in the past allowed us to move forward in a new friendship. We are different people than we were twelve years ago. We have families, careers, new hopes and dreams, and because of that we will have a wiser, more mature friendship this time around.

~Valerie D. Benko

Thank You, Kate

I will permit no man to narrow and degrade my soul by making me hate him.
~Booker T. Washington

he front of the card showed a picture of Jesus standing in front of a rainbow with his arms outstretched and the words, "Jesus Loves You." Instead of the expected note of encouragement, the ugly, sinister words inside frightened me. "Everyone else thinks you're an a**h***." No signature. No return address.

But I knew who'd sent it. The harassment for the past eight years had just reached a new low. This attack came at a vulnerable time for me. I was alone with our two children during the week while my husband worked a new job two hours away. All the other attacks had occurred within the workplace, but this had come to my home, crossing a line that made it feel as though my family were now also part of the vendetta against me.

For the first few years, Kate and I had worked together well. We believed in the mission of our company and the services we provided to our customers. The first inkling of trouble came when an out-of-state inspector made an appointment to review our practices. At Kate's request, I put together a procedure manual in preparation for the visit.

The day arrived. We presented the manual to the inspector. She paged through it and said, "Good work. This is clear and concise."

Before I could thank her, Kate jumped in. "Thank you," she said.

"I wanted to be sure anyone could come in, follow these directions, and produce the same results."

I stood there with my mouth open, but said nothing. While I felt hurt and confused that she would take credit for my work, I chalked it up to the fact that she'd been extremely stressed over this evaluation.

But that incident became a turning point in our relationship. Kate began deflecting conversations, answering with abrupt, one-syllable answers. She neglected to tell me work-related information I needed in order to do my job. At one point, after our boss confronted me about "my" mistake, I discovered Kate had made a serious error and then blamed it on me.

Knowing Kate's difficult home circumstances, I tried to be understanding. I reached out to her with notes, left samples of her favorite tea on her desk, and even wrote an apology for whatever I might have done to offend her. These efforts only seemed to make things worse.

Kate now spoke to me, but only when she wanted to criticize, deride, or humiliate me. One day, I was helping a customer, who Kate had worked with extensively, with some complicated paperwork. She walked by the desk where we sat. "Kate," I said, "could you help this gentleman?"

She fixed me with an icy stare, and in front of the man said, "You should know how to do this," turned on her heel, and marched away.

I began dreading work, which in turn filled me with anger and resentment. Since I'd been a child, this company, this job, had been my dream. Much as I tried to not let it bother me, Kate's hatred slithered under my skin.

The increasingly hostile work environment took me to a breaking point. Quitting was not an option. At the time, my husband was in youth ministry. We were barely making it on both our salaries. But something had to give.

I confided in a friend who had dealt with a similar situation. "Remind yourself of how much Jesus loves Kate."

My gut response spilled out of my mouth. "I don't think I can do that." Her advice ate at me until I realized I had to give it a try. The first time I saw Kate after I'd made this decision, I whispered to myself, "Jesus loves you." At that moment, inexplicable love for her flowed through me. I left work that evening with a lightness I hadn't experienced in a long time.

Whenever I would see Kate, I reminded myself of Jesus's love for her. My reward came as Kate mounted a new campaign to subtly undermine my performance and credibility. This covert harassment brought back the dread of going to work.

At times, I found myself fuming and gossiping about her actions for the rest of the work shift whenever an incident occurred. My growing animosity gnawed away inside me.

Once again, I turned to my friend for advice. "Have you prayed for her?" she asked.

I had not. "Okay, Lord," I prayed when I got home. "You know how I feel about Kate, but I'm going to ask you to bless her." I continued to pray this and discovered it's hard to be angry with someone you ask God to bless.

Something inside me was still not right. That final step happened the day the Lord's Prayer hit me like never before. "Forgive me as I forgive others." In my mind and heart I heard the words, "You haven't forgiven Kate for how she has hurt you."

Stunned and whiny, I thought, "I don't want to forgive her. Besides, she doesn't want my forgiveness."

And then the still, small, voice, said "That doesn't matter. It's what you need to do." Much as I tried to ignore it, I realized if I wanted to be able to live with myself, I had to forgive Kate.

It didn't come fast or easily. When I started saying, "Kate, I forgive you," I felt like a liar. I persevered until one day, when I spoke those words, I knew without a doubt I had forgiven her.

At the end of our transition year, my office threw me a heartfelt going-away party. As I unwrapped the many thoughtful and loving gifts, read messages of well wishes, and laughed and reminisced with my coworkers, gratitude for the blessings of my fourteen years there overwhelmed me.

Yes, Kate was there. True to form, she spoke not one word to me, not even goodbye. It was okay. I now felt only sympathy and compassion for her, and hoped one day she would be able to free herself from hate.

I never saw Kate again. A few years ago, I learned she had passed away. I don't know if she ever came to terms with what had happened between us—or if she even thought about me at all after I moved. But Kate never knew that she taught me one of the most important lessons of my life—how to love and forgive someone who hates you. That lesson has transformed all of my relationships, making me a better, more loving wife, mother, and friend.

Thank you, Kate.

~Elizabeth June Walters

The Apology

Forgiveness does not change the past, but it does enlarge the future.

~Les Brown

I moved to the Phoenix area in my early twenties, and to expand my social life I joined a young adult group at my church. At every gathering I met new friends who helped me to feel more accepted and at home. Because I love music, I started singing in the choir, where I met Lisa. We were about the same age, both a little on the geeky/nerdy side. No matter, our voices blended well together, and soon we began composing songs. Finding people with similar interests helped ease my feelings of loneliness after moving to a new city.

"Are you going to go on the retreat?" Lisa asked. Once or twice a year, the young adult group put on a retreat.

I hesitated. I had little experience with retreats and I still felt like an outsider.

"Come on," Lisa said. "Everyone goes."

"Okay." I reluctantly agreed. After all, some cute guys were in the group. Perhaps I would have an opportunity to get to know one of them better.

As the retreat weekend approached, I learned that the theme was forgiveness. My experience with forgiveness could pretty much be summed up with a heartfelt "I'm sorry!" when I bump someone in the grocery store, or a reluctant non-apologetic "Sorry." This forced apology I learned around the age of four. I hadn't grown much since then.

In my twenties, the world revolved around me and what I wanted. What I feared. What I dreamed. What I hated. I liked being around other people. And, as most people do, I learned how to be pleasant enough without giving in and having to apologize any more than necessary. In short, the forgiveness theme made me uncomfortable. I would attend the retreat, but I planned to sit quietly in the background and watch.

The retreat was held at a camp in Prescott, Arizona, a gloriously wooded paradise that emanated peace and solitude. The first night we gathered in the common room where we also ate our meals. According to plan, I found a spot in the back where I could watch, unobserved. Lisa sat at the front, ending up across from me as we were in a rather disjointed circle. I finger-waved at her, but pretended not to see when she indicated I should sit by her.

The leader, a deacon at our church, got up and spoke about the healing power of forgiveness. His words were motivating and touching.

"Now comes the hard part," he said. "I want to invite you to look into your hearts and if you feel moved to do so, go to a person here in the room and ask to be forgiven for something you've done."

Initially, there was total silence.

Was he kidding?

Who was going to publicly acknowledge that they'd screwed up?

Everyone got busy. Picking their nails. Tying their shoes. Evading the glances of others.

Then Lisa stood up.

We all watched, secretly glad someone else was going first in front of forty witnesses. I was impressed.

My admiration turned to embarrassment, however, as Lisa made her way through the crowd toward me.

Lisa planted her feet firmly in front of me.

I looked down. I couldn't meet her eye.

"Kathleen, I'd like to ask your forgiveness."

I shook my head. Then nodded, not sure how to respond. I felt the heat rise into my cheeks. I could hardly breathe knowing that everyone could hear and see all this. I had no idea what I was forgiving her for.

I wanted her to just go away.

"I have been jealous of you and how easily you joined our group. Even though you became my friend when we worked on music together, I still thought you were doing it for yourself. I've held that against you and I'm sorry."

"It's okay," I choked out. Stunned, I stood up, gave her an awkward hug and then sat back down. Lisa turned and went back to her seat.

Applause broke out and the tension in the room evaporated. All except mine.

Lisa's bravery broke the ice and everyone started to ask forgiveness for various injuries, some big, some small. Echoes of "I'm sorry," and "please forgive me," laughter, and tears floated around as I sat in a fog of incomprehension.

What had just happened?

I mentally reviewed experiences I'd had with the group. Lisa was usually there, and she laughed and joked with the group. But there was a difference. More reserved than I, Lisa always joined the periphery of the group. I hadn't notice her loneliness.

But why had she asked my forgiveness?

I was the one who had neglected to see the situation through anyone's eyes but my own. I was the one who hadn't once thought about what it must be like to be the shy one, the one left out. It had never occurred to me she had a different experience than I did.

Then it hit me.

She needed to ask my forgiveness in order to forgive herself for holding something against me I hadn't even intended. My lack of empathy and compassion had created a dissonance between us.

The world began to change for me. I learned empathy the day that Lisa asked my forgiveness. I had read *To Kill a Mockingbird* by Harper Lee several times. But I realized that I had never understood the message Atticus Finch taught his children: "You never really know a man until you stand in his shoes and walk around in them."

Soon the weekend was over, and my life gained momentum. I wish I could say I had instant empathy. My journey, however, was longer. At first I avoided Lisa because I felt so uncomfortable with the knowledge that I'd hurt her enough that she needed to apologize in order to feel better. How messed up is that? After an uncomfortable apology on my part we reconnected, but our friendship was never the same.

I met and married a man from the group and we moved away from Phoenix. I lost touch with Lisa after I moved, but her actions and words stuck with me. Life's funny in how many chances it gives you to learn a lesson. Each time I found myself unable to sleep, or found myself alone and angry because I couldn't let go of a perceived injury, I would remember.

Lisa's bravery became my salvation.

Through the years my friendships were better, stronger, deeper. I learned compassion and empathy. I apologized and forgave quickly. I watched carefully, ensuring that I never overlooked someone in the same way again.

Lisa allowed me the gift of friendship because her example taught me to forgive.

~Kathleen Birmingham

Coaching the Coach

Anger makes you smaller, while forgiveness forces you
to grow beyond what you are.
~Cherie Carter-Scott

My best friend Billy and I were coaching a twelve-year-old baseball team for competition in open league tournaments. The roster included several ballplayers who'd been pegged as top-notch talent. Our excitement grew with each practice as the boys' skills continued to develop and we realized that this team could compete against the best in the area.

We wanted to add one more player to the roster and held a last tryout for the only boy who came. John Stern, Jr. was an above average player who could help us in situations and provide the backup that every team needs as it goes through a season of as many as sixty games.

We began league play, and in no time the problems began. Only nine players could participate at one time, but all twelve boys wanted to be in the game. Billy and I rotated them so that each received equal time. However, the dads who stood on the hill at games never accepted the fact that their sons would have to share playing time. One of the biggest complainers was John's dad.

These grown men complained and second-guessed Billy and me on our every decision. If their sons failed to get hits, we had kept them from swinging their bats. If they missed ground balls, we had placed them in the wrong positions. Dads expressed their displeasure to sons, and before long, our players were only half-heartedly playing.

Midway through the year, I decided to resign as a coach of the team so that some of the discontent might ease. John Stern, Sr. jumped at the opportunity to fill the vacancy. He moved in and took over the team. Even Billy couldn't stop him from bullying his way in.

Stern's first move was to bench my son. Dallas was a good ballplayer, but Stern meant to send a message to me through my son. In the next several games, Dallas didn't rotate into the line-up; he didn't receive even a minimal amount of time in games. The man benched Dallas with no intention of allowing him playing time in another game.

I held my tongue for a while, but eventually, the injustice of it all got to me. I confronted Stern, and he responded by throwing Dallas off the team! I couldn't believe that my son was kicked off a team I'd help to build. My blood boiled, and words were exchanged between him and me.

For the next couple of years, I couldn't even think of John Stern without becoming so angry that my blood pressure spiked. When I saw him at games throughout the coming seasons, I turned and walked away, refusing to speak to a man that I hated for the pain he'd inflicted on my son.

Dallas moved on to high school baseball. Twice a year, we played against the school that John Stern, Jr. attended. By then, both boys played first base and hit the ball well. That meant they'd spend time together on the base. What I discovered was that they played hard against each other, but they also talked and seemed cordial. Still, the boy's dad had treated my son wrong, and I had no intention of ever speaking to him again.

By his senior year in high school, Dallas had proven himself to be a solid baseball player. He'd hit the ball, made good plays at first base, and pitched against all the teams in the area. That meant he'd faced John and kept him off base with strikeouts, groundballs, or fly-outs.

After one game, my son and I discussed his performance. I mentioned how he'd shut down John, and Dallas said to me, "Dad, it's time to quit being mad. His dad was a jerk, and he hurt me back then, but

I'm okay now and don't care. He can't do anything anymore. Don't be mad."

That Dallas told me it was time to get over this anger surprised me. I realized that for years I'd allowed John Stern, Sr. to sap part of my life's energy whenever I turned my anger loose. My son was right: The time had long since come and gone for me to let it go. I did; I forgave John Stern for the ill that he'd done to Dallas.

Almost immediately, I felt as if a huge weight had been lifted from my shoulders. My mood lightened. Baseball returned to something I enjoyed as I watched Dallas compete. When I saw John Stern, I spoke to him. No, we would never be friends, but I no longer allowed anger and hate to swell inside every time he came around.

Dallas completed his senior year of baseball and moved on to college. He didn't play then because he said other things were now more important. I hope I'm not the reason he gave up the game. I do know that my son taught me about forgiving, restoring my energies, and enjoying life more. I am slower to anger and quicker to forgive because of what he taught me after one baseball game.

~Joe Rector

64

The Power
Is in Your Hands

We acquire the strength we have overcome.
~Ralph Waldo Emerson

I unexpectedly became a widow at an early age. Even though he had been verbally abusive, I was still a basket case when my husband died. Mary, my best friend from school, dropped everything and relocated across the country to be with me in my time of need. I hadn't asked. She was just there. "Don't you worry about anything, I'm here till you get back on your feet again." I was grateful to have her company, and soon her quick wit had me laughing and enjoying life again.

I had a house and she moved in. She was good at everything. She did the yard, the housework and the cooking. I worked. It was nice to have a warm meal waiting for me when I got home. I admit I felt so spoiled. Secretly, though, I wondered if she would ever leave. I couldn't be ungrateful and ask her to go, could I?

She kept insisting she would find her own place as soon as a "real" job came along, although it didn't seem like she was pursuing anything. I paid the mortgage and she worked part-time, covering her minor expenses.

First it was the little things that started to bother me. She'd complain to the neighbors that their dog was trashing our yard. My yard! She'd yell at the newspaper guy when he delivered the paper without a plastic bag. She'd tell my teenage nephew that only bums wore their caps in the house. I may have objected to the cap but wasn't it my place to tell him? To keep peace, I mostly stayed quiet.

To tell the truth, I didn't have the nerve to ask her to leave. The house was large enough so when things got really uncomfortable, I just retreated to my room.

One day I threw a birthday party for my nephew. As soon as the guests arrived she began barking orders: "Take your shoes off. Put them by the door!" A young relative drank a soft drink out of a bottle. "Where are your manners? Take a glass!" "Out of the kitchen everyone. I am trying to cook!" she barked. The youngsters were afraid of her. Older guests secretly referred to her as the Kitchen Nazi. "It's okay, Mary." I tried to defuse the situation. But her retort to me had been so combative that I just let it go.

The next day I sat her down at the kitchen table and gently expressed my dissatisfaction. "Mary, while I appreciate your desire to help me, it's my job to set the rules." She abruptly rose, shrugged her shoulders and dismissed me with, "Sure!"

In no time, her aggressive behavior reared its ugly head again. I allowed the situation to continue. I did anything to avoid confrontation. Yet I was becoming more bitter and angry. I snapped at her. She snapped at me harder. Resentment grew and festered.

When I met Larry and we started discussing marriage, I had a stiff drink for courage and announced to Mary that a couple should have privacy. She promised she would get a place of her own soon. But she never did. She'd argue. She'd fight. She'd cry, "I have no place to go!" Or "I can't afford it. I have no money. I will move out when I have the means." She reminded me that she had been there when I needed her and now I was discarding her like an old shoe. I had a roommate from hell!

I took my dilemma to Larry, who gave me this advice: "Honey, you must handle this problem like the grown woman you are. I can't tell you what to do. The power is in your hands."

I even sought the advice of a therapist. I took Mary with me. After a few visits, to my surprise, the therapist told me she couldn't help Mary. "But I can help you if you listen."

"Help me? But I'm not the one who is argumentative. I'm not the one who uses people and takes advantage of a friend's good nature. I am the healthy one!"

Almost immediately as I spoke these words of protest and denial, I began to see a completely different picture of myself! I had been allowing Mary to take advantage of my good nature, just as I had allowed my first husband to verbally abuse me. I was too timid to take a stand! I had no backbone! I was a wimp!

The next day I smelled smoke coming from Mary's room. This time I walked in bravely. "I have told you a thousand times you cannot smoke in the house!" I shouted. Brazenly, as she furtively dipped the cigarette into a cup she was holding, she retorted, "Who's smoking? I am not smoking! You're crazy." Meanwhile, in full view, the smoke was blowing out of her nose!

That was the last straw. A week later, when she returned from shopping, I had her bags packed by the door. I handed her an envelope and firmly said: "I found a lovely apartment for you. I will pay for it for three months. And here is some cash for any expenses you may have. If you refuse this, I will have you evicted and you will get nothing." It was money I did not have to spare but it was worth it. Her eyes were wide in disbelief as she took it and my offer. She was gone the next day.

It took a while for the bitterness to leave me. I had thought she was my dear friend, but she had taken advantage of me. Eventually I realized that I had contributed to this unhealthy relationship. It was a pattern that I had followed most of my life. In order to keep peace, I allowed people to walk all over me. But the anger had festered inside me. When I realized I would no longer be afraid to say, "No," it was as if a stronger power released within me.

I didn't see Mary again until I ran into her in the supermarket years later. The years had not been kind to her. Her face looked shriveled and resentful. But for old times' sake, we had a cup of coffee and chatted as if nothing unpleasant had ever occurred. We talked about fun times, when life was easy. It pained me that she was not in a happy place. I no longer felt anger toward her. I had forgiven her and was almost grateful to her. Without her, I might never have learned how to become a strong woman in my own right.

We parted for the last time. I kissed her check and we said our goodbyes. As she walked away I think I saw her mouth the words, "I'm sorry." I did see a tear trickle down her cheek. Then I recalled the advice Larry had given me long ago. "The power is in your hands. Use it." The power to forgive was in my hands, also. I still live with these words today.

~Eva Carter

The Power *of* Forgiveness

Lessons from the People You Meet

People have to forgive. We don't have to like them, we don't have to be friends with them, we don't have to send them hearts in text messages, but we have to forgive them, to overlook, to forget. Because if we don't we are tying rocks to our feet, too much for our wings to carry!

~C. JoyBell C.

65

Neighbor from Hell

Today, give a stranger one of your smiles.
It might be the only sunshine he sees all day.
~H. Jackson Brown, Jr., P.S. I Love You

She was determined to make our lives miserable from the moment we met. Edna Strom looked to be in her late seventies. She had a perpetual squint. Her lips curled sourly, as if she had mistaken a bottle of vinegar for soda.

We'd barely moved one stick of furniture into the lower duplex we'd rented next door to her converted two-story home when Mrs. Strom hobbled onto her upstairs front gallery. She glared down at my twelve-year-old son David and then at me, announcing, "You make sure you keep that child out of my yard!"

Since our buildings shared a communal six-foot-high privacy fence that separated our lots, I couldn't understand her concern or hostility. Nevertheless, I replied curtly, "Don't worry!" as I ducked into my entryway with the box I was carrying.

That encounter set the tone for weeks. The next day, while my son was laughing on the phone, we were stunned to hear a loud pounding from the other side of his bedroom wall, which connected our dwellings and ran the entire length of both houses.

"Stop that racket right this minute!"

Mrs. Strom's furious voice filtered right into the kitchen I was painting. I rushed towards David to find him sitting on the bed, eyes wide with shock, his conversation forgotten.

"Mom, I was just laughing!" he protested.

"I know, honey," I soothed, gulping back my own growing anger. "Listen, let's just let this go until we're a little more settled in. I'll deal with it in a few days if it continues, okay?" I promised.

"Okay," he agreed reluctantly.

That same afternoon, he and a friend went out front to play pitch and catch. Within minutes, they both returned, their expressions clearly indicating that they were upset about something.

"What happened?" I sighed, certain our neighbor had struck again.

"She yelled at us from her balcony to go play in the back yard," David complained.

I handed each of the kids a soda, instructing them go out back. Then, I marched out the front door to confront the cranky old woman. This was our home too and I was going to nip this problem in the bud. There was no way she was going to continue scolding my child, especially since he'd done nothing wrong, nor been excessively loud.

I found her sitting ramrod straight in a rocking chair on her front porch, peering out into the street. Her summer dress was crisply ironed, her polished shoes gleamed, and every hair was in place. She wore a pearl necklace with matching earrings. When she saw me approach, she narrowed her eyes, pursing her lips even tighter.

"Is something wrong?" I asked her.

"My boy is coming to visit," she informed me haughtily. "I didn't want to get hit by your son's baseball while I wait for him."

"I'm sure he was being careful," I told her stonily. "He's not a bad kid, ma'am. In the future, if there's a problem, please come to me so we can solve it instead of shouting at him."

Not waiting for an answer, I turned and went back into the house. As I entered the common foyer, I almost bumped into the upstairs tenant who was checking her mail.

"I see you've met Edna Strom." She smiled. "Pay her no mind. She sits out there every day the minute the weather turns warm and waits for her son to visit. He only comes when he needs money. Even then, he's loud, rude and obnoxious, treating her like dirt!"

The apple doesn't fall far from the tree, I almost muttered, but bit my tongue. "Is she always that crabby?" I asked instead.

"Always. Just ignore her. Everyone does."

Edna didn't let up on her tyrannical behavior. She hammered on the walls if we so much as dropped a pot cover or raised our stereo or television to a decibel above a whisper. Even adjusting the ring of our phone to accommodate her couldn't please the woman. We could almost feel her scowl sear into us as she kept her ever-present vigil on the balcony in the pathetic hope that her son might drop in.

Two months later, we were finally settled in and decided to have a cookout for friends and family. I prepared for the event, ignoring the persistent banging whenever I closed a cupboard or refrigerator door a little too hard. By that time, Mrs. Strom was becoming background noise.

The day of the barbecue, as people arrived, I noticed that Edna wasn't at her usual post. Her son had dropped in two days earlier and was every bit as vocal and insufferable as I'd been told, belittling his mother and demanding money. I assumed she wouldn't expect him again anytime soon and was taking a break from her lookout.

As the last guest arrived, we moved to the back yard. I was serving appetizers when a movement from her upstairs window caught my eye. I looked up to see her observing a laughing group of my visitors. Unaware that she could be seen, her usual bitter demeanor was absent. Instead, a combination of sad, wistful loneliness seemed to suffuse her features, and I felt a growing sympathy tug at my heart.

Seconds later, I was ringing her bell. She opened the door, shocked to see me.

"Can I help you?" she asked coldly, and I smiled.

"Mrs. Strom, I was wondering if you'd like to join us since we're neighbors. I'm sure my family and friends would love to meet you."

"Well, I—that is—I—I'm not really dressed to—"

I noticed then that she was clothed more casually than I'd ever seen her.

"You look fine," I assured her. "Everyone is in jeans or shorts. You'll fit right in. Please come."

For the first time ever, I saw her smile, catching a glimpse of the beauty that must have been hers when she was younger.

"Well, if you're sure," she said shyly, patting her hair nervously and straightening her blouse. "I have a fresh cheesecake I can bring—my late husband's favorite. I made it this morning."

"Why, that would be wonderful," I gushed. "Come, let's go."

My husband and son hid their shock, welcoming our neighbor with warm smiles when I escorted her into our yard on my arm.

"Everyone," I called out, "I'd like you to meet my friend and neighbor, Edna Strom."

We never heard a harsh word from her again. In fact, we became close friends, forgiving and forgetting our rocky beginning, and embracing our friendship instead. She no longer sat on her balcony waiting tirelessly for her son's sporadic visits. She was far too busy teaching me her favorite recipes, and joining us for family occasions where she was received with love and respect until she died peacefully five years later in her sleep. Only a week before, she had hugged me tightly and thanked me for being the daughter she never had. I mourned her like I would a beloved relative, grateful that I looked past the thorns to see the fragile flower within.

~Marya Morin

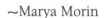

66

Soul Marks

Treat everyone with politeness, even those who are rude to you—
not because they are nice, but because you are.
~Author Unknown

I was heading home after a long day at work and feeling tired and frazzled. I kept thinking about the e-mails I had forgotten to send and the many appointments I had scheduled for the following day.

I was nearing home and navigating a familiar stretch of road with the late day sun glaring off the wet road. I snapped off the radio as the noise was just increasing my tension. All I wanted was to be at home; a warm mug of tea and my cozy couch were just what I needed to put the stressful day behind me. Having to drive those last few blocks felt suddenly, and overwhelmingly, unbearable.

As I approached an intersection, I pulled into the left-turn lane. A small blue sedan pulled ahead of me in the middle lane and then tried to cut in front of me in the turning lane.

With my aggression already high, I determined that I would not let that driver in. I practically kissed the bumper of the SUV ahead of me and stared stoically ahead, refusing to make eye contact. A silly game I had played a thousand times before. The driver continued to try to nudge in but I wouldn't let her. Instead she accelerated forward and merged in two cars ahead of me.

I felt a moment of fury—she had won! It lasted only a moment and then my anger abruptly dissipated. I imagined that perhaps she was a tourist who didn't know that her left turn was coming up so fast. Or maybe she was distracted by her busy day and found herself stranded in the intersection. Or maybe she was late to meet her mother. Any of a million scenarios suddenly flashed through my mind, along with a measure of shame. I had gained nothing through my traffic aggression. The moment would be gone and forgotten quickly, so why make another human suffer, even for a moment, just because I had a bad day? Was that really the energy I wanted to put out in the world?

As I rounded the corner, I moved into the left lane for yet another upcoming turn and saw the little blue sedan inching along in the right lane against a backdrop of office buildings. Traffic in both lanes moved slowly. I took a deep breath before I passed the car and looked directly at her as I drove. Expecting a look of annoyance and anger from her, I softened my heart, smiled and mouthed the words "I'm sorry."

Her response stuck with me. I expected her to express her distaste and frustration but as she took in my remote apology, her face registered surprise. She looked back at me and I saw her start to laugh, as she too recognized the absurdity of the situation and the emotion we attached to it. She waved and I waved back as I continued on my way.

I am grateful I had that awakening. It was a moment of unpleasantness and negativity that would have passed quickly but left just a little mark on my psyche. The type of mark that compounds over time. Instead, I ended up feeling connected and positive in a way that has carried forward. I think of that moment whenever I feel frustrated about commuter life. It inspires me to foster a forgiving approach so that it is kindness and compassion that mark my soul, not anger and ill will.

~Crystal Johnson

Choosing for Myself

Our ultimate freedom is the right and power to decide how anybody
or anything outside ourselves will affect us.
~Stephen Covey

"You're not college material." That's what my eighth grade guidance counselor said to me forty-three years ago and I haven't forgotten those four words. Prior to middle school graduation, it's a requirement to meet with a guidance counselor. In my case, I met with Mrs. Bradleigh to map out my future. Isn't it crazy to think that a practical stranger has so much influence over your choices in life? At thirteen, in a less than fifteen-minute meeting, I was put on a path of taking "business" courses because I was told, "You're not college material."

The courses were chosen for me. I didn't question. My mom didn't argue. So it was ordained. When I began high school I would be taking courses that prepared me to be a secretary. But I had been "playing teacher" since I was in kindergarten. My teacher, whom I adored, had given me a large chalkboard that I dragged home on the last day of school. She gave me yellowed penmanship books, her bell, a pass to the lavatory, tattered jump ropes, and a bunny puzzle (with a missing ear). She beamed. "These are for you for when you're a teacher one day."

Two educators — two totally different mindsets. My kindergarten teacher worded things in a way that made me feel like I could accomplish anything. My guidance counselor labeled me based on standardized tests and average grades.

Four years passed quickly. Prior to high school graduation, my friends visited colleges. I completed my résumé. I began my first secretarial job, working for the government, two days after graduation. For the next few years, I had several interesting jobs as a secretary. I gave it my best shot, but it wasn't something I was passionate about. I might not have been college material, but I certainly wasn't going to do something that I didn't love. It was a powerful realization when I decided that I was accountable for my choices—no one else.

I enrolled part-time at a community college and pursued an associate's degree in science to become a registered dietetic technician. It didn't bother me that I had to backtrack, taking courses most young adults took in high school. I had a three-year goal (since I attended part-time and worked full-time). I graduated two and a half years later with a 4.0 grade point average and a love for my job. Although I wasn't a "school" teacher, I was still teaching patients about nutrition. It was rewarding, and I felt a great deal of confidence, satisfaction, and purpose.

The only downfall of being a dietetic technician was that I had to work weekends and most holidays. As my youngest approached school, my husband said, "Go back to college for teaching. It's what you've always wanted." I looked at him like he had lost his marbles.

"I'm not college material."

"Says who?"

"Says Mrs. Bradleigh." She was still on the tip of my tongue seventeen years later. However, this time I decided to move past her words and take ownership of my life. Five years later I became a second grade teacher.

Mrs. Bradleigh was right. I wasn't college material at thirteen, but she never got to the root of the problem. I lived in Camden, New Jersey as a young child when radical changes were occurring. School was disrupted due to riots. I had six different third grade teachers and don't think I had a math assignment the entire year. My grandfather, who lived with us, passed away and my two brothers were drafted into the Vietnam War—all within a year. The next year, we moved from Camden to the suburbs. The other students were a good two years ahead of me academically.

I didn't have a strong academic foundation from third to fifth grade, but I had great work habits and enjoyed school and learning. If Mrs. Bradleigh had initiated a conversation, I think the pieces of the puzzle would have been put together in my teens instead of my thirties. Mrs. Bradleigh should have asked more questions, but my parents and I also chose to remain silent that day. We were equally to blame.

I've forgiven Mrs. Bradleigh's word choice—those four words—because those words make me think long and hard when I have conferences with my students and parents. I carefully choose words. If someone is struggling, I do my best to come up with a solution, but I do this as a team—student, parent, teacher. Does the child need glasses? Does the child have difficulty processing information and need visual clues? Are there personal matters at home making learning difficult? Does the child feel bullied? Is the child a poor test taker? Grandparents still pass away, wars continue to rage, and it's even harder to keep schools safe. My students' lives aren't much different than my life at their age.

My life experiences have shaped me into the advocate I am today. I think of the people and situations I would have missed out on if I didn't take the detour—the winding roads of career choices.

When I began to forgive, my world got a whole lot wider. My voice became stronger and my experiences became richer. Ultimately, we are responsible for who we are and the contributions we make to others in life.

~Nancy Norton

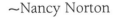

The Love Symbol

Darkness cannot drive out darkness; only light can do that.
Hate cannot drive out hate; only love can do that.
~Martin Luther King, Jr.

Whenever I need to forgive myself or someone else, an image of Laird flashes in my mind. No one would suspect this seventy-four-year-old man in red suspenders had survived five years as a prisoner of war at the Hanoi Hilton in North Vietnam.

Yet there he sat that first day, looking like actor Jack Nicholson, crunching an English muffin in a back booth of the Village Inn. A local magazine had hired me to profile him. As a pacifist studying nonviolent communication, his was a story I didn't particularly want to hear. More brutality. Little awareness.

But who could resist Laird? He must have been something when he became a pilot in the U.S. Army Air Corps at eighteen, I thought, double-checking my tape recorder. And even more of something when at forty-two, he volunteered for combat duty in North Vietnam. That's when a MiG-21, with heat-seeking missiles, shot down his plane.

Moments before his jet crashed in the mountains near Hanoi, he bailed out, landing on a heavily traveled trail, he said. For ten hours, he crouched under a bush amid gunfire and screaming soldiers.

At dusk, he heard girls giggling. One girl needed to pee. Out of twenty-five bushes nearby, she picked his. Reaching her hand around the bush, she felt his face and shrieked.

Laird's captors blindfolded him, tying a rope around his neck, yanking it so that he moved in the rhythm of sudden slavery: taking a few steps, stumbling, sliding, falling over slippery rocks.

The rest of the night he faced a torture known as the rope trick. His captors tied his arms behind his back with his wrists together. They put a rope around his elbows and drew the rope together until it dislocated his shoulders.

They tortured him repeatedly. Over time, he endured five rounds of the rope trick, surviving minute by minute. "Then they completely broke me, physically and emotionally," he said. His eyes never left mine. "I began screaming, agreeing to do anything they asked. I knew I'd throw my kids into a fire to make them quit. I was in a full panic. This was far worse than being tortured and dying."

While in solitary, Laird became overwhelmed by fear, anger, and hatred. He vowed to contact a scientist once released, one who would develop a spray that could kill not only his captors, but all North Vietnamese people.

"These people have no right to live," he recalled feeling after listening to a baby laughing outside while a man inside screamed from torture.

"That's the logic of hate groups," he said. "That wasn't me. I had to drop the fear."

He willed himself to remember his training. Fear is corrosive. In a slavery situation, anger is non-productive. Frustrated anger becomes hatred. Hatred is self-torture, making you bitter and destroying your immune system.

"It's the one thing you can bring home that can continue to destroy the people around you," he said.

He remembered being a child plagued with nightmares. His mom, a Christian Scientist, encouraged him to soften his mind with beautiful thoughts.

"I'd think of pretty angels flying around on wings. If you fill yourself with love, there is no room left for fear. It's like lighting a match in a dark room."

Nice philosophy, but in solitary his heart couldn't grasp love.

Then he remembered the letter his wife sent before he was captured. She'd described gritting her teeth, trying to get their kids to sleep without losing her cool. After bedtime prayers, their little girl threw her arms around her and said, "I love you, Mommy."

Laird sighed, continuing, "All of a sudden the whole world's in its rightful place. God is in the heavens. All's well. I envisioned this, and it was like boom!—somebody took a big weight off my back."

This became his symbol of love, something he visualized repeatedly for months.

"Suddenly, the fear left and along with the fear, the need for the anger and hatred."

Next he realized he needed to learn to love a Power greater than himself.

"I created the God symbol, a sun on the horizon, neither rising nor setting." A line of humanity pulsed from its center enveloping him. "I superimposed my love symbol on top of that symbol. Now I'm loving God."

After reviving his love for God, he practiced "loving the least of My children," figuring "the least of His children" was Big Ug, a particularly sadistic guard. For the next three years, Laird visualized Big Ug with the love symbol over him.

"One day I saw Big Ug and realized I wasn't afraid of him. I felt sorry for the poor slug. Can you imagine going through your life realizing all you did was torture Americans? When I realized he no longer filled me with fear, I realized putting the love symbol on him, in essence, praying for him, paid off. It does work."

Another time, Laird enraged a guard so much, he knew the guard was ready to kick him.

"I'd reached my limit," Laird said. "If anyone touched me, I'd come unglued. It was all I could do to superimpose my love symbol on him. He kicked me, but was so far away, he almost fell flat on his rear. Then he went berserk, turning to swing at me.

"I sat there with this love symbol on him, quaking in my boots. He missed me by two feet and swung all the way around. Now the terrible thing happened."

Another guard started to laugh. The first guard commanded the laughing guard to get a rope to tie Laird to a hook in the ceiling ten feet above. The laughing guard returned with twine too tiny to wrap a decent package. The first guard blanched, beating his hands against the wall in frustration. Then the dinner gong sounded; both guards left.

Laird had no doubt his love symbol invited this moment's grace.

Grace followed him home on March 17, 1973 after the Paris Peace Accords were signed. "You're on cloud nine," said every psychiatrist he saw. "When you crash, they'll hear it from one end of the room to the other."

But he never crashed. He'd forgiven his captors. No residue of hatred ever rose up again. Nothing remained but love and loyalty as he began speaking out for those missing in action.

"Every morning I wake up saying, 'Wow! I've got another whole day.'"

He stopped talking and grinned. I couldn't move. His words had altered the air of this ordinary diner. I didn't want to leave.

So I didn't.

Every Monday for two years we met in this back booth while he shared his life's stories for an autobiography he longed to write. He passed away before we completed the project. But his stories, those I didn't want to hear, continue to shape and reshape me, as I navigate my own past and present pain—divorces, drinking, everyday misunderstandings. I've learned to embrace humanity, my own and others, with loving awareness. My experiences can't compare to his. That wasn't his point. Pain is pain. No matter who or where we are, we have the power—and the right—to release ourselves from it. Forgiveness is a start.

~Jan Henrikson

Rare Gems

Life is an adventure in forgiveness.
~Norman Cousins

It was supposed to be a parent-teacher conference. But Miss Johnson locked her gaze on my junior high son's eyes. During the fifteen minutes she allotted for the meeting, she didn't look at me once.

"Miss Johnson," I began, but she interrupted and addressed my thirteen-year-old son, Rick.

I had worked with Rick on his latest paper, and I felt I had a glimpse of a rare gem—in my own son. He had a gift.

But not according to Miss Johnson. She was saying, "You know, Rick, you just didn't develop your story well enough and you forgot a period here. That's why you got a D on the paper. That brings your overall grade down to a C in English this semester."

Just a few days earlier, when I had reviewed the very same paper, I had told him, "Wow, Rick, you have real talent!" As a published author and writing coach for decades, I had seen a lot of good and bad writing. His skill sparkled. As his character grieved over the loss of his best friend, he pledged to make the dangerous climb to a mountain summit in honor of his buddy. The emotions, scenes, and dialogue were outstanding. As a reading and writing teacher of a hundred students a year just a few years younger than my son, I knew an A when I saw it.

But Miss Johnson didn't think so. The way she ignored me during this conference made me even angrier. It was unprofessional. She should have known better than to deliberately avoid communicating with a parent about her child and his work. For her to ignore my presence was like failing to notice a school-bus-sized Tyrannosaurus Rex in her front yard.

She and I saw each other often enough as teachers at different schools in the same district. But we also served as members of the same committee, which met once a month.

I hated her! I felt her decision to call Rick's work below average—a D—was unfair. So was his final grade of a C. I had worked with both my sons on their final papers. Rick's brother in another class had turned in a paper that had been below average in punctuation and editing, but he refused to work on it any further. He got an A.

But Rick's C would follow him through high school and beyond.

She was unfair, ugly and unprofessional! I felt a hard lump in my throat and anger boiling. At least I only had to see her once a month. I stormed out of the conference steaming over the injustice of it all.

I half-hoped she would be run over by a school bus—or drown in the community pool. But she taught swimming during the summer. Drowning was unlikely.

When summer came, I thought I would have a vacation from Miss Johnson. But when I showed up for the first session of a six-week summer writing class for teachers, she was there too.

Well, it was a pretty big group so I can stay on the other side of the room, I thought. But then the leaders broke us into small teams and guess who was on my team?

How unfair! Three years I've wanted to attend that class, and now she was in the class too. This was going to be a very long summer.

In the small groups, our first job was to write and share personal experience stories. Miss Johnson wrote about family traditions that had brought her, her siblings and extended family close with much fun and laughter. Christmas with everyone making popcorn sculptures. Skits and plays with improvised costumes. Crazy contests. Games. Lots of creativity.

As we laughed with her, I felt my hatred melt—just a little. After all, she did those things with her family for the same reason that I took my sons camping, hiking and skiing in the mountains on weekends and vacations. Our families were important to both of us.

My angry feelings were changing. Over the long days of class together, I realized my respect for her was eroding my hatred.

By the time the school year began again, we had learned to work together. Handling responsibilities on the same committee was much simpler without my harboring hatred. A Young Authors' Day came together with a professional author guest. It took all our teamwork. As we had hoped, the event left the students excited. Teachers learned how to bring writing exercises into every subject.

We on the committee high-fived each other to celebrate the success of the event. Following that was a very exciting five-school writing contest that included Miss Johnson and her students' writing.

Close to spring break the following school year, during a long committee meeting after school, I could only hope the chairman would realize it was time to adjourn.

"Anything else?" the committee chairman asked.

Miss Johnson cleared her throat. "Yes. I just found out this week that I have the big C." She paused a moment to compose herself. "I have to have surgery right away and I will be gone for quite a while. I really hope to see you all in the fall." Uncertainty hung in the air.

The teacher who never missed school, was always on time, and had always been healthy — all of a sudden wasn't. Miss Johnson was in for the fight of her life with her unyielding adversary — very serious cancer.

It would be a tough, discouraging, and long road back to recovery — if she made it. And she was single. Alone much of the time.

As a solo mom with two sons, I knew just what that was like.

Something that I had been doing for years was encourage others going through challenges, illness, loss, or victories. Mostly I worked within our church and community. I used my writing skills and blank notes, cards, and small gift baskets to urge the recipient to persist through the tough roads and trust God.

God prodded me: Do it for Miss Johnson. She needs it.

He laid the thoughts on me day after day. I finally caved in and called the district office for her home address.

Right away, I began sending her cards encouraging her to fight and win. Each week as I urged her on in writing, I realized that I was fighting for her to beat cancer too. No longer did I hate her. I had forgiven her. Hatred changed to respect. Respect changed to like. Like changed to caring. Now I really cared if she would make it.

I wrote from the heart and meant it when I penned the words of encouragement.

I wasn't sure what happened to her for quite a while. The next year, I was hired to work in a different school and district.

Then a former colleague told me, "Did you know Miss Johnson is back teaching again. She's doing better all the time."

"That's great! She survived!"

In a small town like ours, one is likely to run into everyone in town at some time somewhere.

I bumped into Miss Johnson at the community pool. As we enjoyed the warm water in the hot tub, she cried gleefully, "I'm cancer-free now! And I'm getting married! I get to retire this year! God is so good!" She glowed with a smile, then added, "You just don't know how much those notes you sent meant to me. It was a very hard fight for a long time and your words kept me going month after month. Thank you so much!"

I'd come a long way. God and Miss Johnson had healed my heart — moving me from hatred to forgiveness and healing.

Who would have guessed I would one day be her encourager?

And my son Rick? As a sophomore in high school, he beat out all other grades in an award-winning first-place short story.

It turns out that they both were rare gems in God's sight — and mine.

~Jo Russell

What You Do
with Your Pain

To understand everything is to forgive everything.
~Buddha

I didn't even know your name. In 1975, I was thirteen and living in San Diego. Our family had just moved from Ridgecrest, a small naval community in the Mojave Desert where my stepfather had been stationed for three years. I remember being in the courtyard at Horace Mann Junior High School watching two boys play handball against the side of a building. I was mesmerized by the sight of the ball hitting the building's sun-faded surface and bouncing off the blacktop, the swing of a brisk forehand, and the sound of the rubber ball ricocheting off a boy's palm back to the wall.

I was only there a few minutes. The slap to my head came from behind me. It was sudden, unexpected and felt as if someone had pressed the flat of a scalding iron against my face. I turned to see you staring at me with sharp, piercing eyes. There was no expression on your face, but your cold, dark eyes dared me to retaliate. I didn't.

I just stood there, motionless, my right ear and cheek burning from the force of your blow. But the shame inside me at being helpless to defend myself felt even worse.

You did it again that school year — four times, and I never told anyone, not even my parents, because I was too ashamed.

I'm now fifty-one years old, but that courtyard incident is seared into my memory. It never goes away. I don't know why you hit me. Maybe it was because I was Asian and different, an outsider to the school, to the city. I was skinny, not athletic, and a loner. Perhaps I made for an easy target. I probably will never know why you chose to hurt me, but I can imagine you've known pain in your life, a lot of pain, to want to inflict that on someone else, on me.

Did someone slap you when you were a child? Someone older than you? Did you feel alone, powerless to make it stop? And did it happen again and again until you became so angry that you had to take it out on someone else? You needed to make someone, anyone, feel something you'd known throughout your life, didn't you?

I felt that anger when you slapped me and challenged me to hit you back. The humiliation burned in me, molten hot and red, like an acid eating away at the core of my being. You hurt me.

And you hurt me again and again and again, just as you were hurt; that much I understand.

I hope you have made peace with yourself. I hope you have found some healing in your life because rage only leads to more pain, and I'm sure you and I have experienced plenty of that in our lives. Pain is something we share; I'm sure of it. It connects us.

I have felt alone, angry, powerless, as if the world doesn't care, and no one is there to protect me. It's a hollow, lifeless feeling. Nobody understands and nothing matters.

But you see, it does matter. What I do with my pain matters a great deal. If I shut it off and turn away, it will rear up again, unexpectedly, like a blow to the head on a school courtyard. But if I am honest, and I dig deep, and I write, I find I can express my pain. I can share it, and it doesn't feel as overwhelming. I know I'm not alone.

And what you do with your pain matters because it can affect someone else's life. Those slaps occurred almost four decades ago, but I remember them as if they happened this morning.

I hope you have found healing for your pain. I hope there are people in your life to reach out to, someone to listen to you with kindness, understanding, and compassion. I pray for that because it's the only way for the pain to stop.

~Raymond M. Wong

71

What We're Going Through

What we see depends mainly on what we look for.
~John Lubbock

I admit that I've gotten a little scatter-brained while going through this divorce. The blizzard of forms, selling one house, looking for another, packing up, uprooting—yes, I've definitely been addled of late. Which is why, in the express line of a store I rarely frequent, I was anything but speedy.

I handed the cashier a coupon for coffee I hadn't bought; I slid my credit card into the machine the wrong way; I didn't realize I had to push a debit/credit button, and although I pushed the "Accept" button twice, it refused to work until the cashier pushed it. A kind woman, she seemed to have all the time in the world for my ineptitude. But a theatrical sigh to my left told me someone else was less patient. I looked, and the woman in line behind me was rolling her eyes heavenward, a pained expression on a thin face that just missed being pretty.

I wish I had said something like, "I'm sorry I'm so slow. It's one of those days," and her smile made her beautiful as she responded, "Oh, believe me, I know how it goes." Instead, I thought, "Sheesh, sister, give me a break. You don't know what I'm going through."

It wasn't until I had dropped a glove, retrieved it, and was out the door that the thought struck me: I didn't know what she was going through either. It was a revelation. I didn't have a clue what was going on behind that respectable, if annoyed, facade. Most of us go through our days looking more or less normal even when our lives are in turmoil. A sick child, a job in jeopardy, a scary diagnosis, a foreclosed home, and, yes, a divorce... who knows what lurks behind someone's outward appearance?

By the time I put my coffee-less bags into my car, I'd forgiven her, but moreover, I silently prayed that she would forgive my rush to judgment.

And it was then that I remembered something my dad said many, many years ago. "Cut them some slack, Sis."

"Who?" I had asked.

"Everyone."

~Kristine McGovern

72

Pigeonholed in the Park

Everything is just as it needs to be. And if we forgive, our minds and hearts
would open and we could see another possibility.
~Iyanla Vanzant

I hate summer vacation. As the mother of a six-year-old with autism, the four weeks between the end of summer school and the beginning of the new academic year are hell. All children need consistency and routine, but kids on the spectrum thrive on it; if they don't get it, everyone within our visual and auditory range is at risk of suffering from my child's unpredictable behavior. And God help you if you happen to be within his kicking or grabbing vicinity.

As Mom, it's my duty to be in the line of fire; and while I'll happily throw myself in front of any potential victims, I can't control every-thing. A shoe may fly, an errant fingernail may come in contact with a bystander's skin, and all I can do is attempt to contain my son to the best of my ability and express my sincerest apologies. Sometimes it's enough for the inadvertent victim and sometimes it isn't. Unfortunately it's all I can do, and I've had to learn through experience that liking it and accepting it are two different things.

During the ironically termed "summer break" my son Josh and I are on our own until my husband returns from work. It's up to me to come up with activities that won't over-stimulate him, won't involve too much travel time, and won't disrupt the majority of the people around us. I also can't be fully certain that these potential outings will occur on the day originally planned. If Josh's night is bad, a crowded amusement park with long lines is a big no-no. Same goes for museums and petting zoos. On those days we stay local and head to one of the neighborhood parks within walking distance of our home.

"Okay, Josh, let's go!" I said enthusiastically on what was clearly a "park day," hoping my frame of mind would catch up with my tone. I'd packed everything possible: towels, wet wipes, food and water, and made sure that there was enough room in his backpack once his shoes flew off and he insisted on going barefoot because of his sensory issues. I mentally prepared myself to ignore the stares of any passersby and the loud whispers of "why isn't he wearing shoes?" from children to their guardians when we walked down the street. My goal was just to keep moving. Josh never seemed to notice the comments or stares, but every single one made my skin prickle. I'm both grateful for and envious of the cluelessness that autism grants my son when it comes to the reactions of the general public in these instances. I just wish that some of it would rub off on me.

Once we arrived, Josh did his usual running about between the stone frogs spouting water, the slides and the swings. All of a sudden, something caught Josh's eye, something that made him squeal with delight. A large group of pigeons had gathered fairly close to us, simultaneously cooing and pecking at the ground, picking up bits of whatever they deemed edible. Josh immediately began flapping his hands with excitement and charged through the birds, causing them to hop, fly and scatter. Josh giggled and loved the reaction. Once again he charged, and once again pigeon chaos erupted!

It was an amazing moment. My son had noticed his surroundings! He'd created an action and learned the notion of cause and effect. These were huge developmental milestones for him! And not only that, he was genuinely enjoying himself in a completely appropriate way! He was playing with the pigeons, despite the fact that the birds themselves probably had a different opinion of what was happening. This was an amazing moment for us both… until I heard a voice scream "STOP IT NOW!"

I immediately looked up and saw a little girl and her brother each holding a sleeve of crackers. She marched right over to my nonverbal, autistic child, hands on hips and shrieked, "STOP SCARING THE PIGEONS!" I was furious. I didn't care how angry she was; she had no right to yell at anyone. "Stop yelling at him," I replied. This little girl wasn't prepared to deal with another mommy without her own. She turned to a woman who was texting on her smart phone, and commanded, "MAKE HIM STOP CHASING THE PIGEONS!" The woman peered at me over the rims of her sunglasses and told her daughter, "*I* can't make him stop." Meanwhile, my son was still squealing, still running, still having the time of his life.

I wanted to beg her to have sympathy for my son. Couldn't she see that he's not neurotypical? Couldn't she understand that this pigeon interaction was huge for him? That he hadn't said a word throughout all of this because he couldn't? But they just kept glaring, so I said nothing to them. Instead, I said, "Let's go, Josh," as I redirected him to the swings on the other side of the park, and slipped my own sunglasses over my eyes so that the tears welling up remained hidden. Josh happily complied and spent the remainder of our time in the park happily swinging while I pushed him and sang.

When we returned home I ran Josh's bath and released my own frustration by weeping quietly. I wondered if it would always be this way, with people staring and getting angry because Josh didn't notice them when he was involved in something. I understood their frustration. Would they ever understand mine? Would they ever realize the pain that I experience every time they judge him for just "not getting it?"

It was in that moment that I realized the answer was "No." They wouldn't understand my frustration because I let my anger at their response to my child stilt my own response to their offspring. Those who judged my family often did so because of lack of exposure to autism or a lack of understanding. That little girl was having a little girl response and was being protective of the pigeons; and her mother, a mother of two neurotypical children, was having a neurotypical mom response. Maybe she didn't get where we were coming from; if she had, she might have been more understanding. Maybe it was up to me to change my approach to such situations.

I then went back into the bathroom where Josh was luxuriating in the tub. I smiled at my happy boy, rinsed my face and gazed at myself in the mirror. "I'll tell you what, neurotypical mom," I internally stated. "I'll forgive your reaction if you forgive mine. In the future, I'll let you know what's going on so that you have an opportunity to make an educated choice as to how you want to deal with the circumstances at hand. And who knows? Perhaps as a result, our children will reach a respectful understanding of one another, and possibly bring about a better future for all of them."

~Jennifer Berger

Forgiving Notes

A teacher affects eternity; he can never tell where his influence stops.
~Henry Adams

I ran to the bulletin board and scanned the list. I blinked and read it again. Then, I turned away and bit my lip to stem the tears. Mine wasn't among the eight names.

As a shy, sullen sixth grader, I had found the courage to shakily audition for a small singing group our music teacher formed. She envisioned an octet—eight sweet voices lifted in perfect harmony. I envisioned myself singing and swaying in unison with the other seven girls.

I desperately wanted to be one of the group. The octet was invited to the local television station to broadcast their performance. I expected the members would become local celebrities.

I loved music class. Three times a week, our sixth grade class shuffled from our daily schoolroom down the hall to the music room. That room was magical, a place where the daily monotony of math and spelling disappeared for an hour, replaced by the joyful sounds of music.

Alas, my name's absence from the posted list was proof that I was not the pure soprano Mrs. Bleeker sought to balance the group's harmony. I'd flunked the audition.

I raced home after school and took refuge in the limbs of our front yard catalpa tree. Hidden in the dense leaves above the rest of the world, I sobbed out my disappointment and anger. By the time

I climbed down from the tree, I'd decided I hated both Mrs. Bleeker and music.

If Mrs. Bleeker noticed my passive-aggressive flouncing and pouting, she hid it well. Despite my minimal vocal talent, she was determined that I would continue to love music. I was determined I would not. Our wills were constantly at war. I loathed Mrs. Bleeker when she pushed me to enter an essay contest, "What Music Means to Me." Feeling tormented and forced to pick up a pen, I reluctantly poured my musical angst into the composition and forgot about it until months later.

I was shocked when I won the statewide contest. The $50 savings bond was the first time I was paid for writing. Mrs. Bleeker called the local newspaper and the editor sent a photographer to the school. There I was in the next day's newspaper in a grainy black-and-white image on page 3. I was a local celebrity.

Then, the music teacher continued to torture me, insisting I read my winning essay at a PTA meeting. The audience's applause gave me my first taste of the power of the pen.

I was off to a new school the next year, so I didn't think much about Mrs. Bleeker after that. Over the next few decades I grew up and was busy working and raising a family, but I wrote as a hobby. Occasionally, I submitted stories to editors, keeping my fingers crossed that they would publish one. After many rejection slips (none of which caused me to climb into a catalpa tree), I finally sold a piece.

Then I ran into Mrs. Bleeker while I was visiting my hometown. From among hundreds of students she had taught over the years, she remembered me. By then, I was well aware that singing was not my forte. In the middle of a Kmart shopping aisle, in the clutch of her sincere ebullience and warm hug, I surrendered my sixth-grade animosity toward her. We exchanged contact information.

I slipped a copy of my newly published story into Mrs. Bleeker's Christmas card that year and thanked her. Though I never learned to appreciate the difference between a treble and a bass clef, I did learn to appreciate Mrs. Bleeker. I often think about her artful rehabilitation of my wounded soul so many years ago. She refused to let me wallow in self-pity and instead forced me to demonstrate a talent I didn't even know I had. I was too angry and immature to appreciate it until much later.

~Hope Sunderland

74

Finding Peace

He who angers you conquers you.
~Elizabeth Kenny

The midday sun was extremely hot, and our twelve-year-old daughter Kelly grew increasingly concerned. The school had taken the student body to an exciting sports day in the open air and everyone was having fun, but Kelly was jittery. Her sister Judy was undergoing chemotherapy for leukemia and was far more vulnerable to the elements as a result.

We had been warned that even small amounts of sun exposure could cause irreversible damage. When Kelly's entreaties to the supervising teacher elicited little response, Kelly took charge. Bringing cell phones to school contravened school rules, but on that particular day I had equipped her with one for just such an emergency, charging her with keeping an eye on her sister. As the clock ticked on and the sun beat down, Kelly whipped out her cell phone and dialed home. Following a brief exchange with the teacher, my girls were allowed to leave, but not before our daughter had been firmly yelled at and our cell phone confiscated.

Looking back, I should probably have been more organized and taken the trouble of coordinating things with the teacher beforehand, but hindsight couldn't change reality. Our lives at the time were beyond hectic. We had been sucked into a whirlpool of hospital visits, strange medical procedures, painful side effects and harsh emotions. Even though it had seemed to us that we were coping rather well, I realize, in retrospect, that certain things must have fallen through the cracks.

Communication with our daughters' school was one of them. The cell phone fiasco was just one example of how this negatively affected them. While Judy was justifiably absent, more days than not, for close to two years, Kelly was expected to attend as usual. But soon we had to beg her to get up and go. Always a temperamental child, her sister's sickness had intensified her volatile nature. At home we tried to extend as much understanding and support as we could. But at school, instead of enveloping her with warmth and loving attention, the staff chose to focus on every shortcoming. Too often, those perceived misdeeds happened through no fault of her own.

Kelly was sent home, for instance, after arriving at school without a uniform skirt—when I had just spent a week in the hospital with her sister and was woefully behind with the laundry. Her grades slipped—hardly anyone was home to help her with homework! Her attitude was all wrong—you bet she was upset. I don't know why the school staff never contacted us—maybe they realized we were less available or felt uncomfortable bothering us. But our daughter was made to feel like the biggest of sinners instead of being taken for the distraught, lost and emotionally fragile girl she was.

Eventually, despite our fervent entreaties, the school board kicked her out (using a lot of fancy euphemisms) for a list of petty infractions, and that is when our sensitive daughter fell into a steep spiral of deep and genuine suffering. She dropped out of the mainstream school system, digging in her feet at any mention of a standard environment. She ventured into risky company and courted self-destructive behaviors. She hated herself, she hated us, but more than anything—she hated the world.

She has still not completely recovered from the indignities she suffered in elementary school, and for many years my husband and I harbored grievous feelings for the school system's abysmal lack of understanding. I still cannot begin to comprehend why they couldn't have simply cut her some slack. Why couldn't they have made more of an effort to cushion her feelings and focus on her positive side?

We have been through hell and back with Kelly, but the pain of those years has never quite washed away.

By nature I am a gentle, peace-loving person. Never in my life had I been angry with anyone for more than a few hours. For a long, long while, however, I had to come to terms with this crouching beast within me. Sensitivities I never imagined I possessed suddenly reared their ugly head and set me aglow with anger. I was furious. I was deeply hurt. I ached for the Kelly we seemed to have lost, for the unbearable price we had paid for attending to her younger sister. And I seethed with the injustice of it all. We had not been AWOL whilst vacationing in the Caribbean; we had been battling for Kelly's sister's life! How could the school staff have been so very indifferent?

These feelings were unfamiliar and dragged me down terribly. And beyond the sickening sensation of floundering in a maelstrom of negativity, I was shocked by the effect they were having on me. I didn't like knowing I was capable of entertaining so much hatred and disgust. I didn't like knowing there were people on this planet that I simply could not stand to be around. This wasn't the person I had always been. Having already seen the havoc wrought on Kelly's emotional health — I was wary of endangering my own.

There was no precise point of inspiration, nor one particular moment of illumination. It was a process. At some stage I realized I couldn't allow myself to live life like this. I missed my old personality — my casually forgiving nature, my innate tendency to trust and to love. I decided to recover it, and in order to do that I had to forgive. I was determined to put the hurt behind me.

It was tough. Many of the people involved in our daughter's past lived in our town. It was inevitable we would meet some time or other. No sooner had I made that conscious decision than I began bumping into the key players at every turn. At the supermarket. Coming into a parking lot. In line for the ATM. Any time I was near any one of them, my heart raced, I became short of breath, and felt a screaming impulse to put the greatest distance possible between us. But I faced my inner demons squarely, and I told myself they had acted in good faith. They had simply been ignorant, foolish and shortsighted. Above all — they were God's messengers, and as such I should accept the past as past, forgive them for their part in our sorry story and let go.

I cannot say the wound has completely healed. It still has its sensitive spots. But for the most part, I have healed. I have regained a sense of peace and happiness. I have grown in my capacity to love without rancor. And I can face myself and say in true faith, I bear no grudge. I am free.

~Debra Rosehill

Chapter 8

The Power of Forgiveness

When a Crime Has Been Committed

Most of us need time to work through pain and loss. We can find all manner of reasons for postponing forgiveness. One of these reasons is waiting for the wrongdoers to repent before we forgive them. Yet such a delay causes us to forfeit the peace and happiness that could be ours.

~James E. Faust

75

The Greatest Gift

Never does the human soul appear so strong as when it foregoes revenge
and dares to forgive an injury.
~Edwin Hubbel Chapin

Whenever a stranger hears my accent and asks where I'm from, I want to answer: I was born in Paradise. For me, growing up in Rwanda *was* paradise.

My tiny African homeland is so breathtakingly beautiful it's impossible not to see God's hand in her mist-shrouded mountains, lush green hills and sparkling lakes. But it was the beauty of the people that made Rwanda so idyllic to my young heart.

Everyone in our little village got along like a big, happy family. As a youngster I wasn't even aware our country had two tribes—the majority Hutu (then numbering 7 million of Rwanda's 8.2 million inhabitants) and the minority Tutsi, of which I was a member.

I never felt unsafe or threatened when I was out playing and was the happiest girl in the world at home surrounded by the warmth and affection of my three doting brothers and the most loving, protective parents imaginable.

My parents were teachers and looked up to in the community. There was always a place at our table for anyone in need, and people traveled from miles around to seek my parents' advice and counsel.

But things were not as they seemed. My parents had shielded me from the simmering ethnic tensions in our land. When I was twenty-four years old those tensions erupted in a storm of violence that forever swept away the paradise I knew as a child.

On April 7th, 1994, the Rwandan's president's plane was shot down and extremist Hutu politicians unleashed a diabolic plot. All commerce was shut down and it was announced on the radio that the business of the nation would be killing Tutsis. Seven million Hutus were commanded to pick up a machete and carry out the following orders: *Kill every Tutsi you know, kill every Tutsi you see, kill every Tutsi man, woman, child, and infant—kill them all, leave none alive.*

Hatred enveloped the hearts of people I had known and trusted all my life—neighbors, teachers, schoolmates and friends.

When the killing began, hundreds of terrified Tutsi families swarmed to our home seeking sanctuary. But when my father saw the heavily armed government militia surrounding our property, he feared the worst and hurriedly pressed his rosary into my hand.

"Run to the pastor's house," he urged, "he is Hutu, but he is a good man and will hide you. Go, Immaculée... go *now!*"

I spent the next three months crammed into a 4 by 3-foot bathroom with seven other terrified Tutsi women as the slaughter raged outside. I heard the screams of those being hacked to death just beyond the bathroom walls.

I lived in constant fear of death—or worse. I prayed day and night with my father's rosary pleading for God to spare my life, but I would learn there was a difference between being spared and being saved. Hatred began taking hold of my heart, just as it had in the killers. I wished them dead; I wanted them to suffer like they were making so many others suffer. Had someone given me a loaded gun, I might have crawled out of my hiding place and tried to kill them all.

When I said The Lord's Prayer, the words "forgive those who trespass against us" simply would not form on my lips. How could I forgive the unforgivable, forgive those I wanted to kill myself?

The sickening thirst for revenge was foreign to me; my parents raised me to love my neighbor and live according to the Golden Rule. I grew more terrified of what was happening to my soul than what the killers might do to my body—I did not want to survive the slaughter if it meant living with a spiteful heart incapable of love.

I prayed for God to show me how to forgive those I had grown to hate. Suddenly, I saw an image of Jesus in the moments before his death, crying out to God to forgive those who were crucifying him.

In that instant, I realized the killers were children of God who had lost their way. I prayed: "Forgive them Father, they know not what they do." The hatred drained from me and my heart flooded with God's love. For the first time I was aware of the power of forgiveness to heal and transform—it was the greatest gift I have ever received.

When the killers were finally driven from the country, I emerged from hiding and learned of my family's fate. Thank God my eldest brother survived because he was studying abroad. My father had been shot protecting the families who had come to him for help, my mother was hacked to death on the street when she ran out of hiding to help a child, and my youngest brother was machine-gunned to death with thousands of other unarmed Tutsis corralled in a sports stadium. My elder brother had his head chopped open by family friends; I heard that before he died he forgave his killers.

In all, more than a million innocent souls were murdered during that bloody nightmare.

Discovering the details of my family's murder reignited my struggle to prevent anger and hatred from taking hold of my heart, but I had also discovered the one way to win that struggle was through forgiveness… and I knew what I had to do.

Several months after the genocide, a politician friend arranged for me to meet the man who led the murders of my mother and elder brother.

When I arrived at the jail I was stunned by what greeted me. A sick and disheveled old man in chains was shoved onto the floor at my feet.

"Félicien!" I cried out. He had been a successful Hutu businessman whose children I'd played with in primary school. Back then, he was tall, proud, and handsome—with impeccable manners. In front of me now, he was a hollowed-eyed specter in rags covered in running sores. His hatred had robbed him of his life.

The jailor kicked him in the ribs yelling, "Stand up, Hutu! Stand up you pig and tell this girl why you murdered her mother and butchered her brother!"

Félicien remained on the floor, hiding his face from me in shame. My heart swelled with pity. I crouched down beside him and placed my hand on his. Our eyes met briefly and I said what I had come to say: *I forgive you.*

Relief swept over me, and a sigh of gratitude slipped through Félicien's parched lips.

"What the hell was that about, Immaculee?" the furious jailor demanded as Félicien was dragged away. "That man murdered your family! I brought him here so you could spit on him. But you forgave him! How could you do that?"

"Because hatred has taken everything I ever loved from me," I said, "Forgiveness is all I have left to offer."

I turned and walked out of that prison free of anger and hatred and I have lived as a free woman ever since.

~Immaculée Ilibagiza with Steve Erwin

Not Guilty

You can't forgive without loving. And I don't mean sentimentality.
I don't mean mush. I mean having enough courage to stand up and say,
"I forgive. I'm finished with it."
~Maya Angelou

The bailiff opened the large courtroom doors and stepped into the hallway. "The jury has reached its verdict," he said. I gasped. The buzzing crowd instantly hushed. The jury had spent three hours making its decision — three hours that, to me, seemed like days.

I gripped my husband's hand as we shuffled into the courtroom ahead of our two sons and the rest of our family and friends. Sitting stiffly on the hard benches, no one spoke.

"Rise," the bailiff said with authority in his voice.

I held my breath. My heart pounded. We were about to hear the final verdict. Finally, finally, we'd see justice carried out!

The phone had rung late at night a year earlier. In moments, our middle son Jeff raced into our bedroom shouting, "Joe's been hurt!" We frantically pulled on the clothes from the day before and rushed out the front door. We arrived at the hospital minutes after the ambulance, but we received only one small piece of information. "They're working on him."

It was surreal. "This isn't happening to us," I repeated silently over and over again.

In the midst of our anguish and desperate prayers, the doctor walked in. "Are you the parents of Joe Eckles?" he asked.

I jumped to my feet. "Yes, how is he? Where is he? When can we take him home?"

Then came the crushing news. Our nineteen-year-old son had not survived the multiple stab wounds he had received.

I crumpled under the weight of his death.

"These things don't happen to good boys!" I wanted to shout. The light of my life had been snuffed out. My husband and I sobbed. Questions of what had happened, how, and why mixed with the pain. Joe was the captain of his football team, captain of his lacrosse team, witty, handsome, a leader in every way. How could this happen to him?

I prayed, not with words, but with cries only God could hear as they came from the depths of my soul. I asked for strength, for direction, and comfort.

Weeks crawled by, and perhaps slower than I wished, peace trickled in. And it was God's grace that sustained me enough to move forward through daily routines. A year crawled by slowly.

"I got a call from the prosecuting attorney," my husband announced with a somber tone. "The trial will begin next month."

The day the trial was scheduled to begin was October 27th, which was my fifty-first birthday. "I'm not sure if I'm ready," I confessed to my husband.

He gave a pained sigh. "I don't know myself, but we need to see justice served."

The trial began. And although we sensed the support of our family and friends around us, that courtroom was an odd, uncomfortable place, cold and harsh. We were the victims, and sorrow intensified the unwanted experience. The grief in our hearts blurred the details of the legal proceedings. Each witness was called to relate his or her side of the story. An altercation had caused our son Joe and the other driver to exit their cars. A fight broke out and Joe didn't know the man was armed with a knife.

"Help me, God!" my heart cried out. "I don't know if I can bear to hear one more detail of that dreadful night!"

But the torture continued. The medical examiner's report of each of Joe's twenty-three stab wounds reached my heart with almost the same force they had entered Joe's body. Once all the testimony was heard, the judge read the instructions to the jury.

After hours of deliberating, they called us back into the courtroom.

"Jury, did you reach a verdict?" the judge asked.

One of the jury members stood. "We have."

I held my breath as he read the three charges. Most of the words were a blur to me, but what I heard was, "Not guilty on all counts." A gasp of horror burst from our side of the courtroom. Shouts of glee and cheering came from the other side. They celebrated his acquittal. We were horrified by the injustice. The man who took our son's life had pled self-defense and was found innocent on all counts.

The process of picking up the pieces began all over again. The lash of injustice compounded the heartache of his loss. We held each other night after night while my husband and I prayed.

One evening, he paused after our prayer. "You know," he said with a soft voice, "God may forgive this man. We need to forgive him too."

"I agree," I said.

Like a wet, heavy blanket off my back, the heartache lifted. That was exactly what we needed to do.

Once we chose to forgive the man who took Joe's life, our world changed. The darkness of our pain was dispelled like the blackness of night by the morning sun. We never saw the man again. But had we encountered him, a word of forgiveness would have been extended instead of vengeance or rage.

Through prayer, we had asked God for comfort, but He gave us more than that. He gave us the ability to feel peace.

"How can you forgive something like that?" a friend said to me back then.

My answer has always been: "If we had not forgiven him, we would be the prisoners, trapped inside the bars of bitterness. We made the choice to be set free, to live in the liberty that forgiveness brought."

In that freedom, Joe's memories are sweeter. In that freedom, our wisdom is greater—to recognize the gift he was to us for nineteen years. And once free, we invited joy and laughter back into our lives.

That joy is sometimes accompanied by tears. But those tears are different now. They carry gratitude for our sorrow that turned to healing. For the injustice that turned to acceptance, and for the anger that turned to peace.

~Janet Perez Eckles

Silencing the Boom

It's not an easy journey, to get to a place where you forgive people.
But it is such a powerful place, because it frees you.
~Tyler Perry

I woke from a September nap to a voice on the radio. "George Russell Weller has not been charged with a crime," the National Public Radio commentator said. Two months earlier, the eighty-six-year-old man had confused the gas pedal for the brake and sped through the Santa Monica Farmer's Market. He struck seventy-three people. Ten pedestrians died. I suffered severe injuries: multiple fractures, a ruptured spleen and a brain injury.

The commentator was interviewing an eighty-nine-year-old man who admitted he did not do well on the written test in a recent driver's safety class, but would continue driving. "I've been driving for seventy-five years and I've been careful," he said. "It's other people's turn, let them be careful." I glared at the radio's red blinking light as if I could stun the arrogance out of the old man's grating voice.

His disregard for the tragedy ignited my resentment toward Russell Weller. If he hadn't been driving, I'd still be working as a nurse. But in order to return to nursing, I had to focus my energy on healing. So I let my resentment ferment.

Six years later, it still fermented. I unearthed the news articles I had collected about Russell Weller, hoping to discover something that would allay my resentment. I read a bystander's account of what he heard at the scene: boom, boom, boom. Metal slamming into people.

I desperately wanted to forgive Russell Weller, otherwise boom, boom, boom would continue to haunt me. But I didn't know how to forgive him. How do you forgive someone you've never met?

The more I read about Russell Weller, the more confused I felt. A reporter quoted him saying, "If you saw me coming, why didn't you get out of the way?" Why would someone who mowed down a bunch of people say that? Other articles referenced his friends' claims that he was a gentle and concerned person. His attorney said his client was "deeply sorry." My eyes stung from all the reading, from all the searching for answers as to why Russell Weller had been driving when he had a history of accidents. I wanted to ask him why he had insisted on driving to the post office that day to mail a letter, rather than listening to his wife, who begged him to stay home and wait for the postman to pick it up.

I realized I couldn't forgive Russell Weller by reading words on paper. I needed to see him in person, up close. I needed to hear a genuine apology from Russell Weller.

I decided I would return to Santa Monica with my husband to visit Russell Weller. I had tried calling him, but his number was disconnected. I called his pastor, who asked his family for permission for us to meet. They said he was too ill. I believed them, but I did not give up. I called a private investigator. "If you insist on going to his house you should hire a police escort," he advised.

On Valentine's Day, my husband and I rolled up to Russell Weller's house. I couldn't think of a better day to forgive him. I cautiously walked up the long driveway to the front door, holding a sweetheart rose plant. I crouched down and placed the plant on the step. I did not leave a note. I believed Russell Weller would know that the plant came from me. As I stood up, I glimpsed bright red letters pasted across the black mailbox: NO SOLICITORS.

I ran back to the car, my heart pounding. "You did it!" my husband yelled. Tears fell down my cheeks. "Do you think you can let go now?" he asked.

"I don't know." I wished I could have said yes. I wished I could have said I forgave Russell Weller.

Ten months later he died.

The boom, boom, boom still haunted me. I tried convincing myself that I had forgiven him. I told my therapist it was an accident, and that Russell Weller must have suffered too. I told family and friends that I had forgiven him. "You're so strong," a friend said. "I'm not sure I could forgive someone who brought so much harm to so many people."

A year passed, and I still struggled to truly forgive Russell Weller. After coaxing from a friend, I called the head deputy of The Santa Monica Farmer's Market. Within a week, I received a videotape of Russell Weller speaking to police investigators one hour after the crash.

I slid the disc into the DVD player. Silver specks blotted the screen for many seconds before he shuffled, with his cane, into the fluorescent-lit room. He sat down, tapped his cane and picked at his bruised arm—the only injury he sustained in the accident. He scanned the faded white walls, then gazed at the peeling ceiling. He raised his arm up and said, "Can you imagine?" Who did he think he was addressing?

An investigator walked into the room, and Russell Weller immediately said, "I'll tell you everything that happened." He spoke with urgency, as if he needed to make sure the investigator knew the accident wasn't his fault. He did not cry. Somehow, crying leads you to believe that someone is truly sorry so I wished he had cried. He spoke about his work as a food broker, and his time served in Korea. Shouldn't he have asked about the pedestrians he had rammed into an hour earlier? I found myself disliking him. Then he looked straight ahead, his voice loud and clear, and said, "All of a sudden the car accelerated." It was as if he believed the car was to blame. His speech slowed, and his southwestern twang lowered to a whisper: "I'm in trouble with my heart and soul." I scooted closer to the television. A long moan rose from his throat. "God almighty, those poor, poor people. What a tragic ending, and I contributed to it."

In that moment, I forgave Russell Weller.

More than a decade later, I still feel the swelling on his bruised arm. I still hear sorrow seep from the steady tap of his cane.

But I do not hear, boom, boom, boom.

~Melissa Cronin

From Revenge to Peace

Forgiveness is like faith. You have to keep reviving it.
~Mason Cooley

"A unt Rachel and Uncle Harold have been murdered," my mom said softly over the phone. "An employee who did their yard work beat them to death and has been arrested."

Immediately, shock and disbelief overwhelmed me. I didn't know his name and never asked. Knowing that would make it real. Since I lived 1,300 miles away from the publicity, I was shielded from the details but not the reality. At the funeral, the spicy sweet smell of carnations brought no peace or comfort as we buried my aunt and uncle.

Everyone has people they dislike or avoid, but I'd never had a reason before to hate someone. Nightmares plagued my dreams when I fell asleep. In the worst one, a hooded figure sat restrained in an electric chair. A large switch on the wall glowed as a judge encouraged me to pull the lever. At first, I hesitated. But as the dreams continued night after night, I gleefully yanked that bar, relishing the outcome. I'd wake up in a cold sweat, my heart pounding, and then I'd cry because I had become inside what I hated most—a killer.

I found it difficult to concentrate, and day-to-day tasks became almost unbearable as if I were trying to swim through mud. Any joy evaporated from my life, and nothing brought me peace or pleasure. I'd grown up in a religious home, but this shattered everything I'd ever known about forgiving. He'd beaten my dear elderly loved ones to death with a baseball bat! How could I let someone off the hook for a crime so heinous? Trapped in misery, I only managed the prayer, "Oh God, I can't stand this!"

One day, my husband was cleaning the car with our two-year-old son playing in the front seat. Like a typical boy, he pushed every button and turned every knob he could find. Later, I crawled into the car for a trip to the grocery store. I started the engine, and the radio blasted at full volume: "MOST PEOPLE CONFUSE PARDON WITH FORGIVENESS." I turned down the volume and collected my wits as the preacher continued. "When someone is pardoned, the consequences for their crimes are removed. Unless you are a governor, the President of the United States or God, you can't pardon anyone!"

I backed out of the driveway and kept listening as I drove. "When you forgive, you give your right for revenge to God. The person who wronged you is still accountable for what they have done. The wrong is now between the wrongdoer and God. If you've been badly hurt and can't forgive, it's okay. Ask God to make you willing to forgive. That's enough for now."

I pulled over as tears streamed down my face. "God, I can't let go of this. You'll have to make me want to." I dried my eyes and went on with the day. That night there were no dreams, just sleep.

As weeks went by, a thought followed me around. Whose capacity for vengeance is greater, mine or God's? Who would a murderer fear more, Him or me? God could hurt this man more than I ever could, so I gave the Lord my right for revenge. It wasn't because I was being kind or loving—it was survival forgiveness. I forgave just for me, putting this situation in His hands. Even with my vindictive motive, the nightmares stopped completely.

When the court deliberated on the murderer's fate, I was at peace because his destiny was not in my hands. He was given a life sentence. Part of me was relieved because it was finished, and part of me wanted to be angry. He will live; they are dead. I placed it into the Lord's hands again. Peace returned. Joy and pleasure trickled slowly back into my life as my heart healed. I pushed it all out of my mind, relieved, thankful for normalcy, and ten years flew by.

When an offender is given a life sentence, he comes up for parole every ten years. Parole was denied him, but it brought me questions: What if God forgives him? What if someday I'm in heaven, he walks in and the Lord says that it's okay for him to be there? I decided that if the Lord lets him in, he must have changed. I gave up my right for revenge, so if my Father says it's okay, then I'll trust Him. At that point, I thought forgiveness was completed, but it resurfaced again a few years later.

Our church started participating in a new prison ministry, and they needed people to bake cookies for the prisoners. Baking the cookies included praying for the inmates who would eat them. So as I baked, I prayed that the Lord would change their lives. I asked that they would become new people who would know and love God. And then He whispered in my heart, "Pray for that other prisoner you know."

"For him, Father? You want me to pray for him?"

Reluctantly I began. First, I prayed that someone would bake cookies for him. A power began to flow into me as I asked my Lord to change his life and make him a new person. Something began to break inside me, like a dam that first cracked, then leaked, and love broke through in a torrent. "Father, I want to meet him in heaven someday." Did I say that? And then I continued, "Please, it will be such a waste otherwise."

I used to worry about walking into heaven and facing the people there whom I've wronged or hurt. Praying for him made me understand that our Father pours love into all of our hearts, even for those who hurt us. Others will want me in heaven with them, just like I want him there. It's liberating to know that when I extend forgiveness and pray, my heart opens to receive more of it from the Lord, others and myself.

Forgiveness was a process for me. I needed God's help to even be willing to give up my right for revenge. Trust in the Lord's justice nurtured acceptance of whatever the outcome might be. I have grace in my life again and I received a love for a man I believe I'll meet in heaven. I'll keep praying for him.

~Susan Boltz

A Mother's Lesson

Our sorrows and wounds are healed only when
we touch them with compassion.
~Buddha

Back in June 1987, my brother was killed in a car accident. He was twenty-six years old. The phone ringing in the middle of the night woke me. Shortly after that I heard my mom wailing. I walked into my parents' bedroom and Dad said, "Bully died in a car accident earlier this evening."

My world stopped. I was twenty-two and had just graduated from college. My brother was the one person in the world who accepted me exactly as I was. He was my confidant, my sounding board and my best friend.

Mom seemed to age overnight. I overheard her telling people on the phone, "I'm a wreck. I miss him already."

As the days went by we learned more about the accident, which happened on Maui (we lived on Oahu). Turns out the driver was my brother's boyfriend. They were drinking and had gotten into a disagreement. Angry, my brother climbed into the bed of the truck instead of the cab. The driver was speeding and driving erratically. As he moved to pass a car by driving on the shoulder of the highway, he lost control and the truck flipped. My brother was tossed clear but then the truck landed on top of him.

On the day of the funeral, Mom was pale and thin. Already a svelte woman, her grief curbed her appetite, making her appear skeletal.

As we loaded into the car to go to the funeral home, she said, "I was hoping this day wouldn't come."

During the viewing we were surprised to see the driver's mother, father and sister there to pay their respects. They hugged each of us tightly and we all cried together. I watched through wet eyes as my mom clung to his mom, the two ladies giving each other strength through their grief. It seemed his family loved my brother as much as we did.

We survived the funeral and burial and did our best in the following months to get back to our normal routines. Days and months passed.

Eventually my brother's boyfriend was charged with drunk driving and manslaughter. He pled guilty to all charges. Having passed the stage of grief, many of us were firmly in the anger stage and several family members expressed their satisfaction that the driver would be punished.

At sentencing, Mom sent a letter to the court asking for leniency for the driver. She explained that she had accepted her loss and an incarceration would not bring my brother back. Further, she said the driver would live the rest of his life knowing that his poor judgment caused the death of someone he loved and she hoped he would seek mental health counseling to help him get past it.

Her letter surprised everyone. The judge read it out loud to the open courtroom, and there wasn't a dry eye in the room. The judge stated that Mom's letter swayed his decision and he hoped the driver would use this event to seek counseling, change his ways, and change his life.

Days after the sentencing, Mom and I talked. I asked her how she could send such a letter and how she could not want that man punished for taking Bully away from us.

Through tears she told me something I have kept with me all these years. She said, "I am sad for your brother. He was my artist, my wanderer, my gentle soul. I miss him every day. But I cannot hold hate in my heart for anyone or for what happened or it will eat me alive. I have to forgive or I will not be able to live."

And with that we closed the chapter.

Forgiveness is a powerful weapon in healing. Love for all.

~Danielle Lum

A New Beginning

Forgiveness is not something you do for someone else;
it's something you do for yourself.
~Jim Beaver

They say rape is murder of the soul, and they are right. Unfortunately, I know this truth all too well. When I was eight years old, I was raped by a family friend. My innocence, purity, and zest for life were stolen from me. The vivacious, energetic little girl who loved life and people instantly disappeared, and in her place was a broken, scared child who immediately became shy and afraid of strangers. I went from being a talkative kid with many friends to a quiet wallflower who kept people at arm's length. I learned how to be in a room filled with people without anyone ever knowing I was there. I became a different person.

I wish I could say I immediately went to counseling and got the help I so desperately needed, but I didn't. It was a time when sexual abuse was taboo, and few people talked about it, let alone believed it could happen in their families. My parents knew something was wrong, but I never uttered a word about the horror I had lived through, so they were clueless as to the enormity of what had occurred.

Like many children, I blocked out the rape and forgot the man who hurt me. Yet the effects of that moment were far-reaching and followed me into adulthood. I became so depressed that I put myself into counseling during my sophomore year of college. It took a couple of years, but eventually, I began having flashbacks to a time my mind had turned into a black hole. My mind did such a thorough job of blocking out the rape, I could hardly remember anything about my elementary school years. But with the help of two good counselors, I began to put together the pieces to the puzzle.

Although remembering was vital to my recovery, it was the hardest thing I have ever endured, even more so than the actual rape. Flashbacks aren't like normal memories. They transport you back to a time and place you don't want to be. Your body may stay in the present, but every other aspect of you is somewhere else. You can see, hear, taste, smell, and feel everything as if it were happening to you all over again. My flashback was so real I even felt the physical pain of being raped for days after I fully recalled what I'd been forced to endure.

With that remembrance, I was filled with the most intense anger I've ever experienced. Gone was the kind, peace-loving woman and in her place was someone I didn't know, a person whose every waking thought was consumed with rage and hatred towards everyone I blamed for my pain—the man who raped me, my parents for being friends with the man, and God for allowing it to happen.

Suddenly, it didn't matter what I'd learned from my parents and Sunday school teacher. I didn't care about doing the right thing and letting go of my anger and bitterness, and I certainly didn't care about forgiving those who wronged me. They deserved my wrath. I couldn't go back in time and change what happened to me; I couldn't make the person who raped me pay for his brutality; I couldn't wish away the trauma of the past and present. All I could do was hold onto the emotions of reliving that terrible moment. It was the only control I had.

For a time, everything in my life seemed to stand still. I still went to work, spent time with family and friends, and said and did the things that were normal, but inside, I was frozen in time. I had hidden from the truth for so long, I was afraid to let go of the raw emotions the rape caused for fear it would negate the truth. I thought moving on and forgiving those who hurt me would be like an ostrich hiding her head in the sand.

To this day, I'm not sure what caused me to reach that conclusion, but it was one of the most profound moments of my life. I realized the thing I was so desperately fighting for—a semblance of control—was the very thing keeping me from it. Refusing to forgive my rapist, parents, and God was destroying me. It was stealing my joy and destroying my relationship with my parents. Even worse than that, it was giving a rapist even more power over my life than what he'd already taken. The first time he stole from me I had no choice, but holding onto my hatred and being unable to move on with my life was my decision.

Once I realized this, I did the only thing I could do. I forgave him. It wasn't easy. It took countless hours of counseling, journaling, and praying, but in the end, I beat him. I won the victory over my rapist by forgiving him. He may have stolen my innocence, my sense of security, and my self-confidence for a time, but he didn't get to keep them. The moment I made the choice to forgive him, I got everything back. Gone was the sense of foreboding, the fear that continually plagued me, and mistrust of strangers.

That day, I became a new person. I was finally able to move on with my life and get the new beginning I so desperately needed. And though that time in my life was the hardest thing I've ever faced, I learned a valuable lesson. Forgiveness isn't weakness, and it doesn't mean the one doing the forgiving has been defeated. On the contrary, it is one of the greatest acts of courage and strength a person can ever do, and when one forgives someone who doesn't deserve this kindness, it is the sweetest victory one will ever know.

~Erin Elizabeth Austin

An Orchard of Forgiveness

*All major religious traditions carry basically the same message,
that is love, compassion and forgiveness... the important thing is
they should be part of our daily lives.*
~Dalai Lama

A wave of memories and emotions swept over me as I wandered the apple orchard. I had come face to face with one of my greatest fears within the walls of the orchard store. Nothing had prepared me to look into the eyes of the man who had permanently altered virtually every aspect of my son's wellbeing when he violently shook him.

It had been eight years since we had presented our victim impact statement at his sentencing in the district courthouse. On that day, he was taken into custody to serve a limited prison sentence for the felony charge of shaking my son. My son faced a lifetime sentence of severe and profound disability. I didn't view this as justice.

I thought back to the day prior to Ryan's shake when he proudly showed off his new crawling skills. I bubbled with pride as I watched him explore his new mobility. The next day, I saw the same child suffering from a traumatic brain injury, locked in a coma, and living only by virtue of a miracle, extensive brain surgery, and a ventilator. The days and nights in the pediatric intensive care unit were long and brutal as I watched for signs of life amid all of the sensors, lines, and monitors.

On top of that, my husband and I were being investigated for causing his injury and already convicted by the staff of a crime we didn't commit. Meanwhile, the perpetrator, a once loved and trusted daycare provider, protected his own self-interest and refused to admit guilt.

In time, Ryan awoke from his coma. Around the same time, we were ruled out as suspects. The journey of parenting a medically fragile, quadriplegic, cognitively delayed, nonverbal child began. When we took Ryan home from the hospital, his head control was that of an infant, he could not move any of his limbs, and he was fed through a g-tube. He was neurologically agitated and experienced grand mal and complex partial seizures with a frightening regularity that took away all sense of calm and control. We did not feel equipped to handle the magnitude of his care, yet we had no choice. By the grace of God and the assistance of very skilled and supportive medical, therapeutic, and educational communities, we not only survived but thrived as a family. Ryan was our inspiration. We were continually encouraged by his grace, perseverance, and positive disposition.

An integral part of our family journey involved the grief process and anger resolution. We knew early on that we could not hold ourselves hostage to our own victimization. The crime committed against our son could never be undone. In order to promote a healthy and loving environment for Ryan, we had to let go of what happened and focus on how we could provide the best possible life for Ryan. Focusing on what could have been only caused pain and regret. Living the life presented to us to the fullest was the healthiest and happiest way to live.

Forgiveness occurred early on. My faith encouraged it, and the ability to move on demanded it. Simply, I needed to forgive to live. I did not want to raise Ryan in a fabric woven with anger, hate, and resentment. Forgiveness paved the way for hope, joy, and immense love. Forgiveness did not lessen the wrongness or impact of the act, but Ryan deserved a positive life and a mom who focused on the beauty of the person he was instead of the devastation that permanently changed him.

Returning to the apple orchard, I strolled among the trees to catch my breath, revisit the memories, find my balance, and pray. Once centered, I returned to the orchard store where I saw him again. This time I smiled and waited in the wings while he and his wife carried on a conversation with the orchard owner. He shared happy memories of visiting the orchard as a child and the continued annual tradition of returning to his roots.

The ease and simple pleasure with which he spoke indicated that he, too, had moved on from that dark day. He had rebuilt a life filled with new hopes and dreams. He had served his time in prison, struggled to find employment as a convicted felon, divorced his first wife, and lost all visitation rights with the daughters who were his world when we knew him. As a man of faith, I have no doubt that he probably faced his own demons of guilt and sadness for the crime committed. For the first time since the shake, I saw the man we had so carefully chosen to be the caregiver to our son. I was able to look beyond the betrayal and pain and see the qualities that initially made us believe that he was a faithful, kind, and nurturing individual. As I watched, I did not seek to make myself known. It wasn't my place to guide the moment. It was time to let "our" story rest.

Unexpectedly seeing our former daycare provider at the apple orchard was a test of the authenticity of my forgiveness. It was important to realize that it was genuine. I do believe that we are all capable of facing life's unpredictable but defining moments with grace when we allow love and compassion to be our guide.

I have no doubt that Ryan would not have stopped at a smile. He would have said "hi" and fully embraced the moment with his abundant grace and unconditional love. While I could not go that far, I realized that I did not begrudge the man a good life. I believe that our lives were meant to cross paths in that moment for the sake of healing, but I also acknowledged that he will never be a part of our lives moving forward. I have forgiven, but I will never forget. I will, however, continue to live life in God's ongoing promise of hope and joy, displayed in the daily affirmation of my son's beautiful smile.

~Kirsten Corrigan

Notice of Release

*The practice of forgiveness is our most important contribution
to the healing of the world.*
~Marianne Williamson

T he impetus to learn about my mother's killer came from an outsider, a virtual stranger. It came twenty years after the murder, quietly camouflaged like the army of other unexpected emotional blitzes I had experienced since her death. They would catch me by surprise, following seemingly inconsequential events such as a simple lunch with a friend and her mother. Like falling into a foxhole, I'd wait for the attack to finish, and then climb out, a fatigued survivor.

My husband Michael and I were attending an informal meeting at a church we were thinking of joining as a place to spiritually anchor our family. We sat in the back of the room. Within a few minutes, a man named Gary stood up to address our group of about fifteen. The head of a prison ministry, he spoke to us about his work at a local men's prison and the positive impact forgiveness had on the lives of the inmates.

"It's amazing to see how some of these men commit themselves to doing God's work after the terrible things they've done. They turn their lives around," he said. I felt myself twinge, feeling viscerally annoyed.

While I basically believed that forgiveness was a good thing for mankind, it wasn't something I thought much about. I had never considered forgiving the man who killed my mother. That brand of forgiveness was for extremists who went on *Oprah*. I had no interest in having a positive impact on a cold-blooded murderer. In fact, I was silently bitter that my mother's killer had only received a life sentence.

This drug-crazed gunman had entered a convenience store where my mother worked evenings. He held her at gunpoint while she emptied the register. He fired a single shot that hit her squarely in the chest, killing her instantly. Two days later he was apprehended and sentenced to life in prison at Angola State Penitentiary in Louisiana. I was a freshman, away at college, brought home for the funeral, half out of my mind and in shock.

Gary continued, but my mind drifted. I wondered if my mother's killer ever stopped to think about her or what he would say to me if he ever had the opportunity. How could I ever forgive the man who had so thoughtlessly and irrevocably changed the course of my life? Gary was describing the unthinkable. But surprisingly, Gary had tapped into a deep vein and I was afraid of what might happen next, the thought of forgiving the murderer startling and alarming me. The more afraid I felt, the more I cried. It was another unexpected blitz. The experience rattled me, leaving me unsure of what had happened.

Gary's talk changed the dial on my radio. He turned it to a new frequency. I couldn't change it back. Articles in newspapers, magazines, shows on television, and conversations with people all kept circling back to the topic of forgiveness. Unable to block it out, sickened by the thought of it, I was a little curious too. Having been spared the horror of the trial, I knew nothing of him, not even his name. Who was he?

I spoke to relatives, made phone calls, read old news clippings, and researched the case like it was a job. I placed my notes into an unnamed manila file folder on the side of my desk. Over the course of a restless year, I periodically added new pieces of information, names and phone numbers, slowly developing a mental profile of my mother's killer, Nathan Wolfe.

At some unknown point, Nathan began to inhabit my dreams. Restlessly, I turned the dilemma over a thousand times in my mind. How could I forgive him? And why? One afternoon, while writing an article in my study, I came across my file. I was casually leafing through the pages when a piece of paper fell out. It was the telephone number of the chaplain's office at Angola State Penitentiary. I stared at it for a second and then dialed the number, with no thought of what I'd say. A man with a soft voice and Cajun accent answered. "Chaplain's office, Father Demereaux speaking."

I hesitated. "Hello. My name is Marta."

I felt ashamed of lying to a priest, substituting my middle name out of fear. Only a partial lie, I thought. "I'm calling to inquire about one of your inmates who killed my mother twenty years ago. I wonder if you could help me."

Now he hesitated.

"What is it you want to accomplish?"

"Well," I sank deeper into my chair, "I'm trying hard to find a way to forgive him, but I'm afraid of being identified in case he's ever pardoned. I also want to find out whether he feels any remorse."

"Does it make a difference if he feels remorse?"

"I'm not sure," I said. What did remorse have to do with it? I had no way of knowing, but felt, somehow, that it shouldn't.

"This is a very brave thing you are attempting. You are unburdening yourself and walking in the path of our Savior." Although I tried, I couldn't deny my Catholic upbringing as a hidden force in all of this.

"Let's talk about how I can help you." His soothing voice calmed me. "Would you like me to deliver a letter from you to him?" I felt my stomach tighten at the thought of something so tangible between us, as if her killer could touch me through a piece of paper. Father Demereaux interpreted my silence. "Or perhaps you can simply tell me what to say and I'll personally deliver the message." My stomach relaxed slightly.

"That would be better," I agreed. "How about if you say, 'The daughter of the woman you killed in 1980 wishes to forgive you. Do you have anything you want to say in return?'" It sounded so simple and to the point. He repeated it back to me. "That's it," I said.

"Let's do this," said Father Demereaux. "Can you call me next Friday night around 8:00?"

"Yes, that's fine. Thank you." He gave me his home telephone number. I gave him Nathan's name. After hanging up, I realized I'd perspired through my shirt. Breathing quickly, I thought, what have I done? What if he's released and comes after my family and me? What if I'm not really ready to forgive? What if, what if, what if? I wept, choking on my own anxiety, feeling desperately unsure of myself.

Twenty years had been a long time. But the following week seemed even longer. I kept myself busy, trying not to think; but at night, my head on the pillow, that's all I could do. I thought of every possible scenario, mostly worst case. The panic rose up, throbbing in my chest and head, leaving me uncertain if I could navigate these violent waters.

Friday was orchestrated around the phone call that evening. Michael came home early to work on a small used boat we purchased to explore the Loxahatchee, the river on which we live. My two daughters, full of excitement, were helping him out on the dock. After an early dinner, he lured them back out to work on the boat, offering me the space and time I needed. I returned to my study, switched on the light, closed the door, sat at my desk and took a deep breath before dialing. Father Demereaux answered.

"Ah yes, Marta, my dear. You're calling about Nathan." Time and space disappeared. "After we spoke last Friday, I went to him on Saturday morning, never having seen him before, as he doesn't attend the service I lead every Wednesday evening. I introduced myself and delivered your message. I asked if he had anything to say in return. Perhaps you can imagine that after twenty years he was taken aback. After a few moments, he said he needed time to think about it. I told him I'd be back in touch with him in a few days."

Father Demereaux continued. "The following Wednesday, during my usual service, I saw him sitting in the back of the room. After I finished, I went to where he was sitting. Before I say anything more, my dear, I need to tell you something important." Father Demereaux, almost whispering, said, "Nathan is dying of cancer. He doesn't look well at all. I'm struck by your timing, my dear. That over a twenty-year period, you call now. A year ago, he was not sick and might not have received your message so openly. Six months from now he'll likely be dead. It only confirms my faith in the workings of a Holy Spirit."

Of all the scenarios I'd imagined, it never crossed my mind that I'd be forgiving a dying man. In that moment, I realized that things were unfolding just as they were intended. Trembling, the tears streaming down my cheeks, I found myself smiling, even laughing. How could I be laughing at the news of a dying man? Was I that vengeful? But it was something entirely different. It was the realization that for the first time since 1980, I felt at peace, that I had nothing to fear.

He continued, "Nathan wishes me to convey how grateful he is for your forgiveness. He asked me to tell you how deeply sorry he is for what he did, that he could never make excuses for it, but that it was a bad time in his life, that he was out of his mind on drugs. He conveys his deepest regrets to you and your family."

And so I sat there, not knowing what to say. My clothes were soaked from perspiration and tears. Feeling immeasurable gratitude, I thanked Father Demereaux and hung up. I sat at my desk, allowing the tears of relief, sadness, gratitude and closure. I felt my mother's presence. This was what she would have wanted.

The next day I sent Father Demereaux flowers and a note that read:

Words cannot express my gratitude.
Sincerely,
Stephanie Marta Cassatly

He told me later that he was teased by the rest of the Chaplain's office — a Catholic priest receiving flowers from a mystery woman.

Two days after Christmas, a thin white envelope with blue lettering arrived from Angola State Penitentiary. Addressed to me, it read:

Notice of Release
Pursuant of Department regulation, this office is required to advise you of Nathan Wolfe's release. He expired on December 23, 2000.

I stood in the driveway holding the letter to my chest. I closed my eyes to the warm sun, thinking about the word "release." We both had been set free. How strange now to grieve her killer, for the life he never had, the bad choices he made and the love he probably never felt.

My daughter called me from the dock. "Come and take a ride with us, Mommy." Michael and my girls were waiting for me, ready to take a ride up the river on the boat they'd been refurbishing over the past few months. The last coat of paint was finally dry. I smiled, put the note in my pocket and walked toward them.

~Stephanie Cassatly

A Heart Restored

Forgive all who have offended you, not for them, but for yourself.
~Harriet Nelson

The front door banged open. Breathless, my two youngest children, Joe and Bethany, rushed in. "Mom. Mom. Ben's in trouble. Come quick." I plunked down my teacup and grabbed my purse. Houses flashed by as we drove several blocks. Bethany pointed to a grassy lot off Main Street. "He's over there." The car lurched to a stop. I leaped out and rocketed toward a jeering mob of high school kids.

A blond-haired sixteen-year-old boy jumped in front of me. Inches from my face, he launched into a slew of profanity. Two kids darted from the scene. A red pickup peeled onto the grass. The driver yelled, "Come on. We gotta get out of here." Amidst a squeal of tires he roared off.

I dodged through a crowd of a dozen or more kids running away, until I spotted my fourteen-year-old son. Ben lay motionless on the ground, arms folded over his head, knees pulled tight against his chest. Knocked down from behind, they had kicked him repeatedly. I knelt beside him. "Mom?" He lifted his head.

Bruised and beaten, blood streamed down his chin. I gasped. Inner sobs racked my body as tears flooded my eyes. "They're gone. Can you get up?"

"Yeah. I think so." He groaned as I helped him to his feet.

Everything seemed a blur. I couldn't think what to do. We piled into the car and drove three blocks to the police station. An officer took a lengthy report while another called paramedics, and then photographed Ben's injuries. We headed to the nearest hospital, thirty minutes away. By the time we arrived, a sack of blood bulged from behind Ben's left ear.

Shaking his head, the emergency room doctor ordered multiple X-rays. "This violence among young people is out of control. Somebody has to do something."

Nurses cleaned Ben's wounds while we waited. X-ray results showed he had a dislocated jaw, broken nose, and a skull fracture. A nurse gave us follow-up instructions as I signed release forms. While I helped Ben on with his jacket, the doctor said, "I'm going to send you and the police department a letter detailing the serious nature of these injuries. The kids involved should be fully prosecuted."

Beginning his investigation the next morning, an officer interviewed students at the high school. From all accounts, the police determined Ben's attack was totally unprovoked.

Medical bills poured into our mailbox, along with the ER physician's letter. I made copies and hand-delivered them to the police department as request for evidence.

Several weeks later, Ben complained he didn't feel well. The doctor discovered a rampant infection caused by his broken nose. He warned us the infection could spread through the thin nasal cartilage and penetrate Ben's brain. We spent the next four months running back and forth to appointments. Tears streamed down my cheeks the day the doctor said, "The antibiotics have done their job. He's in the clear."

Months had passed and we wondered why no word came from the county prosecutor until one day a friend on the city council flagged me down on the street to relay rumblings within city hall. "I can't say who's saying what, but word has it the kids involved are 'good boys from good families.' No one connected with the city government wants to see them serve time for an assault, or have their reputation tarnished by a felony."

Anger burned inside me. The injustice singed my very soul. While life continued as normal for everyone in our small town, our family struggled to recover from the shock of what had happened.

Two years later a friend who worked for the county prosecutor happened across Ben's file. When she asked why they hadn't prosecuted the case, her supervisor said, "Lack of evidence. No medical records or photos were submitted with the police report."

Betrayed by people trusted to execute justice, I grew cynical and hard. Until one day my dad said, "You can't let this ruin your whole life. You need to let it go."

Of course no one knocked on our door pleading for forgiveness. No one apologized for our suffering. But I'd seen people who refused to forgive. They clung to hatred like their worst best friend. Bitterness seeped in and, like a gangrenous wound, spoiled their hearts from the inside out, polluting all their relationships. I didn't want that to be my story.

My father's words haunted me. Though I wanted justice, I knew he was right. Would I allow this horrible event to sour my whole view of life or would I forgive? It was clear the only way to restore my own heart was to lay down my anger. But how could I forgive?

On my knees alone in my room, tears streamed down my face and onto my bed. "Lord, please show me how to forgive." As if God laid his hand on my shoulder, his gentle voice whispered in my ear, "Pray."

I realized prayer was my key to freedom. Each day I prayed for our family and the kids involved. God gave me strength to battle through a tangle of emotions, breaking down the wall of protection I'd built. Before long, the icy cynicism that gripped my heart began to melt. In time I forgave the youths who, in a wolf-pack frenzy, lost their own measure of innocence that day they crossed the line of decency into violence.

The most difficult for me to forgive were those granted authority to serve the public, those meant to be our guardians. Only in God's strength could I let go of my anger and see them as God does. People, who for whatever reason are broken themselves, making wrong choices.

I plowed through my heartache. Praying for the police, I asked God to give them courage to stand for what is right regardless of who they encounter. I prayed for them to have wisdom as they carried out their duty to the community.

Sometimes there is no justice, but for the sake of my own spirit, I let go of my pain, fear, and anger. I accepted the fact I have no control over other people, however I always have the choice to forgive.

For a year I replaced every angry thought by giving thanks to God for his many blessings, and I prayed for people in our town. One morning I awoke, and I felt like myself again. Instead of anger, joy filled my heart. And I remembered there are still a whole lot of good people in this world.

Today friends say I have a bright, generous spirit with an easy laugh. What many don't realize is that it's because twenty years ago I opened my heart and made a choice to forgive.

~Kathleen Kohler

Forged by Fire

In order to hold on to thoughts of anger, bitterness, revenge, guilt,
and shame, we have to use a lot of energy.
~Edwene Gaines

House fires happen for many reasons. Faulty wiring. A candle left unattended. A cooking accident. But the fire that damaged our home had a different and terrifying reason.

We woke to the ear-splitting scream of smoke detectors at 1:00 a.m. Flames danced across the carpet, throwing thick black smoke. I grabbed the dog while my husband and our children ran outside to wait for the fire department. We watched helplessly as the blaze grew brighter.

The next day we surveyed the damage. Two rooms in our modest home were charred while the rest of the house sustained heavy smoke damage. Heat made drywall nails bulge from the walls. I thought the experience of watching our house burn couldn't get worse, but I was wrong. The fire marshal told us the fire started when someone cut my daughter's bedroom screen, broke the window, and tossed a Molotov cocktail inside. Given the late night attack, it was evident someone intended not only to damage our home, but to hurt or even kill us.

Almost immediately, investigators operated on the theory that a disgruntled youth was to blame for the fire because of my job as a juvenile probation officer. The thought of being targeted terrified me and I anxiously awaited word on who could have done it. Although the police interviewed dozens of people, no leads panned out. When a detective told me there wasn't anything more they could do, I couldn't believe it.

Our family stayed in a rental apartment while the restoration company worked to put our home back together. I spent half my time replacing possessions and the other half worrying about what might happen next. Since I had no answers, I tried to calm myself by making up my own. I formed an image of the perpetrator as a dangerous but transient stranger. I told myself he'd surely have left town by now, and that he knew better than to ever return.

More than three months later, we moved back into our completely restored home. The scent of new paint made it seem brand new, but that didn't remove the old memories and fear. At bedtime my eyes stayed wide open. Every time a car drove down the street I ran to the window and peeked out. We decided to put security lights all around the house and I left the porch light on every night.

It's impossible to maintain a high level of anxiety forever. When no new calamity occurred, my fear subsided but unfortunately it was replaced by something else — rage. I dreamt about someone trying to set our house on fire again, but this time setting himself ablaze. I didn't try to save him. I fantasized about the perpetrator being caught and me testifying against him in court. I demanded the judge make him suffer the way we had suffered.

Macabre fantasies colored each of my days, but the hues were dark and disjointed. They seeped into nearly every thought I had. My feelings scared me almost as much as the fire. Then on a beautiful Sunday morning, our minister preached a sermon on forgiveness. I fidgeted while he spoke about bearing no malice until two sentences made me sit stock-still.

"It's possible forgiveness could prompt a wrongdoer to turn over a new leaf. But the person you really change when you forgive someone is yourself."

I chewed my lip. I knew how much my anger festered, but hadn't a clue how I could forgive a nameless, faceless person. I wasn't even sure I wanted to try. There had to be another option. I thought about therapy. I considered hypnosis. I wondered if I could simply banish my anger through sheer force of will. But nothing made sense until I remembered how holding a pen in my hand and putting my thoughts on paper helped unburden me when I had a problem. That's when a light bulb went off. I decided to write a letter to the person who firebombed our house.

I wrote about the destruction of both irreplaceable family photographs and my husband's high school ring. I described my daughter's tears, my son's wary expression, and the nightmares that haunted me. I poured out every detail of how the fire impacted our family. When I had no words left, I put down the pen and took a deep breath. My shoulders felt lighter than they had in months.

I put aside the letter for one week. Then I picked it up and read what I'd written. It surprised me to notice how many questions filled the pages. Why did you do it? What did you hope to accomplish? Do you regret what you did? I sighed, knowing the answers would never come. Then my eyes widened. It really didn't matter who set the fire, what we lost, or how it damaged our home. What did matter was how I let a paralyzing event take ragged bites from my soul. I knew what I had to do and smoothed the letter to add a postscript.

"Since the night of the fire, all my thoughts were entwined with what you did. I felt helpless and angry. I wanted revenge. People often strike out at others when they're hurting. I wonder if you felt damaged and broken on the night you came to my house with hate in your heart. Though the fire didn't destroy me, it did change me. I've been forged into a stronger and more resilient person. I've learned to find peace. Although I'll never understand what drove you to such a reckless act, I want you to know I forgive you. I hope you've been able to heal and find peace, too."

Nothing can change what happened to our family on that dark and frightening night. But by choosing to forgive, I've been able to relinquish the role of victim. I don't dwell on the fire anymore. The past has no power over the present now that I've finally let it go.

~Pat Wahler

A Precious Gift

Yes, this is what good is: to forgive evil. There is no other good.
~Antonio Porchia, Voices

I wanted to spit on him. I wanted to spray spittle across his face, since I was unable to spew the venom that overflowed my heart. I wanted to shriek and hiss about what the assailant had done to my best friend's son—because of him, an entire family was shattered.

No, my friend told me. She insisted that was not the way to go.

Two years earlier, Darice's youngest son had been startled by a home intruder. In the struggle over the gun, three bullets ended up in Aaron; the slug that the surgeons left there remained in more ways than one. Too close to his spine, physically, it was going to stay there forever. And it was a constant reminder of that awful morning, because from that day on, Aaron was a paraplegic.

During the first year following the shooting, the focus was on rehabilitation and renovation. While Aaron was learning how to drive with hand controls and getting quite skilled with his wheelchair, his family and friends painted walls and scrubbed tile and planted bushes around a new home for Aaron and his wife. Unable to forget that awful morning, they had to get a fresh start if there was any hope of continuing their lives without constant nightmares. Unable to do the complicated jobs—like creating a wheelchair accessible shower stall or installing lower sinks—I dug up unwanted bushes, cleaned out the garage and painted. And while an army of loved ones donated their time and effort, Aaron scooted along the floor as he painted the lower sections of the house and helped install laminate floors.

During the next year, the focus was on what Aaron had not lost. Becoming paralyzed had not affected his sunny disposition. He still had a dazzling smile and could still make strangers warm up to him with his easy, friendly style. Aaron still had a zest for life. He filled his weekends with wheelchair basketball tournaments and volunteering with other disabled people. He also finished his college graduate work and rolled across the stage to get his master's degree.

And for most of those two years, the young man who had shot Aaron was in jail awaiting a hearing. A few months after he'd broken into Aaron's home, the intruder turned himself in to the police. We all breathed a sigh of relief. Before the young man had surrendered to the authorities, only the immediate family could visit Aaron in the hospital, which eventually became the rehab center. Wanting to be supportive of Darice, I'd go to the hospital and call my friend, who would come down to the lobby and chat for a few minutes. Now that the felon was safely behind bars, I finally was allowed to go upstairs to his room. There was my friend's son—surrounded by a circle of laughing friends—popping wheelies in his wheelchair and cracking jokes.

Once Aaron was released, he and his wife settled into their new home and things seemed good. Darice and James got their son a van retrofitted with hand controls. Aaron was having trouble finding a job, as were most kids in their mid-twenties, so he started volunteering at a disability center. They had gotten their home decorated the way they wanted—the only thing that stood between them and closure was hearing a judge say, "You're guilty and now you're going to prison," to the man who almost killed Aaron.

As the court date got closer, I was insistent. "Darice, I'll take the day off work to sit next to you," but she wasn't even sure if she was going to go. Seeing the young man who had tried to end Aaron's life in person, having to watch him stand up and walk around while her own son would never walk again—she didn't know if she'd be able to handle it.

The day of sentencing passed—apparently it was rescheduled, but Aaron didn't tell his mother until the day before. He also was having trouble deciding if he would attend, already dealing with too many bad memories. The last time he had seen this guy, the two of them were in a life-or-death struggle over a pistol. Seeing him again—would it bring some closure or open old wounds?

The day of the sentencing Aaron, his mother and his father were there. When the young man spoke to the judge about how sorry he was, he spoke so quietly Aaron had to wheel right up behind him to hear. When Darice and James were given a chance to say something in the courtroom, they sat there silently, unable to put into words how their world had crashed down upon them that spring morning.

And when Darice met the intruder's mother in the courthouse hallway, she hugged her... and both women cried.

Darice told me later that evening about the hearing. "Why didn't you tell me, Darice? I would have gone with you." She explained she hadn't decided until the last minute.

When I heard what had happened, I asked, "How could you? How could you embrace that kid's mother? Why didn't you get angry?"

Looking down at her folded hands, Darice said, "We both lost part of our boys on the day that Aaron was shot. My son lost the ability to walk, but her son is going to lose most of his youth because he's going to be in prison for a long time."

All the words in the world spoken by either woman couldn't alter the facts, but a tearful embrace between mothers spoke volumes. I realized that wanting to spit and shriek prevented me from moving forward. Darice had given herself the gift of forgiveness, and now she was able to move on with her life. Now, she could celebrate what her son still had—and all that he had never lost.

Forgiveness. It's a precious gift to give to yourself.

~Sioux Roslawski

Forgiveness Practice

Courage doesn't always roar. Sometimes courage is the little voice at the end of the day that says I'll try again tomorrow.
~Mary Anne Radmacher

After a drunk driver killed my son Shawn on his high school prom night, my life fell apart. My vibrant charismatic nineteen-year-old had perished and in his place stood only broken dreams.

Searching for hope, I gathered memories seeking to keep them alive. I shared my feelings with friends and family on a daily basis. We reminisced about the sports Shawn played, the fish he caught, the hijinks with friends. I searched old photo albums, watching his progress from towheaded toddler asleep on Dad's chest to his senior picture in cap and gown. I reread sympathy cards detailing Shawn's impact on his friends' lives.

All those sweet memories faded when I saw his killer in the courtroom. For the first time in my grieving process, I was angry. The young man appeared stoic, devoid of emotion or remorse. Why was he alive and my son dead, his future gone? Shawn had a plan for life after high school—two years in community college and a part-time job with a carpet company.

Our son loved children and coached a youth flag football team where he patiently led small boys who idolized him. He wanted a future with a family and was fond of saying, "When I have kids, mine will be dressed in babyGap!" The world lost a good father. I lost an opportunity for grandchildren.

After several years of struggle, I began my journey up the steep hill of forgiveness. The theologians are correct: Progress cannot be accomplished if one is dragging the chains of anger and hatred.

The first step involved pondering a Sunday repetition of The Lord's Prayer: "Forgive us our trespasses as we forgive those who trespass against us." I had trouble saying the words.

During my daily walk, I wrestled with this dilemma. I shook my fist and told God I wasn't ready. Wisely, God didn't answer. Maybe I could forgive in increments, or practice forgiveness in percentiles. I began by saying, "God, I can forgive him ten percent." Daily I repeated this mantra. Shawn always defended the underdog, didn't he? The scabs on my soul began to soften.

Some days I managed to add another point or two, others another five. Two months later, I stalled before fifty percent. Why would I want to admit that I was halfway to total forgiveness? Not me, Lord!

Eventually I crawled across the fifty-yard line. Relieved at this milestone, I believed success was possible. Progress accelerated until I arrived at the ninety percent marker. Only ten points separated me from total forgiveness. The light at the end of the absolution tunnel beckoned, but my face turned away.

Spring passed, including what would have been my son's twenty-fourth birthday and the fifth anniversary of his death. I longed for completion of my task. What an accomplishment that would be—and an accomplishment I needed. Instead, I plodded into summer while still stuck at ninety percent. Depressed, I wondered if I'd make the final victory.

One morning in the fall, I awakened to the words, "Come into his heart Lord Jesus." Did I dream the phrase or did the voice speak to my innermost being? I believed the latter. The elusive 100 percent arrived, and with it relief and journey's end. At last, sounds were more musical, colors more vibrant, tastes sweeter.

The following May, a letter arrived from the drunk driver. The killer's note was composed two days before he was released from prison. At his sentencing hearing three years prior, the judge had directed him to write an apology to us. It began simply: "Undoubtedly, this represents the most difficult letter I have tried to compose… the content is derived solely from the inner-workings of my heart."

Why now? Why did this communication arrive after completion of my tortuous journey toward healing? The last line summed up my spiritual travels: "Be well in the meantime and may God give you guys the courage, strength, and wisdom to light your path."

The timing of the letter did not go unnoticed. May was the great equalizer—May 1st, the date Shawn died and the following week Mother's Day. Now perhaps I understood God's plan. Until I'd reached the 100 percent marker, I wouldn't have accepted the apology.

A scripture came to mind: "Thy word is a lamp unto my feet, and a light unto my path." Peace arrived in increments. I provided the math. God, through forgiveness practice, became the teacher.

~Rita Billbe

I Am a Survivor

Forgiveness is the experience of peacefulness in the present moment.
Forgiveness does not change the past, but it changes the present.
~Frederic Luskin

To My Uncle:

I'm writing this letter to tell you that I forgive you for all the things you did to me as a child. I don't need to remind you what those things were. You already know. I have another reason for doing this, and that is I want you to know how your abuse has affected my life, both good and bad.

To forgive you doesn't mean that I forget. That old cliché is such a lie. Once those memories are imprinted on your brain, you cannot erase them no matter how hard you try. I am a survivor, and survivors always carry with them the events and circumstances that brought them safely to the other side.

I had no recollection of your abuse for nearly twenty years. My mind completely blocked it out. It was having my own son that brought that forgotten child within me back into focus and I began to remember. I don't know why my mind chose to block out what happened. But I truly believe my mind was protecting me, keeping those memories locked away deep inside until I had reached some level of emotional maturity where I could better deal with them. I have vivid memories of a happy childhood up until around age five. But from age six to ten or so, things are a bit blurry and I have entire blocks of time, years even, that I don't remember much. That particular timespan coincides directly with the years that you came to visit us.

As a pedophile, you fed off our family for decades. I know there are others because I've spoken with them, and all of their stories are eerily similar to mine. I cannot imagine a more hurtful act than to steal the innocence of a child.

There are no words to describe the amount of pain that you have caused me. Your abuse has affected nearly every part of my life. I can't speak for the other victims in our family, but I know that the emotional toll must be great, especially for those who, although very young, didn't block out their abuse and can recall vividly the acts you committed against them. I know because they told me.

For many years I've battled depression and anxiety. I've tried various things to ease the pain, not knowing where all this emotional turmoil was coming from. Then after recalling the abuse, enduring years of helpful but painful therapy, and seeking God's guidance in my life, I can look back and say that most of my life has been, to some degree, shame-based. And it's all because of you.

Ashamed as a child because no matter how hard I tried, I never felt quite good enough. Ashamed of my changing body during puberty, then later using my budding sexuality by acting out with boys, and beating myself up emotionally for years because of it. Even now, I still deal with issues concerning body image, intimacy, trust, inadequacy, and a profound fear of failure.

I give that shame back to you. It is not mine. It's yours.

Now for the good stuff. As hard as it is for me to admit, many of the traits that are deeply engrained in me to this day are, I believe, a direct result of your abuse and its aftermath. I have a strong empathy for others and can sense the emotional pain of others. I hate to see anyone suffer, which is probably why I chose to become a registered nurse. My career choice has been greatly rewarding. I would like to think that in the twenty-four years I've been practicing, I've helped in times of need to those I've ministered.

My mother told me that around age six I began to develop a strong creative streak and vivid imagination. I couldn't do enough arts and crafts, and I would make up stories about heroes rescuing young kids from all kinds of perilous situations. That creativity and imagination, along with a passion for music, would follow me all my life. Several years ago I discovered the joy of writing. I am happiest when I am being creative. But it's my writing that has truly been my salvation. It does for me what no amount of Prozac could ever do. And no one can take that from me.

I have a wonderful husband who loves me despite my many issues and flaws. He has stood beside me through everything, always encouraging me to do whatever it is I need to heal. He loves me even when I'm difficult to love, and he's the greatest blessing the Lord has ever given me.

I'm also a better mother because of what I've gone through. I was always vigilant, admittedly maybe too vigilant, about where our son went and with whom he came into contact. We encouraged him to talk to us, no matter what the subject matter. And when he was old enough to understand, we talked about good and bad touching and what to do if anyone, no matter who, touched him inappropriately. We have an open, honest line of communication to this day because of the foundation we laid all those years ago.

Why am I telling you all this? Because I want you to know that you didn't break me. I am a vessel with scars and cracks, but God still uses vessels like me.

There is a verse in I Samuel 16:7 that reads, "...for the Lord sees not as man sees; for man looks on the outward appearance, but the Lord looks on the heart."

I've heard this verse numerous times over the years, but the power of that passage never really made an impact on me until recently.

It was such a random, uneventful day as I pushed my shopping cart across the parking lot of our local supermarket. I've battled with my weight for most of my life, and I was feeling especially "unpretty" that day because I had stepped on the scale that morning to find I had gained back ten of the thirty pounds I had lost over the past few months. My self-esteem plummeted, and I decided it wasn't worth the effort to do my hair or put on make-up before I left the house.

After loading my groceries into my car, I got into the driver's seat and turned the key. I caught sight of my reflection in the rearview mirror and I stopped dead. I pulled off my sunglasses and stared at the unkempt hair beneath my husband's old baseball cap. I looked down at the sweatpants that felt a little tighter today and the ratty gardening sneakers I had on, and I felt that familiar wave of shame start to wash over me.

Then that particular verse popped into my mind and before I even realized what I was doing, I looked back at myself in the mirror and said, "God thinks you're beautiful."

I cried like a baby all the way home because, for the first time in my life, I truly knew what it felt like to be unconditionally loved.

That day was a catalyst for me. I am finally learning to love myself, and in doing so, I have come to the realization that I have to let go of all the anger and hatred I've had for you all these years. Only then can I be truly free.

I am no longer a victim. I am a survivor. And God thinks I'm beautiful.

Sincerely,
Your Niece

~Cheryll Snow

Peace After the Storm

The motto should not be forgive one another; rather, understand one another.
~Emma Goldman

I t was a big decision for a ninth-grade dropout and mother of seven to make. The death of our three-year-old Laura had created a desire in me to go to medical school. The summer I turned thirty-two, my family and I had embarked upon that journey.

Now the last semester's term papers were upon me. There were articles I couldn't get from our local area, so I needed to make a trip to Oklahoma City. Two of my classmates and I decided to go and get the trip behind us.

I felt strangely uneasy the morning we left, but chalked it up to fatigue. We got what we needed and headed home. All of a sudden I had this sick sensation in the pit of my stomach that something was wrong. We stopped so I could call. I knew something was not right, but all they would tell me was, "Come on home."

Three hours later we pulled into the driveway. It seemed like the entire property was frozen. The silence of death was on everyone's face as I entered the front room. Grandpa? Grandma? I quickly scanned the room for the children. Randy? Where was Randy? No, it couldn't be Randy... he was over at Jay's house. They were going to band practice. I turned to Doug and asked through uncontrollable tears, "Is it Randy?"

"Yes."

My heart felt a squeeze so tight I thought it would crush me. My tears were unstoppable.

Doug had taken the car apart. He had been busy working on it. Leeanna needed lunch bags for the kids' lunch the next day. Randy volunteered to ride his bike to the store. Jay went with him. The boys were seconds away from turning into the store parking lot when a drunk driver topped the hill at 75 mph in a 25 mph zone, hitting Randy and throwing him several feet in the air. Jay was cut by the glass. Randy was dead.

Randy was fifteen and the light of our lives. He always added that extra sparkle of laughter and excitement to our everyday lives. The funeral was amazing. People came from everywhere — many we didn't know, but they knew Randy. I felt an unbelievable pride in my son when a little crippled lady came to the door bringing a dish of food. She shared how much it had meant to her to have Randy cut her yard every week and take out her trash. She told us when she tried to pay him he'd smile and say, "Oh, I don't take money for this kind of thing." Randy left us thousands of memories to laugh at and cherish.

There's no way to adequately explain the grief, the guilt, the questions, the "what ifs" that torment your mind and heart in those early days. I finally got far enough along that God helped me understand that the other family was suffering as much as we were, plus they carried the burden of having caused the death. The situation was even more complicated by the fact that the drunk driver was the father of one of Randy's best friends.

We made the decision to visit the driver. The tragedy they were suffering was intense. Changes were taking place in the family for the betterment of all. Perhaps, with the passing of time, the changing of habits and the help of friends, the Lord would be able to put their lives back together.

The beginning miracle was the spirit of forgiveness that God placed in my heart. A spirit of unexplained peace engulfed me. Randy was safe in the arms of God; I knew his battle was over. It would take many miracles to keep this other family from being totally destroyed.

From that moment, and with the passing of time, I realized it is the experiences of life, rather than age, that brings about maturity.

Several years passed before our paths were to cross again. Miracles had indeed happened. A once drunk driver was now free from alcohol and busily involved in serving God. A marriage once threatened to become a divorce statistic was firmly grounded on the Lord. The children had grown up with the love of both parents. For me, this brought a sense of personal peace to my soul. A thankfulness for God's mercy welled up within my heart. All had not been lost.

~Patricia Williams

Chapter 9

The Power *of* Forgiveness

The Importance of
Self-Forgiveness

It's toughest to forgive ourselves. So it's probably best to start with other people. It's almost like peeling an onion. Layer by layer, forgiving others, you really do get to the point where you can forgive yourself.

~Patty Duke

Finding Honesty

Honesty is the first chapter of the book of wisdom.
~Thomas Jefferson

I had a friend. We were like sisters. Given that we are both only children, that's saying a lot. We were together so much that people thought we actually were sisters. We knew each other's hopes, dreams, secrets, good traits, bad traits, and accepted each other no matter what. One truly amazing thing about our friendship was that we could talk about anything, including when we had a problem with each other. We definitely had our fair share of fights, but we always solved them, whether it was through talking, yelling, or writing notes back and forth because we were too angry to speak. We always made up, always fell right back into our comfortable sisterhood, our four-hour phone conversations resuming as if nothing had happened.

When we each chose different universities to attend after high school, our goodbye was physically painful. My chest and gut ached with having to leave our everyday friendship behind and face an entire new world without her. We visited each other as often as we could, e-mailed daily, and ran down our cell phone plan minutes in record time.

And then the inevitable happened. We grew apart. Made new friends. Chose different life paths. Things that shouldn't have mattered but that seemed so important in our twenties. And we stopped doing the most important thing that we had always done, that made our friendship unique from others: we stopped being honest with each other. Rather than allowing the friendship to change with us, we tried to fit our new selves into our old friendship. Square pegs, round hole. It just didn't work.

One sunny, spring afternoon, we met for lunch. A life changing moment. I had written what I thought was a private e-mail to a mutual friend. An e-mail about my now-former best friend. Containing my very strong opinions and doubts about the man she had chosen to date and wanted to marry. In the past, I would have gone straight to her to talk about it, but I no longer felt comfortable doing that. So of course, as these things go, she found out. So did many other people. Without intending to, I hurt her more deeply than either of us thought possible, and irreparably wounded our relationship. She didn't understand why I spoke to anyone but her about something so personal, and I didn't understand why she couldn't see the reasons why I couldn't.

We didn't speak for six years. We tried to talk about what happened right after, but the trust was gone… completely lost. I missed her wedding; she missed the births of my children. We missed out on everything. Because of something I did. Or was it?

I blamed myself for so many years for what happened. I was sick to my stomach over the loss of my wonderful friend, and weighed down with the knowledge that it was my fault. But after many years, and putting it into perspective with everything else we both went through during those lost years, I stopped beating myself up for it. The truth is, our friendship, in its previous capacity, ended long before the e-mail. Yes, I made a mistake and should not have betrayed our old trust. But that wasn't the only reason the friendship died. With that realization, I forgave myself, and found peace.

Many years later, I reached out to my friend. I wouldn't have been brave enough to do that if I hadn't first forgiven myself and then realized that perhaps our friendship deserved another chance. To my surprise and joy, she had forgiven me and also wanted to contact me. Almost like old times, we were able to talk about what had happened, forgive each other, and move forward with a new friendship. When we finally spoke on the phone, we cried at the familiarity of each other's voices.

Is our friendship just as it used to be? No, absolutely not. Life is not a fairy tale. It is a new friendship, and it is slowly growing. And it is, most importantly, a forgiving friendship. And I am okay with that.

~Sara Springfield Schmit

We Did Our Best

Forgiveness is beautiful and it feels good when someone gives that gift to you.
But it's one thing for someone you wronged to forgive you.
It was another to forgive yourself.
~Kristen Ashley, Fire Inside

The door slammed. I yanked it open and watched my husband of almost thirty years tromping across the front lawn. As he opened his car door, he looked back and saw me silhouetted in the doorway.

"You're wrong, you know," he said so quietly I had to strain to hear him. "There was never anyone else but you. No one. Ever." With those words, he disappeared into his car. Perhaps as emphasis, the car sputtered and shook before the engine turned over and he pulled away.

Tears ran down my cheeks. I became the twenty-year-old who fell in love with a slender young man with curly black hair, soft brown eyes, a tender but tentative smile, who was exactly a year older than me. A birthday wasn't the only thing we shared. We were both hard working, loved our families, espoused similar political beliefs, loved children and knew how to live on a tight budget.

In four years, we had bought our own house, had three of our four children and established a comfortable, if frugal lifestyle. We agreed that I would be a stay-at-home mom and he would be the breadwinner. We made a good team. On our ninth anniversary we conceived our fourth child, who joined our family nine months to the day later. It was also our shared birthday.

My husband gained prestige and acknowledgement at his job while he pursued a college degree. He became the first college graduate in his family. When I expressed pride in his accomplishment, his eyes flattened and darkened with something I couldn't identify. This was the first time I suspected all was not well.

Our children grew and thrived, we became more financially secure, but the seeds planted earlier cast shoots of discontent through our relationship. Our children attended college or secured jobs and I stepped back onto a road I had abandoned when I married and gave up my dream of a college degree. People often refer to stages in failing relationships as pounding nails into a coffin. Although I don't believe it was my intention, that stage of my journey added nails.

Once begun, there seemed to be no turning back. Again, relying on hindsight, I wondered that fateful day in the doorway why we had ever fallen in love and how we had stayed together as long as we had.

When I described our meeting and what we shared in common, I failed to point out where our paths diverged. I was gregarious, outspoken, and loved a good conversation, especially one with a suitable amount of controversy to jack up the interest level. I was quick to say I love you, never able to stay angry, and optimistic to an annoying fault. My husband was my polar opposite—quiet, introverted, someone who refused to discuss religion or politics and was content to sprawl on the couch and watch sports during the few hours he wasn't working, going to school or playing sports. I found it difficult to engage him in a conversation of any length.

John had a guttural laugh that seemed reluctant to emerge. I tried to make him laugh, but he withheld his laughter and I began to wonder what else he was withholding.

We argued about disciplining our children, what they could and couldn't do. And we blamed each other when we didn't approve of their behavior. The tenuous thread that held us together showed serious signs of fray. Angry words replaced words of love.

We made deals to get through activities. My studies intensified as I neared graduation. When I began working, I continued to prepare microwaveable meals, but we ate separately. I began to wonder if he had found someone else.

"Are you having an affair?"

"Yeah. What's for dinner?" he replied, head buried in the refrigerator. I never knew if it was true, but I realized later he was trying to tell me our relationship was over.

We battled endlessly through the long divorce. Each of us took steps to move on but we never forgave each other. All the paperwork that accumulates in a divorce serves as one big tally sheet of wrongdoing that each partner carries in his or her head, sometimes for years. It makes for a major roadblock in moving on.

I joined a divorce support group. Although the support helped, I felt stuck. One of the speakers hit the nail on the head for me.

"Repeat after me," she began. "In my marriage I did the best I could." I did as requested and heard my words echoed by others in the room.

"Now, say my spouse did the best he or she could." This time there was silence. The heck he did, I thought, and imagined others saying the same.

Because she had oozed compassion and understanding when she began her talk, the occupants of the room stayed in their chairs, albeit in silence. She continued to make the case that, up to that moment, all of us had done the best we could. "After all," she asked, "who would choose to do the worst?"

It took a while before I could embrace that idea and forgive my husband and myself. He wasn't the best husband for me and I wasn't the best wife for him. But I had loved him and had really intended to do my best. And I believed he would say the same.

And my past, sorry as my efforts might have been, was the best I could do at that time. The speaker reminded us not to use the past as an excuse for poor future behavior. Seeing the limitations of my past is a strong motivation to do better in the future. My past is indeed made up of all my best efforts.

~Judythe A. Guarnera

The Mistake that Wasn't

Love yourself—accept yourself—forgive yourself—
and be good to yourself, because without you the rest of us are without a
source of many wonderful things.
~Leo F. Buscaglia

Giving birth should be one of the happiest times in a woman's life. However, when it's the mid-60s and the woman is single, it can be one of the worst things imaginable. I hadn't planned on getting pregnant, but I hadn't done anything to prevent it either. Since the baby's father denied any responsibility and my parents were disinclined to help, the options for dealing with my pregnancy were few: I could have the baby and try to raise it on my own (unheard of in those days), I could seek an abortion (illegal in those days) or I could have the child and give it up for adoption.

Early in my pregnancy, my parents instructed me to stay away from their house. "We don't want all the neighbors knowing."

I moved in with a girlfriend, but as time went by and I continued to grow larger, she suggested I live elsewhere. "My boyfriend feels uncomfortable having you around."

I checked out some homes for unwed mothers, but I was in my twenties and the idea of living with a bunch of pregnant teenagers left me cold. I contacted my pastor and he suggested an adoption agency that would not only help me find a place to live, they would also pay all my medical expenses. All I had to do was agree to allow the agency to place my child "in a loving home" once he or she was born. I could see no other solution.

Rather than accept the offer of living with a host family, I continued to work and lived in a motel. It was an expense I really didn't want, but it had a small kitchen area so I saved money by not having to eat in restaurants. On the day my water broke, I was having a rare lunch with my mother who, instead of driving me to the hospital, told me to "Get in your car and go." The hospital was twenty miles away but, trying to hold back the contractions, I drove myself, stopping only long enough to fill up the gas tank.

When I arrived at the hospital, an attendant helped me from my car and a nurse put me in a wheelchair and headed for the elevators and then to the labor room. Alone in the room, I wondered about everything that was going to happen. Would I experience a lot of pain? Would my child be a boy or a girl? What would happen if there were complications and my child didn't survive? No one answered my questions; no one held my hand; no one heard my screams.

After my son was born, I was moved into a room with three other women who had also just given birth. One, like me, spent a lot of time crying; the other two could only talk about what they planned to do when they got out. An elderly nurse brought in some papers for me to sign and asked if I wanted to see my child. Signing those papers meant I was voluntarily giving up my firstborn child. I wouldn't see him take his first step. I wouldn't walk him to his first day at school. I wouldn't see him graduate, get married or have children. How could I, as a mother, do such a thing? How could I just turn my back and look away? I bit my lip, shook my head and signed the papers.

Upon being discharged from the hospital, I drove back to the motel, collected my belongings and moved into a small studio apartment. Although the doctors had advised me to take six weeks to recover, my funds were running short and I needed to return to work immediately. Luckily, I found a job close to the apartment and spent my days leaning over a typewriter and my nights crying into a pillow. Where was my son? Was he being cared for? Did anyone comfort him when he cried?

As the pain of losing my child lessened, another grew. Even though society and my parents frowned on the idea of illegitimate children, I was the one who had given up my son. I had signed the papers. I had walked out of the hospital without him. I could have kept him. I could have found a way. But no, I took the easy way out and gave him up. Everything that happened had been my fault. I knew I would never forgive myself.

Over the next years, I went from one relationship to another. No one could ease my pain. I eventually married but, as might have been expected, even that ended in divorce. I couldn't love myself and therefore couldn't love anyone else. The only thing on my mind was my child. A day didn't go by that I didn't think about him. What did he look like? Was he happy? Did his parents love him?

Shortly before my son's twenty-eighth birthday, I received a telephone call from the adoption agency stating that the child I had given up for adoption had been making inquiries about me. "He wants to know if you would like to meet him."

"Would I like to meet him?" Never had I thought anyone would ever ask me such a question.

"Of course I would," I replied. However, after going over all the details and hanging up the phone, I began to worry. Why did he want to meet me? Was he sick? Did he need money? What if he just wanted to tell me he hated me? After all, I had never forgiven myself for giving him away... why wouldn't he hate me?

We met at the agency, shook hands and fell into an immediate embrace. We cried, we talked, we shared pictures and we hugged some more. He had been placed in a home with two brothers and two sisters, all adopted, and his parents had been kind, understanding and loving. Instead of condemning me for giving him up, he thanked me. "I know it must have been hard, but you did everything you could to make sure I had a good life."

My son had forgiven me... it was finally time for me to forgive myself.

~Margaret Nava

The Man
Without a Face

Holding onto anger is like drinking poison
and expecting the other person to die.
~Buddha

Walking home one night, I turned up the alleyway to enter my apartment building through the back door. I knew I shouldn't be walking alone after dark, but it was a quick two blocks from my favorite bar to my door, and I had done it a million times before. On this night, however, there was a faceless man standing halfway down the alley. This was not unusual as my downtown neighborhood had its share of the homeless. As I neared the door, my key in hand, he moved toward me. I realized, registering fear for the first time, that he would beat me to the door. Then my world went black.

The next thing I consciously remember is being under bright lights in the hospital, naked under a scratchy blanket, being told I had been sexually assaulted. My mind was thick with cobwebs as I tried to understand what they said. Through the fog of painkillers and a concussion, the horror of calling my family, and the humiliation of a sexual assault kit, my only glimmer of hope was that the man responsible had been arrested and was being held on a million-dollar bond. I had something to hang on to: that justice would prevail. That kept me going in the long weeks and months that followed. I was assigned a court advocate who took my place in the courts. She told me that nothing would happen quickly and she was right.

But the court system failed me when the man was found to be mentally ill, and all I was left with was anger. I wasn't going to get the closure I so desperately needed on this horrible chapter in my life. I moved away from the city where this tragedy struck me, but I couldn't leave it behind. The nightmares kept coming. I felt entitled to a resolution. I felt entitled to all the rage and anger I kept bottled up inside. The only solace I felt was when I drank. While my friends and family acknowledged my "right" to my anger, they couldn't stand to see me destroy myself this way. I spent more and more time alone.

When things couldn't possibly get any worse, I was arrested for a DUI and forced to wear an ankle monitor that prohibited me from drinking. I was also required to get counseling. This blessing in disguise allowed me to learn about resentments, anger, and the pain that it causes inside. I couldn't get better until I let go of my anger and started forgiving those who had hurt me. Only then could I hope to stop drinking for good and start healing. I had to begin by making a list of people to forgive: old friends, family, colleagues. But I knew who would be the toughest man to forgive; a man whose face I didn't even know.

Forgiveness, for me, began by realizing that I wasn't blameless for the events in my life. I had lost friendships, and had to start by recognizing that I had played a part in the loss of those friendships. Granted I may have been hurt by people, but I may have been to blame for causing hurt as well. This shift in perspective was eye opening for me. It allowed me to move forward and start rebuilding relationships that had been broken. I was able to repair some friendships, but some were too badly damaged. All I can do for those friends is pray that they can forgive me and move on. My family relationships may have suffered the most. Over time, we were able to work through our hurts and anger and into new, stronger relationships. It hasn't been easy, but it's been worth it. My relationships today are fewer in number, but more honest, and are better and stronger than the ones I had before.

The lingering question was how to forgive a man I didn't know and didn't want to know. Was he even a man if he was capable of such an act? I couldn't go to him as I had with the other people I had forgiven. It was entirely possible this man didn't even want my forgiveness. But I knew I couldn't move forward without forgiving him. And then I realized I was mad at myself too. I was blaming myself for walking alone that night and for using the back door of the building instead of the front door. I thought maybe God was inflicting a punishment on me. I could forgive other people in my life, but I was still carrying resentments toward the man, God, and myself.

Sometimes healing just takes time, and so it was with me. I realized if I wanted to be free of this man, I had to forgive him. In time I came to pity him. He is clearly not a well person. I hope that he will never harm anyone again, but he is no longer my burden to bear. I don't think of him, and he doesn't plague my sleep. After all, he doesn't even have a face. Most importantly, I had to forgive myself. It wasn't my fault what happened to me that night. Nothing I did caused that to happen. Nothing I could have done would have prevented it. Allowing myself to believe that allowed me to trust in myself again. Finally, I had to stop blaming God. I learned to find a different God in my recovery; a kinder, gentler God than the one of my youth. A God who would never abandon me in an alley. A God who doesn't dole out punishment. And this God is the one who taught me how to forgive. And when I found this God I could love and trust and believe in, all my anger slipped away.

I choose every day to focus on the good in my life and in the world, and there isn't room to focus on the past and the bad things that have happened. Sometimes bad things happen to people, but I choose to focus on the good things. This decision keeps me happy, healthy, and sober. My life is full of peace now, in a new city, with supportive friends and family—thanks to the gift of forgiveness. And I know I wouldn't have this life today if that faceless man had not walked into my alley that night.

~Stacey Wagner

I Forgive Me

Forgiveness is a gift you give yourself.
~Tony Robbins

I was fifteen, a sophomore in high school, and thrilled about the evening ahead. My classmates had elected me to the Homecoming Court and tonight was the celebration. Excitement filled the room as girls primped for the presentation. Dressed in a beautiful gown, I felt like a princess at a ball. Unexpectedly, my mom walked through the door with a troubled look on her face. She came directly over to me and softly said, "Stan won't be able to make it tonight. He was in an accident and is in the hospital." I burst into tears, although I had no specific details. Stan was my boyfriend.

"What happened?" I asked. She said he had fallen at his gymnastic meet. Homecoming festivities were about to begin, so I composed myself and smiled as if everything was fine.

After homecoming, my parents drove me to the hospital and I rushed to the ICU waiting room. Stan's immediate family was there. His dad kept crying, which deeply upset me. As they told me what happened, it took a while to sink in. I just wanted to see Stan. The hospital policy allowed only family in the ICU, but an exception was made. We were restricted to only ten minutes and I was taken in to see him.

He looked the same, except for the breathing tube. He tried to talk but no sound came out, only moving his lips. I don't remember anything I said, only the awful sounds of machines and the feeling of helplessness. I assume I told him about homecoming. I definitely recall saying, "I love you." Even at fifteen, I understood the prevailing comfort of knowing someone loves you and is pulling for you. I was there for him and would be by his side while he recovered.

The reality of Stan's accident was that he would never recover. He had broken his neck by falling off the still rings at his gymnastic meet. His first and second vertebrae were broken, and he was a quadriplegic. His condition required a tracheotomy to keep him breathing and alive. His vocal cords were paralyzed but he could move facial muscles, so communication was by lip reading. His mind was 100 percent whole. He was truly imprisoned in his paralyzed body. No words can describe the mental and emotional anguish he endured.

I was devoted to Stan and he knew I loved him. After school, my mom would drive me to the hospital to visit him for those emotional ten minutes. I didn't miss a day. He was on a specialized bed that would rotate him, so sometimes he would be face down with his head in a brace. My most difficult memories are when the swelling in his brain was at its worst. He was unresponsive, staring at the floor with tears falling from his eyes. I would sit on the floor and look up at his swollen face and tell him about the day at school and the friends that sent their love. My heart broke as I saw the boy I loved endure such agony. I cried myself to sleep at night thinking about the horrible sights and sounds I had experienced that day. I prayed desperate prayers, "God, let Stan live, let him recover, heal his broken body."

As weeks passed and his muscular body atrophied, everyone accepted the reality that he would never recover. Unbeknownst to me, Stan and his family were quietly and lovingly strategizing about my place in his life. I had turned sixteen and was driving myself to visit him. Now in a private room, we could talk freely; he would ask me to hug and kiss him and hold his hand. It was gut wrenching to watch his face as he would concentrate so hard trying to feel my hand holding his. His family bought flowers and cards for him to give me for our monthly "anniversary" of dating. Becoming proficient at reading his lips and understanding what he wanted to ask or tell me brought more joy and laughter for both of us.

Nine months passed and Stan invited his best friend George to visit him. Multitudes had visited the hospital, yet no one had actually seen Stan after his accident except for his parents, sister, brother-in-law and me. I was so happy about this positive step. Stan was getting better, I thought. After their visit, Stan tenderly told me I needed to move on with my life and that he was breaking up with me. He said that he wouldn't recover and I shouldn't spend my teenage years visiting him and missing high school experiences. He said, "I asked George to invite you out on a date." I was shocked, saddened, and conflicted, although I agreed. Though somewhat relieved, I was completely unprepared for the overwhelming feelings of guilt that would plague me in future months and years.

George honored Stan's request and invited me to a football team party. The party was fun and new possibilities appeared. In time, I found a new wonderful boyfriend, but continued to visit Stan every other month. He had moved home with all the medical equipment and full-time care that he needed. I had indeed moved on in my life, but was shackled with a heavy burden of guilt. I felt guilty living a happy life while Stan suffered. I felt guilty that I dreaded visiting and seeing him suffering. I felt guilty that I cared about Stan's wellbeing although I had a boyfriend who might feel hurt because of my loyalty to another. I obviously would have benefited from professional counseling, but in the 1970s there was a stigma to counseling so no one suggested it.

After four years of suffering as a quadriplegic, Stan died peacefully in his sleep. Someway, somehow, at some point in time, I found a way to eradicate all the guilt and move forward, living productively. I forgave myself. That may sound strange because I didn't do anything to cause or create this tragic situation. In fact, I may have even gone beyond what was expected of me. Why would I need to forgive myself? Simply put, I forgave myself for not having all the right words, actions or decisions. I forgave myself for not being the perfect friend or girlfriend. I forgave myself for not being enough. No one made me feel guilty. I brought that all on myself. Forgiving myself has been survival for me as a daughter, wife, ex-wife, mother, and friend as I have made more mistakes than can ever be counted. Forgiving myself has enabled me to forgive hurtful words and actions of others. Forgiveness comes in many sizes, shapes and forms. Forgiveness is personal. Most of all, forgiveness is powerful.

~Julie Kinser Huffman

The "Other" Woman

And you know, when you've experienced grace and you feel
like you've been forgiven, you're a lot more forgiving of other people.
You're a lot more gracious to others.
~Rick Warren

M e? Forgive her? No way. She was the woman who put my marriage in jeopardy, the one who flirted with her coworker and let it go too far. How could I forgive such a foolish and selfish person? She was the reason for my heartache. If I forgave her, she might do it again to another husband or another coworker. I was afraid to forgive her. She might betray me again. What made it more unforgivable is that "she" is me.

I was the one who betrayed my husband. I was the one who lied to my parents and friends and coworkers. Strangely enough, they had all forgiven me, but I could not forgive myself. How had I wandered so far from my values and morals?

I would often think about the "what ifs." What if I had not let our office friendship drift into the danger zone? I justified my need for male friends because my husband Ron had become distant, critical and cold. I was lonely and in need of reassurance, and Jake was more than willing to accommodate my needs. Each small decision to let Jake get closer was something I needed to forgive myself for. As first, we just sat next to each other when a group went out for lunch, but then we started going to lunch on our own. Then one day, dinner after work, which required a lie to Ron about where I was going. Next, we would meet after work in secret locations. Each progressive step was small, but led to a large cliff.

I knew it was wrong to deceive Ron and the guilt weighed heavily on my heart. My emotions told me to run away with Jake, but my rational mind knew that it was not right to leave Ron without giving him a chance to save our marriage.

After a conversation with my parents and their wise advice to talk about the problems in our marriage with Ron, I decided to see if it could be saved. Surprisingly, Ron was very open to working on our relationship and he confessed that he had been distant and impatient with me. But when I told him I'd been having an affair, his answer was even more surprising. He said, "I knew something was very different about you. You felt so far away and disconnected. So now I know why."

I told him that I was willing to walk away from Jake, if we would go to counseling and try to rebuild our marriage. He said, "I want to stay married. Please end it with him. We have both done and said terrible things to each other. Our marriage was a mess—and a lot of it was my fault. You have betrayed me, but I choose to forgive you."

After I told Jake it was over, and quit my job, Ron was able to begin again—miraculously. He let go of the pain. I, however, got stuck in the sorrow of regret. Receiving and believing in my forgiveness was tedious, treacherous. One step forward, two steps back. The memories kept haunting me, surprising me—triggered by the scent of a stranger's cologne or the melody of a song. The shame of past pleasures followed me.

My lies had been so tangled with truth that I wasn't sure which was which. I slowly began to untie the knots of my life. I was relieved to be done with deceit, but because its shadows, exaggerations, and half-truths had been my companions for months, the light of the whole truth seemed harsh.

I was full of self-doubt and couldn't believe how easily I'd been swept away by my feelings. I didn't plunge into adultery—I drifted in and I had to use all my strength to pull my heart back.

Eventually though, I came to see that I would have to surrender to the forgiveness in order to free myself from the prison. I already had the keys, but I had refused to use them. Finally, one day, I did.

I found victory through surrender as I prayed: "God, I give up. I cannot carry this anymore and today I choose to receive forgiveness. Now I ask for strength as I let go of the guilt, the shame, the sorrow, and choose to walk in the light of truth."

I refused to entertain the stray thoughts anymore. Instead, I replaced them with images of the new life that Ron and I were building. I also discovered that encouraging others with our story of forgiveness gave a purpose to our pain. This summer, decades after my affair, we celebrated our thirty-sixth wedding anniversary and our marriage is strong, loving, and healed.

~Nancy C. Anderson

95

The List

We are products of our past, but we don't have to be prisoners of it.
~Rick Warren

M y list really wasn't all that long. While I could not read anybody else's, I sat close enough that at a glance I could tell the guys around me had longer lists than mine.

This was a special time for my fellow inmates and me, and the men who came to spend the weekend showered us with the love of Christ. We were expected to participate in every activity and today's focus was on forgiveness. They talked to us about God's forgiveness of our sins, and our need to forgive others — that forgiveness cleaned the slate and provided motivation to serve God.

Now that the talks were over, we were given a sheet of paper and a pen. The lights were dimmed and it was very quiet. The very air felt holy, somehow. Set apart by God for this special moment with him.

"Your forgiveness list is between you and God," the group leader explained in a quiet, sincere voice. "Nobody but you and God will see it. We don't see it, and the guards aren't allowed to look at it. Be real. The names you write down on that list are for your eyes only. God knows your heart, and any names you leave off for your forgiveness list, well, that's between you and Jesus. But just so you know, Jesus said in Mark 11, 'And whenever you stand praying, if you have anything against anyone, forgive him, that your Father in heaven may also forgive you your trespasses. But if you do not forgive, neither will your Father in heaven forgive your trespasses.'"

Silence.

I knew this was an important moment for me. I already had a few names written down, though going into this activity I had already forgiven them all. I had been wronged. I'd been abused, neglected, used and offended in many ways, but I never was much for holding grudges against anyone. And I'd never been one to blame others for my own mistakes.

Perhaps that's why my list wasn't very long. But that was also why the last name on my forgiveness list was the most difficult to write down. I took the exercise seriously, and I knew God did as well. I could hear him calling my name. It was my name he was telling me to write down on the piece of paper.

I'd hurt a lot of people in many different ways. I ruined my life, and in some ways, that of my family too. I had sinned against God, against my country, against my family and friends, and against myself. God offered me forgiveness for my sin, but could I forgive myself?

Everything was my own fault. I had made the wrong decisions. I went to Sunday school. I knew right from wrong, and I was without excuse, regardless of what the contributing factors were in my life. I learned one of life's hardest lessons—actions have consequences. And now God was willing to forgive me, so why was it so hard to forgive myself?

Tears blurred my eyes as I sat and stared at my little list. I was aware that everybody else—all forty-one other inmates—had already completed their lists and were in line. Nobody could burn his list in the fire until all of us were done, so everyone waited quietly for me.

I broke the silence with a bitter-sounding chuckle as I considered how some of the others were probably thinking I must have a lot of people to forgive. I shook my head, and with tears splashing onto my paper I wrote my own name in big letters.

"Okay, God, there it is," I prayed, preparing myself to stand and join my peers in line. "If you can forgive me, then I forgive me too. But I'm gonna need your help."

I didn't bother to pick up the pen when it fell to the floor. I was on a mission, one that was long overdue. I had to burn this list. I felt a sudden panic attack coming on as I approached the line. I'd taken so long, I feared the fire might go out before I got there to burn my list.

The group leader intercepted me halfway across the room. He hugged me and told me everything was going to be okay. He was the speaker whose talk focused on the need for forgiveness. And rather than lead me to the line of men that stretched down a hallway to the front door of the chapel, he led me past it. I didn't know where we were going, and I don't recall exactly what I was thinking, except that I had taken too long. I had held up the program, and I feared I would not be allowed to burn my forgiveness list.

I noticed that several of the men in that long line were crying too, and almost all of them were smiling either in encouragement or understanding at me.

When we had passed them all, and stepped out of the front door of the chapel, I saw the little fire there, struggling to survive. I had it in mind to toss the list on the flame as we passed by—I had to burn it.

But my scheming was foolish. The group leader stopped me right in front of the flame, squeezed my shoulder and spoke softly in my ear, "Do it, brother. Free yourself."

It's really true. When the burden was lifted from my heart, the air smelled cleaner, the sky looked bluer, and the future looked brighter. "And when (Jesus) had said this, He breathed on them, and said to them, 'Receive the Holy Spirit. If you forgive the sins of any, they are forgiven them; if you retain the sins of any, they are retained.'" (John 20:22-23 NKJV)

The act of forgiveness had set my spirit free.

~Robbie Freeman

96

The Final Forgiveness

Only after we can learn to forgive ourselves can we accept others as they are because we don't feel threatened by anything about them which is better than us.

~Stephen Covey

For a moment following the initial noise and confusion of the crash, a deep stillness returned to the Maine woods. Then a friend in the back seat broke the silence. "How does it feel to be a statistic?"

Slowly, there was rustling, groans. Each sound seemed to be amplified as we sat thirty feet off the country road where our car came to a rest after being broadsided.

A disembodied voice echoed for a split second, seeming to come from all directions at once, which, of course, was impossible. The voice was strangely light and upbeat, carefree almost, despite the fact that the owner of the voice turned out to be the driver of the car who had just hit us. One of the passengers in my car, who was unhurt, got so angry when he heard the guy laughing he almost went over and decked him, but he couldn't get out of the car.

At least this is the information I was given when I awoke from my coma thirty days later.

It's strange how, even after almost forty years, and granting forgiveness to so many people, the idea of forgiving that other driver, the person who did this to me, has not crossed my mind until I started thinking about writing this.

I was so busy trying to regain and recapture the things I had lost that I never looked back to the event that caused it all. In fact, I was strangely disconnected from the events of that night, in much the same way my traumatic brain injury (TBI) removed me from my own life.

Deep down I became angry, not about the crash itself, but about how people treated me after the coma when I was struggling to get my life back. Quite a while passed before I could get over the slights that I attributed to my friends in college, who I felt weren't there for me when I finally returned to school. I couldn't understand why people acted the way they did toward me. Sometimes ignored, often misunderstood, I would beat myself up because I didn't understand what was going on and felt it must be my fault. This caused a great deal of pain and resentment as I tried to make my way through a world that had become confusing and alien to me. Often nothing made sense and I felt like I was going crazy.

With difficulty, I graduated from college a semester late and tried to move on with my life. Although confused and unsure about my abilities, and prone to beating myself up for not performing or for making dumb errors, I was able to return to work in my family's business. Soon after that, I was married and had two terrific children, but I was not at peace, always looking for my place. Lingering doubts, anger and frustration were still with me. I used to refer to myself as an "angry little boy," stuck at age nineteen. Even though I knew it all went back to my car accident, I had no idea what to do about it.

At one point, nearly twenty-five years after the car accident, I had a revelation of sorts. Although in my mind I had forgiven those who I felt had wronged me, I decided that wasn't enough. To make it mean something more, I needed to go the next step by looking up my old friends and talking to them. One lived in the next town, and I made an effort to contact him. Eventually, I connected with each of my friends and found a wonderful weight lifted, as well as a return to a bit of normalcy. I learned that, of course, my friends weren't the demons I had made them out to be. Forgiveness freed me from the angry chatter in my head. And in the process, I also learned we had all become different people. I didn't feel the need or desire to resume a relationship with them, and I was at peace with that.

What I did finally see was that each of us carried regret and hurt from that time period. I also learned I needed to take responsibility for some things and not go looking for ways to place blame. By getting to a place where I could forgive, I began to see that I had unrealistic expectations and that I had, in one way or another, played a role in the way things happened. I also saw that blaming other people reduced my personal power by saying, in effect, that my life was not in my control. By blaming others, I was letting them have control over me.

Forgiving my old friends wasn't about "giving in" or "giving up" or "compromising," it was about growing and taking responsibility for my own life. I was making a statement that I was powerful enough to live on my own, without using blame as a crutch when things didn't go right.

About a year passed and I began seeing a neurologist for the first time since my coma. My coma was in 1975, and there weren't MRIs or CAT scans then, so my doctor suggested I have a current MRI. Even though we all knew I had a brain injury, I had never actually "seen" the damage.

The results came back showing areas of damage as well as areas of dried, twenty-five-year-old blood products in my brain. The news, which I had expected but was not prepared for, brought back the memory of years of rehabilitation, anger, confusion and resentment. But it also provided me with a conclusion, an ending, of sorts, for my journey. On the drive home from the doctor I was overcome by the strength of the truth and had to pull over.

For the first time, I grieved the events of that night and forgave the other driver. At that moment, I not only understood how hard I had been on myself all these years, I saw what I had done to myself by not giving myself a break. The MRI was clear; my brain had real damage, and I shouldn't blame myself for the way I was. Sitting in my car on the side of the road, sobbing, I knew I had to finally let myself off the hook. First, I forgave myself for the unrelentingly negative way I had treated myself. And then I acknowledged myself for all the battles I had fought, and the good things I had accomplished.

A great wave washed over me as that nineteen-year-old boy from 1975 finally became the forty-two-year-old man who sat behind the wheel of that car. Forgiveness of myself, the final forgiveness, had healed me, and allowed me to move ahead with my life.

~Jeffrey Sebell

Uncle Ron's Laugh

To forgive is the highest, most beautiful form of love.
In return, you will receive untold peace and happiness.
~Robert Muller

Memories of my childhood in Washington, D.C. are sweet for many reasons, but mainly because of family. There were six kids in mine, plus Uncle Ron and Aunt Lois lived down the street with their three girls. We attended the same school and had the same friends.

In the summer we'd barbecue, with Dad and Uncle Ron drinking beer and grilling. I imagined that Aunt Lois and Mom traded gossip as they prepared side dishes. In the winter, the grownups ate in the dining room while the kids stayed in the kitchen. We'd crowd onto a pink Barbie banquette that I loved, kicking each other under the table.

With nine kids, trips to the Smithsonian and the spring cherry blossom festival probably strained everyone's nerves, but they were unforgettable. Summers were crammed with swim team and camp. Fall meant jumping into piles of leaves after school. Winter was my favorite season because of Christmas and snow.

This past January, I watched snow falling, cocooning me within a false peace. My nerves were shot. I'd been fortifying myself with numerous cups of hot tea and grilled cheese sandwiches, hoping that comfort food would provide a peace that had eluded me for a year.

Finally, I picked up the phone and dialed one of the few numbers that I'd ever memorized.

Aunt Lois answered on the third ring. I imagined that she'd been in her garden, basking in the quiet of roses and other flowers. I couldn't remember what it looked like. It had been too long since my last visit to her new home in California.

"Hello Auntie." My voice shook a little.

"Hi Karla." Her voice trembled, too.

Suddenly I was a little girl again, running down the street to play with her daughters. She'd scold us and shoo us outside to run off our youthful energy, and then take the sting out of her words with a plate of cookies.

Aunt Lois had been the Bluebird's troop mother. We met at her house one Saturday a month, seriously recited our pledge and did Bluebird stuff. Amidst the songs and games, Uncle Ron would swoop in with hugs and jokes.

"Ron, we're busy," she'd say, waving him away like he was a big kid.

"Bye, girls," he'd say, winking at us and snatching a cookie from the plate.

His hearty affection was different from the formality of my home. I knew that my parents loved me, but sometimes I wished my dad would laugh like Uncle Ron and call me his chickadee.

I closed my eyes against the onset of tears. If only life included a do-over card to be used in extreme emergencies. Memories of Uncle Ron filled my dreams, waking me up with tears and regrets. I'd lost a precious opportunity to see him before he died, to my everlasting regret.

"I couldn't call you during the holidays. I couldn't bear not hearing his voice." Despite my good intentions, I sobbed my apologies into the phone.

"I know, dear. He loved you too." Her sweetness made me feel worse. Her husband of fifty-one years had died a year ago. I should've been comforting her, yet here she was comforting me instead, reaching out with loving warmth that hadn't faded over the years.

I stumbled through the conversation, told her that I'd call again soon and hung up. I leaned my head against the receiver. Pippin, our newest cat, curled against my legs in silent sympathy. I curled up on the bed, nesting among the rose and white comforters like I used to when I was a kid. I wished that life could be that simple again, with cookies and Bluebirds, and family just a hop away.

I hadn't forgiven myself for not seeing him before he died. For the last two and a half years, I'd been a flight attendant for a regional airline. I could manage short trips that took two hours or less, but any longer and I got sick. The thought of being on a plane over four hours made me get dizzy and run for the nearest bathroom.

I'd tried to force myself to do it. I even made a list of reasons why it was silly not to. I didn't have to pay for a ticket. California was sunny. We could sit in the garden and laugh.

I'd desperately wanted to see him, but now it was too late. One of his constant comments floated through my misery. His gravelly voice with its hint of Southern whiskey and bawdy humor always cracked me up. Throughout the years, he'd listened to my dating stories, ready to run to my rescue.

"Tell old Uncle Ron what's on your mind. If some fella is bothering you, tell him that I may be old, but I still got a can of whup ass for him."

In between the laughter and talking ran a thread of love that made him so special to me. He was the father behind my dad, the father I could talk to about anything. I confided my worst fears, as well as my most laughable moments to him. He'd regaled me with stories of all of us growing up together.

That night, I dreamt of him. I was standing at the grill in the back yard of our old house in D.C. cooking hamburgers. He walked through the smoke, eyes twinkling like he'd just told an off-color joke. I almost didn't recognize him, so young and handsome he appeared. Behind him, I caught a glimpse of another man, gray eyes smiling, just as tanned and fit. My father.

"Uncle Ron," I said, taking a step toward him. "Daddy?" The bright sunshine touched us all with gold, almost too intense for me to see. I squinted, shading my eyes with my hand. Raising his hand in farewell, Daddy disappeared, like his job was done.

I couldn't move forward. I strained futilely to reach Uncle Ron, but the golden light restrained me. He shook his head, a small smile playing about his lips.

"Hey, good looking, I'll see you again. Then you can hug me as much as you'd like. Figure you'll need me around to talk about all the fellas whose hearts you broke."

I laughed along with him. And, just like that, he vanished.

I woke up, gray morning light filtering through the bedroom curtains. I watched as it brightened slowly. As it touched my face, I closed my eyes, imagining the gentleness of sunlight and hearing Uncle Ron's laughter one more time.

In that moment, I forgave myself, just as he had.

~Karla Brown

The Support of a Family

We all have regrets from past experiences. You've got to learn to forgive yourself, to put one foot in front of the other and go forward.
~Rashida Rowe

I forgave the boy who permanently damaged my finger in elementary school with his discus-throwing dodge ball technique. I forgave Dad whenever he was too stubborn or opinionated. I even forgave my corporate nemesis who did his best to destroy my reputation. Whenever I forgave someone, my pent-up resentment lessened. But the hardest person to forgive was myself, for falling in love with a chameleon.

I was in my thirties when we met. One year older than I, he seemed perfect — fun loving, bright, charming, and considerate. A nature lover like me, he introduced me to sailing and I introduced him to skiing. After seven years together, his hidden evil twin slowly emerged — the liar, the alcoholic, the adulterer, the skillful manipulator who knew just how to present himself to any audience for the desired effect. At first, I believed the man I fell in love with was the real one and this new creature was a temporary aberration. But as his behavior deteriorated over several years and he admitted that he had lied from the very beginning, I was forced to accept that the new him was the real one and I ended the relationship. Only then did my family tell me the rest.

It turned out that he had learned where my widowed mother hid her cash and had stolen thousands of dollars. Because she knew I loved him at the time, she kept the thefts secret and allowed this man to spend weekends with me at her home again and again until I cut him out of my life. Because of me, he shared two days at my cousin's house and stole from him too. For eight months, my cousin kept this secret, only revealing it after I told him about the theft at my mother's house. Even then, my cousin only said "something" disappeared. He never told me what.

I had allowed a conman to fool me. Because I brought this toxic person into our family, the hurt he caused was my fault. No matter that he fooled countless others—I should have known better. His affairs, the money he took from me, and the lies he told me paled in comparison to the anguish he caused my family. What he did to them could not be undone. The unknown "something" stolen from my cousin could not be replaced. When Mom told me about her missing money, I was too shocked to offer to repay her.

Later, she refused my repeated attempts to reimburse her.

"It isn't right, Mom," I said. "It's my fault."

"What he did is not your fault. The money is not important. What's important is for you to put this behind you and heal."

We hugged, I shed a few tears, and my cloud of guilt began to lift. Within two months, the cloud disappeared. Because Mom could forgive me, I could forgive me.

~Janet Hartman

Pen and Paper

It takes a strong person to say sorry, and an even stronger person to forgive.
~Author Unknown

I was seventeen and a freshman in college. My boyfriend attended another school in a different state, and I'd even considered transferring there as a sophomore. When his father realized ours might not be infatuation, and his plans for his son's graduate education might be altered if we were serious enough to marry when I finished college, he insisted the relationship end. It did... right before New Year's Eve.

Earlier, I'd dated a young cadet from the U.S. Merchant Marine Academy not too far from my Long Island girlhood house. His depth of affection for me and his gentle manner had made my mother comfortable enough to telephone the cadet about my "broken heart," and I instantly had company. Being young and self-centered, I took my upset out on the cadet, who only offered whatever comfort and kind words he could and listened. But I was so devastated that even at midnight I would not let the cadet kiss my cheek to celebrate another year. I cried and cried and used a young man, who loved me, as if he had no feelings.

Many decades later, my daughter and I were discussing people we'd hurt that we wanted to apologize to, and I mentioned the cadet. I wanted to thank him for his kindness, and I wanted to tell him I was truly sorry for hurting him. My daughter encouraged me to make amends, and told me to write the academy and have my letter sent to that alumnus if he was still alive. I did that, and in the letter mentioned my enduring marriage to a man I'd met right before I went to grad school, and that this letter was an overdue apology and a thank you and not a let's-get-together. The letter found him; he wrote back, accepted my apology, and said that I was important in his life and he was glad I was well and happy.

Several years later, I received a note from a man with the same last name: his son. The cadet had died, and in his personal items was my letter of apology. His son, seeing the address, wanted to let me know his father was dead and that this letter must have been important for his father to keep it. The son returned the letter to me.

I thanked my daughter for encouraging me to make amends for a situation that had happened when I was only seventeen but had been on my conscience. I was glad that I'd let a once-young cadet know, before he died, that I was sorry for caring only about my own emotional anguish when he was so kind to me. I regretted hurting his feelings. My husband clasped my hand, approving of my reaching out to apologize to someone I'd hurt. And I was able to forgive myself, finally.

~Lois Greene Stone

My Guilt Collection

The years teach much which the days never knew.

~Ralph Waldo Emerson

"Please! What should I do?" she begged.

"I've already told you," I answered, suddenly aware of the burnt macaroni and cheese odor that hung in the air. "Darn it! Hang on for a second," I muttered, dropping the phone down on the cluttered counter. Armed with a hot pad holder I quickly rescued my over-done dinner and set it to cool, while in the background my four-year-old's crying reached a new crescendo.

Even though my girlfriend always called at the worst possible times, I never had the heart to turn her away. On this night, however, I wasn't in the mood for it all. Unfortunately, I grabbed the phone and continued in a not-so-nice tone: "You fear for your life and yet you stay with him. You're not married so you could leave. I'm scared he might kill you—but if you won't help yourself..." My voice trailed off and then it was silent.

Suddenly, my phone crackled. Through the static she repeated her usual words: "But, I love him."

"Listen," I paused, as the phone hiccupped again, "Can you hear that?"

"Yes," she whined, "so tell me what to do before the line goes dead."

"Leave him," I snapped. "We've had this conversation for almost a year and nothing's changed. I'm sorry I can't help you right now, but my little one is crying and I've burned our dinner." At that moment the phone line roared and then disconnected us, which frequently happened during our conversations. At this point, one of us always called the other one back, but this time neither of us did.

Although I still cared about her and thought of her often, it wasn't until I found an old photograph of us together that I realized eighteen years had passed since that last conversation. My kids had grown, and hopefully she had found happiness. It seemed like a perfect time to call and rekindle our friendship. I was confident that she would forgive me for losing my patience the last time I had talked to her. At least I hoped she would.

While searching for her current phone number on the Internet, I discovered she had married. Minutes later I was excited when a familiar photograph popped up. When I clicked it I found this: "Our beloved, daughter, mother, stepmother, grandmother, aunt, and friend, departed from this earth much too soon."

"Oh no," I moaned. "What have I done?" Never in my wildest dreams had I imagined this tragic scenario. I was so sad, and also felt so guilty. I hated myself for what I had done. I closed my door and wept. Alone in the darkness I created the perfect hell where I tormented myself with every "what if" or "if only" my mind could concoct. Deep down I would never forgive myself. Because of me, my sweet friend had died believing that I didn't care about her.

"You blame yourself for everything," said my husband. "You collect guilt like others collect stamps. You had a family to care for. Her constant calls took time away from your family—a lot of time. You also worried constantly about her."

"But, she's dead," I cried. "I feel so bad about the way things ended."

"That's not your fault, either," he replied.

In truth, my husband was right about my collection of "what ifs" and "if onlys." However, this was more horrific than anything I'd collected so far. As my anguish deepened, I yearned for comfort, but found none. Days later, desperate to find peace, I went for a long hike through the forest where instead of talking out loud to myself—something I'm well known for—I spoke to my girlfriend.

"Wherever you are, you know how I feel. I was all you had—and I let you down. There's no doubt in my mind that you've forgiven me, but you know I can't carry this load. I need to find a way to forgive myself." When I finished speaking, I felt completely whipped. There were no goose bumps, no signs from beyond—only a strange, empty, numbness.

That evening, I decided to read her obituary one last time. Usually, the bitter memory of our final conversation raced through my head, but this time I found myself laughing hysterically as memories of our escapades flew through my mind. Some made me laugh so hard I cried as I remembered everything—including the first time we had met. Our time together flashed before my eyes and with it, all of the times I had been there for her. At that moment, I knew in my heart that I had come through for her as a friend, and that my plea for forgiveness toward myself had been heard. I finally felt at peace.

Hopefully, someday, I'll forgive myself for the rest of the "what ifs" and "if onlys" in my collection, but for now this is a start.

~Jill Burns

A Poem that Says It All

The Road Ahead

Anger
Begets anger.
Rage
Rumbles forward,
Steamrolling
Good as well as bad
On the road ahead.
Forgiveness
Begets forgiveness.
Peace
Shines from above,
Nurturing
All that is precious
On the road ahead.

~Christina Galeone

Meet Our Contributors

Nancy C. Anderson is the author of *Avoiding the Greener Grass Syndrome: How to Grow Affair-Proof Hedges Around Your Marriage*. She and her husband Ron have been married for thirty-six years and encourage other couples to love each other in thought, word, and deed. Read more on her website/blog at NancyCAnderson.com.

Erin Elizabeth Austin is the founder of Broken but Priceless Ministries, a nonprofit organization which helps people suffering with a chronic illness. In her spare time, she loves to spend time with family, friends, and build forts with her nephews. Her goal for each day is to have an adventure, laugh, and eat chocolate.

Valerie D. Benko is a frequent contributor to the Chicken Soup for the Soul series and has more than two dozen essays and short stories published in the U.S. and Canada. Visit her online at valeriebenko. weebly.com.

Jennifer Berger currently resides in Queens, NY with her husband Aaron and their seven-year-old son Josh. A former editor and freelance writer who loves to read and write, Jennifer is now a stay-at-home wife, mother and full-time advocate for her child.

Rita Billbe is a retired high school principal from Oklahoma City. She and her husband own a resort, Angels Retreat, on the White River in Arkansas. Two of her passions are fly fishing and singing in her church choir.

Kathleen Birmingham works as a ghostwriter, convincing her steadily expanding list of clients to share their deepest, darkest secrets with the world. A regular contributor to national magazines, Kathleen is also a member Writers and Critters, an all-women group comprised of writers from around the world.

Susan Boltz is a retired medical lab technician and basic logic assistant. She stays young by teaching Sunday school for high school students. Writing devotionals and humor, biking, and baking cookies for Kairos Prison Ministry keeps her busy.

Karla Brown attended St. Joseph's University in Philadelphia, PA and is happily married. She loves swimming, nature and reading. She also hopes to one day publish her middle grade, young adult and romance manuscripts. E-mail her at karlab612@yahoo.com.

Linda Bruno is a speaker and writer. Her current project is a devotional (*All God's Creatures*) based on how our interactions with our pets mirror our relationship with God. She and her husband Guy have one grown daughter, five grandchildren, and two furkids. Linda can be reached via e-mail at lfbruno@cfl.rr.com.

John P. Buentello is the author of several books and numerous essays, short stories, and poems. E-mail him at jakkhakk@yahoo.com.

Jill Burns lives in the mountains of West Virginia with her wonderful family. She's a retired piano teacher and performer. Jill enjoys writing, music, gardening, nature, and spending time with her grandchildren.

Twelve years ago, stifling sobs, **Diane Caldwell** boarded a plane to Greece. She hasn't lived in the U.S. since. She currently makes her home in Istanbul, where she dances with gypsies whenever possible and writes when the muse whispers. Her stories have appeared in eight different anthologies and on numerous websites.

Eva Carter was born in Czechoslovakia, raised in New York, has lived in Las Vegas, NV and is currently in Dallas, TX with her husband Larry and their cat named Squeaky. After a twenty-three-year stint in finance for a long-distance company, she enjoys writing, creating greeting cards and photography. E-mail her at evacarter@sbcglobal.net.

Stephanie Cassatly earned her MFA degree in Writing at Vermont College of Fine Arts. Her work has appeared in various publications. She teaches writing part-time at Palm Beach Atlantic University, speaks publicly on the topic of forgiveness and resides with her husband and two daughters in Jupiter, FL on the Loxahatchee River.

Kitty Chappell is an international speaker and award-winning nonfiction author who has appeared on radio and television discussing the power of forgiveness. Her autobiography, *Soaring above the Ashes on the Wings of Forgiveness*, is being developed into a feature film. Kitty welcomes your comments at www.kittychappell.com.

Jane McBride Choate has been writing since she was a child entertaining friends at school with stories featuring them. Being published in Chicken Soup for the Soul is a dream come true for her.

Helen Colella is a freelance writer and retired teacher. Published works include educational books/materials, articles/stories for adults and children, anthologies, parenting magazines, and the new *Explore & Discover National Parks: Just Follow the Signs*, a family-oriented activity book. Helen is also a consultant for blue13creative in Denver.

Kirsten Corrigan received her B.A. degree from Luther College and her M.A. degree from The University of Iowa. She retired from a career in finance to focus on being Mom to her son, Ryan. Kirsten enjoys photography, running, teaching fitness classes, freelance writing, and singing. E-mail her at kirsten.r.corrigan@gmail.com.

Melissa Crandall cut her professional writing teeth on media tie-in novels (*Star Trek, Quantum Leap*, and *Earth 2*), then branched out into short stories and essays. Recently, she was chosen as one of only twelve writers in the state of Connecticut to participate in *The Great Connecticut Caper* hosted by Connecticut Humanities.

Melissa Cronin holds an MFA in creative nonfiction from Vermont College of Fine Arts. Her work has appeared in online journals and in *Chicken Soup for the Soul: Recovering from Traumatic Brain Injuries*. Melissa has written a memoir. She and her husband live in South Burlington, VT where she writes for a local newspaper.

Annalee Davis earned a Master of Divinity degree and graduated *summa cum laude* from New Brunswick Theological Seminary. She has been published in *The Secret Place*, the *Pentecostal Evangel*, Chicken Soup for the Soul books and other compilations. She loves to speak, write and play the harp. E-mail her at reverendannalee@comcast.net.

Kalie Eaton is currently pursuing her Bachelor of Arts degree at Mercer University in Macon, GA. She is a member of the esteemed Zeta Phi Beta Sorority, Inc. She enjoys photography and plans to enlist in the U.S. Navy post-graduation. Her Instagram handle is @_kamaea.

Neither blindness at thirty-one, unthinkable tragedy nor painful injustice defeated **Janet Perez Eckles**. Rather, in spite of adversity, she has become an international keynote speaker for Spanish and English-speaking audiences. She is a #1 bestselling author, radio host, life coach, master interpreter and Christian ministry leader.

Terri Elders, LCSW, lives near Colville, WA with her dog Natty and three cats. Her stories have been published in nearly a hundred anthologies. She now has two dozen stories in the Chicken Soup for the Soul series. She co-edited *Not Your Mother's Book... On Travel.* She blogs at atouchoftarragon.blogspot.com.

Holly English enjoys horseback riding, hiking, and beach combing. She also plays the piano, guitar and banjo—very badly—and never plays them when others can hear. She is currently writing a western romance novel.

Steve Erwin is an award-winning journalist and wrote the New York Times bestseller, *Left to Tell: Discovering God Amidst the Rwandan Genocide* with Immaculée Ilibagiza. He was an NYC correspondent for the Canadian Broadcasting Corporation and writer for *People* magazine. He's written seven nonfiction books and is finishing his second novel.

Beverly Fox-Jourdain was born in Ontario and graduated college in England. She currently resides in British Columbia with her husband, three children and a menagerie of dogs and horses. She is the author of two inspirational novels to date.

Robbie Neil Freeman is an inmate in the Texas state prison for crimes committed in his rebellious youth. He has had to grow up in prison and learn that actions have consequences—good or bad. He's learned that his Heavenly Father is the perfect role model and tries to follow His example. Robbie will be eligible for parole in 2024.

Sally Friedman is a longtime contributor to the Chicken Soup for the Soul series. A graduate of the University of Pennsylvania, she has contributed to *The New York Times*, *The Philadelphia Inquirer*, *The Huffington Post*, and numerous regional and national publications. Her favorite subject is family life. E-mail her at pinegander@aol.com.

Christina Galeone is a freelance writer from New England. She enjoys writing regularly for Beliefnet, *The Catholic Free Press*, *Community Advocate* and the *Telegram & Gazette*. She also writes screenplays. She is excited to be included in this Chicken Soup for the Soul book!

Judythe Guarnera connects with people through her volunteer work as a mediator and through her writing. Her first novel, *Twenty-Nine Sneezes*, is in the final editing stage. She has been published in a variety of venues, including a previous Chicken Soup for the Soul anthology.

Charles Earl Harrel pastored for thirty years before stepping aside to pursue writing. He has 510 published works. His articles, stories, and devotionals have appeared in thirty-two anthologies, including four stories in the Chicken Soup for the Soul series. Charles enjoys playing twelve-string acoustic guitar. E-mail him at harrelce@aol.com.

Janet Hartman left New Jersey with her husband and Terrier to telecommute from her sailboat, following the sun along the East Coast for six years. She began writing about sailing and the liveaboard life. After moving ashore in North Carolina, she added land-based subjects and flash fiction to her repertoire. Learn more at JanetHartmanWrites. com.

Jan Henrikson writes, hikes, edits and dances in Tucson, AZ. Her stories have appeared in a variety of anthologies from Chicken Soup for the Soul to A Cup of Comfort. Every day she is thankful for her adventures in the Sonoran desert with her friends, her love, Louis, and their future dog, Beau.

Born into poverty, **Ruthy Herne** believes in the power of faith, hope and love... and the greatest of these is love! A bestselling author, she's married to a wonderful man, has great kids and grandkids, and loves God, family, her country, chocolate, dogs and cappuccinos.

Ann Hoffman is a retired lecturer of English Literature and Music. Her hobbies are singing in a choir, quilting and writing. She has five children, eleven grandchildren, and lives with her husband in the small coastal town of Nelson Mandela Bay in South Africa. She writes short stories, poems and children's books.

Vanessa Hogan, B.A. B.Ed, is an elementary educator and literacy mentor. She resides on scenic Cape Breton Island, Nova Scotia with her husband Liam and their young daughter Veglia. Vanessa has always had a passion for writing and aspires to publish children's literature in the future.

Georgia A. Hubley retired after twenty years in financial management to write full-time. Vignettes of her life appear in various anthologies, magazines and newspapers. Once the nest was empty, Georgia and her husband of thirty-six years left Silicon Valley in the rear view and now hang their hats in Henderson, NV. E-mail her at geohub@aol.com.

Julie Kinser Huffman grew up in Nashville, TN and currently works as a property manager in Houston, TX. She has three grown children: Viktoria, Lindsay and Stefan. Stories that bring value, hope, and encouragement are her passion and Julie is honored to be a contributor. E-mail her at juliekinserhuffman@hotmail.com.

David Hull received his Bachelor of Arts degree from SUNY Brockport in 1986. He has published numerous short stories in magazines and Chicken Soup for the Soul books. Retired from teaching in 2013, David enjoys reading, gardening and spoiling his great-nephew. E-mail him at davidhull59@aol.com.

Jennifer Hunt has loved writing since she was very young. She finds peaceful expression in her writing. Her favorite job is that of mother to her three beautiful children. She thanks her best friend for supporting her in writing and submitting something so personal, and hopes it can help even one person.

Immaculée Ilibagiza is the author, with Steve Erwin, of several books including the New York Times bestseller *Left to Tell: Discovering God Amidst the Rwandan Holocaust*. A recipient of the Mahatma Gandhi International Award for Peace and Reconciliation, she travels the world speaking about forgiveness. Please visit her website: www.immaculee.com.

M.M. Jarrell is an academic advisor at a university. She has volunteered as a leader with several ministries for divorced/widowed. Her passions are ballroom dance, writing, and reading. She finds joy in her ability to help others reach goals, discover hope, and find purpose.

Crystal Johnson is a counselling psychologist and speech language pathologist in Vancouver, BC. Writing is her creative outlet and method of processing the challenges of life. She is grateful for the support of her family in all that she does.

Anne Jones is a pseudonym. The author of this story wanted to remain anonymous, but she thought that her story might help other people who are struggling to forgive.

Sheila Kale is a mother to four and grandmother to eight beautiful children. She is a life coach in Central Texas helping creative people stop procrastinating, see with new perspective, and accomplish what they have always wanted. Known for incorporating stories and humor, she is a sought-after inspirational speaker.

Sheridan Kee received her associate's degree in 2014. She plans to continue her education by getting her bachelor's degree in social work to help children in need. She enjoys riding horses, baking, and church activities. For if you forgive people their wrongdoing, your heavenly Father will forgive you as well (Matthew 6:14).

Lois Kipnis has forty years of experience as a drama teacher and arts administrator. Her publications include a one-act play, *Things Can Always Be Worse!*, and three books for teachers: *Together We Can Improvise*, *Volume 1* and *Volume 2*, and *Have You Ever… Bringing Literature to Life Through Creative Dramatics*.

April Knight collects antique valentines and love letters written in the 1800s and has many framed and hanging on the walls in her home. She believes e-mails have killed romance. Her latest published books are a romance titled *Sweet Dreams: 50 Romantic Bedtime Stories…for Big Girls*, and a mystery titled *Nobody Dies in Kansas*.

Kathleen Kohler writes stories about the ups and downs of family life for numerous magazines and anthologies. She and her husband live in the Pacific Northwest and have three children and seven grandchildren. Read more of her articles or enter her latest drawing at www.kathleenkohler.com.

Linda LaRocque is the author of several award-winning plays. Her numerous short stories have appeared in *Guideposts*, *Signs of the Times*, Chicken Soup for the Soul books and various other anthologies. Her plays are published by Playscripts and ArtAge Publications. Linda writes from her South Haven, MI home.

Deborah Lienemann lives in Iowa with her husband and daughter. She has three grown sons and a granddaughter. She enjoys writing and sharing messages of hope, inspiration and her Christian testimony with others. She is currently an aspiring writer, and journals and writes daily.

Born and raised in Honolulu, HI, **Danielle Lum** is a writer, soul searcher, teacher, business woman, aunt, friend and lifelong student. She loves animals, sunsets, traveling, photography, sake, and hanging with friends. Her kids have four feet and tails. She misses her mom but is grateful that her lessons will live on forever.

Cecilia Heather MacDonald has three published children's stories to her credit along with social commentaries and has been a ghostwriter. She's currently working on several novels/scripts in varying genres for children, young adult and adults. She welcomes your comments at writedimensions.wordpress.com or chmtwinb@gmail.com.

Kathryn Malnight has been published several times before, and this is her second story in a Chicken Soup for the Soul book. As of right now, she lives with her four awesome siblings and parents. She enjoys film, reading, writing (obviously), Broadway musicals, and working with kids with special needs.

Kristine Robbins McGovern has a degree in philosophy from the University of Colorado and was a print journalist for twenty years. Her short plays have been performed across the country, and her paintings have appeared in several national shows. She recently moved to Florence, CO, where she is rehabbing a house built in 1903.

Cynthia Mendenhall is a nonfiction writer and Certified Christian Life Coach who works with single-again adults. "True Forgiveness" is part of a yet-to-be-published instructional guide to creating a great life after divorce. Cynthia is available for speaking engagements. E-mail her at cmendenhall2011@gmail.com.

Susan Méra grew up in the UK. She believes that peace comes from within and that only if we live in a state of peace and love can the world itself be peaceful. A former journalist, Susan and her French husband Henry live in Australia and share mutual interests in history, literature, philosophy, culture and fine cuisine.

Marya Morin is a freelance writer. Her stories and poems have appeared in publications such as *Woman's World* and Hallmark. Marya also penned a weekly humorous column for an online newsletter, and writes custom poetry on request. She lives in the country with her husband. E-mail her at Akushla514@hotmail.com.

Sherry Morton-Mollo teaches Advanced Placement English and has a master's degree in English Literature. She received her B.A. degree at the University of California at Los Angeles. She believes wholeheartedly in the power of forgiveness and its transforming power.

Margaret Nava writes from her home in New Mexico where she enjoys sunny days, beautiful weather and green chile. In addition to her stories in the Chicken Soup for the Soul series, she has authored six books and written numerous articles for Christian publications.

Daniel Nester is the author of *Shader: 99 Notes on Car Washes, Grief, Making Out in Church, and Other Unlearnable Subjects.* Other books include *How to Be Inappropriate* and *The Incredible Sestina Anthology,* which he edited. He teaches writing at The College of Saint Rose in Albany, NY.

Diane Nichols is the author of the worldwide memoir *Prison Of My Own... A True Story of Redemption & Forgiveness* as seen on ABC's *20/20* and *The Montel Williams Show.* She is also an award-winning newspaper reporter, a magazine journalist and a budding novelist. She invites you to visit her website at www.dianenichols.com.

Nancy Norton received her Bachelor of Arts degree from Rowan University in 1999. She has three grown daughters and teaches second grade in New Jersey. Nancy enjoys traveling with her husband, spending time with her grandchildren, and being walked by her two dogs. She plans to write character education books for school children.

Kay Conner Pliszka has twenty-two stories in eighteen Chicken Soup for the Soul books. She uses her stories, both humorous and dramatic, to touch the hearts of audiences as she gives motivational and inspirational speeches in various parts of the country. E-mail her at kmpliszka@comcast.net.

Connie Pombo is a freelance writer, author and speaker. Her stories have appeared in several Chicken Soup for the Soul books and numerous publications. Connie enjoys traveling, running and swimming. She is working on her first novel, based in Sicily. To contact her or learn more, visit www.conniepombo.com.

Joe Rector has published three books, along with several other pieces for magazines and newspapers, and writes a weekly personal column for *The Knoxville Focus*, a weekly newspaper. E-mail him at joerector@comcast.net.

JoAnn Richi, MC, LPC, holds a Masters of Counseling degree and has been in private practice for over twenty years. She is currently working on a series of eBooks on mental health. Ms. Richi is also the Clinical Consultant for The Psychology of Bliss Seminars in Arizona and Italy. For additional info, visit JoAnn's website at joannrichi.com.

Mark Rickerby is a writer, screenwriter, singer, voice artist and multiple Chicken Soup for the Soul contributor. His proudest achievements are his daughters, Marli and Emma. He released a CD of fifteen original songs for them, and co-wrote his father's memoir. For info on these and other projects, visit www.markrickerby.com.

Sallie A. Rodman has her Certificate in Professional Writing from California State University, Long Beach, where she is currently teaching writing to adult seniors. She loves to share unique personal experiences. Her work has appeared in numerous Chicken Soup for the Soul anthologies and various magazines. E-mail her at sa.rodman@verizon.net.

Sioux Roslawski is a full-time third grade teacher, a part-time freelance writer and an occasional dog rescuer. Currently she's working on a novel, and in the process, doing more deconstruction than construction. You can read more of her writing at siouxspage.blogspot.com.

Award-winning author, speaker, blogger **Jo Russell** shows by example how to cope in all stages of life and stay sane. She posts a humorous weekly blog on www.button-to-god.com. Jo is a retired reading teacher. Her inspirational stories, devotionals, and humor span more than forty years in magazines and anthologies.

Beth Saadati, a high school English teacher, has invested her time and heart into the lives of hundreds of teenagers. She is currently teaching writing classes, homeschooling her son and daughter, writing two books, and sharing a message of truth, courage and hope in the aftermath of her beloved firstborn's suicide.

Karen Todd Scarpulla, graduate of Towson State University, spent nienteen years in Chicago raising her two children. She currently lives in California. She has a passion for cooking, entertaining and traveling. She continues to write books and speak to audiences, encouraging them to find forgiveness. Learn more at www.walkingbeyond.com.

Sara Springfield Schmit received her Bachelor of Arts degree in Communication from Southwestern University in 2003. She has two boys, a husband, and two crazy dogs. She plans to get her Master of Art degree in English from The University of Texas at San Antonio.

Jeff Sebell experienced a traumatic brain injury in 1975. Through his book, *Learning to Live with Yourself after Brain Injury*, published by Lash & Associates, and his blog, Jeff addresses core issues of self-discovery for those who have had a TBI. His blog can be read on his website at www.TBIsurvivor.com.

Yvonne Curry Smallwood has been writing and publishing inspirational stories for more than twenty years. But her absolute favorite pastime is traveling with her family and friends. When she is not writing, you can find Yvonne in a craft store purchasing yarn for the many crochet items that she donates to local charities.

Michael T. Smith lives in Caldwell, ID with his lovely wife Ginny. He works as a project manager and writes inspiration in his spare time. Sign up for a weekly story at visitor.constantcontact.com/d. jsp?m=1101828445578&p=oi or read more stories at ourecho.com/ biography-353-Michael-Timothy-Smith.shtml#stories.

Cheryll Snow is a wife, mother, grandmother, writer, and registered nurse. This is her second published piece in the Chicken Soup for the Soul series. She is currently seeking representation for her inspirational novel, *Sea Horses*. E-mail her at cheryllsnow@yahoo.com.

Now retired from local government, **Joyce Stark** travels widely across Europe and the U.S. She continues to write anecdotal stories and travel articles from her past and those she meets.

Robert Stermscheg, now a retired police officer, enjoys reading as well as writing. His passion is researching and writing historical fiction. When not writing, he enjoys traveling with his wife. Contact him through his website at www.robertstermscheg.com.

Lois Greene Stone, writer and poet, has been syndicated worldwide. Her poetry and personal essays have been included in hard and softcover book anthologies. Collections of her personal items, photos, and memorabilia are in major museums including twelve different divisions of the Smithsonian.

Lynn Sunday is an artist, writer, and animal advocate living in Northern California with her husband and senior rescue dog. Her most recent publications include: *Times They Were A-Changing: Women Remember the '60s and '70s*; *Chicken Soup for the Soul: The Dog Did What?*; and *The Noe Valley Voice*. E-mail Lynn at Sunday11@aol.com.

Hope Sunderland is a retired registered nurse with a B.A. degree in Psychology who hung up her bedpan and enema bucket to write. She writes from the South Texas Gulf Coast. This is her third contribution to the Chicken Soup for the Soul series.

Kara Sundlun is an Emmy Award-winning television news anchor and host of *Better Connecticut*. Her series *Kara's Cures* is a mainstream guide to health and spirituality; she is also a contributor for *The Huffington Post*. Kara is married and mom to cherished children Helena and Julian.

Willow Swift is a blogger, mother, and poet... not necessarily in that order. She writes to help herself, and others, explore and enjoy the journey of life, and to make sense of the stones so often in the path.

Annmarie B. Tait lives in Conshohocken, PA with her husband Joe Beck. She enjoys cooking and many crafts, along with singing and recording Irish and American folk music. Annmarie has contributed several stories to the Chicken Soup for the Soul series, *Reminisce* magazine, and numerous other anthologies. E-mail her at irishbloom@aol.com.

Stacey Wagner currently lives in Seattle, WA. She has an MBA and B.S. degree in Business Administration from Black Hills State University in South Dakota, where she was born and raised. She enjoys traveling and not staying in one spot too long.

Pat Wahler is a grant writer by day and award-winning writer of essays and short stories by night. She is proud to be a contributor to five previous Chicken Soup for the Soul titles. A lifelong animal lover, Pat ponders critters, writing, and life's little mysteries at www. critteralley.blogspot.com.

Elizabeth June Walters is the pen name for a writer who lives in Pennsylvania. She has two grown children and lives with her husband and dog. In her spare time she enjoys reading, crafting, Bible study, and practicing hospitality.

Kate White is a thirty-one-year-old writer who lives just outside of the Detroit area. She has been previously published in the Chicken Soup for the Soul series as well as in *Floating Bridge Review* and *The Linor Project*. Kate is currently working on publishing her memoir, which she plans to release late 2015.

Arthur Wiknik, Jr. served in Vietnam with the 101st Airborne Division and fought in the Hamburger Hill battle. He has appeared both on the History Channel and the Military Channel. Arthur frequently shares his military experiences at schools and civic organizations. Visit his website at www.namsense.com.

Patricia Williams lives in Lakeview, AR. She is a senior citizen and loves having had the time to write and share many other people's stories. Currently she is homeschooling five children, ranging from four years old to thirteen-year-old twins. She has a wonderful church family and loves what she does.

Ferida Wolff is the author of three essay books for adults and seventeen books for children. Her essays appear in anthologies, newspapers and magazines. She is a frequent contributor to the Chicken Soup for the Soul series and also writes a nature blog at feridasbackyard.blogspot. com.

Raymond M. Wong earned an MFA in Creative Writing at Antioch University LA. His writing has appeared in *USA Today*, *U-T San Diego*, *San Diego Family*, *Small Print Magazine*, and *Segue*. His memoir, *I'm Not Chinese: The Journey from Resentment to Reverence*, was published in 2014. Learn more at www.raymondmwong.com.

Meet Our Authors
Amy Newmark &
Anthony Anderson

Amy Newmark was a writer, speaker, Wall Street analyst and business executive in the worlds of finance and telecommunications for more than thirty years. Today she is publisher, editor-in-chief and coauthor of the Chicken Soup for the Soul book series. By curating and editing inspirational true stories from ordinary people who have had extraordinary experiences, Amy has kept the twenty-one-year-old Chicken Soup for the Soul brand fresh and relevant, and still part of the social zeitgeist.

Amy graduated *magna cum laude* from Harvard University where she majored in Portuguese and minored in French. She wrote her thesis about popular, spoken-word poetry in Brazil, which involved traveling throughout Brazil and meeting with poets and writers to collect their stories. She is delighted to have come full circle in her writing career—from collecting poetry "from the people" in Brazil as a twenty-year-old to, three decades later, collecting stories and poems "from the people" for Chicken Soup for the Soul.

Amy has a national syndicated newspaper column and is a frequent radio and TV guest, passing along the real-life lessons and useful tips she has picked up from reading and editing thousands of Chicken Soup for the Soul stories.

She and her husband are the proud parents of four grown children and in her limited spare time, Amy enjoys visiting them, hiking, and reading books that she did not have to edit.

Anthony Anderson has appeared in over twenty films, and his performance on *Law & Order* earned him his fourth consecutive NAACP Image Award nomination for Outstanding Actor in a Drama Series for the 2010 season. Before joining *Law & Order*, Anderson starred in the New Orleans-based drama *K-Ville*. Over the years, he has displayed his bountiful talent in the DreamWorks' blockbuster *Transformers*, directed by Michael Bay; as well as in Martin Scorsese's Oscar winning feature, *The Departed*, alongside a stellar cast including Leonardo DiCaprio, Matt Damon and Jack Nicholson.

Anderson is star and executive producer of ABC's sitcom *Black-ish*, which premiered this Fall alongside co-stars Tracee Ellis Ross and Laurence Fishburne. He plays the main character in the series who is a family man that struggles to gain a sense of cultural identity while raising his kids in a predominantly white, upper-middle-class neighborhood.

Most recently he has been seen in the Sundance film *Goats* and 20th Century Fox's *The Big Year* starring Jack Black, Owen Wilson and Steve Martin, directed by David Frankel.

He first gained attention as one of Jim Carrey's sons in *Me, Myself, and Irene*, and has subsequently appeared in such films as *Scary Movie 3*, *Barbershop*, *Kangaroo Jack*, *Exit Wounds*, *Cradle 2 the Grave*, *Two Can Play That Game*, and *Malibu's Most Wanted*. He also starred opposite Eddie Griffin and Michael Imperioli in *My Baby's Daddy*, opposite

Frankie Muniz in *Agent Cody Banks 2* and had a cameo in *Harold and Kumar Go to White Castle*. Anderson brought his talent and humor to the small screen in his own WB sitcom *All About the Andersons*, which was loosely based on his life. Anderson appeared in the police-drama television series, *The Shield*, opposite Michael Chiklis and Glenn Close and in NBC's *Guys with Kids*.

Anderson grew up in Los Angeles. While pursuing his acting career, he continued his education by attending the High School for the Performing Arts, where he earned first place in the NAACP's ACT-SO Awards with his performance of the classic monologue from *The Great White Hope*. That performance, along with his dedication to his craft, earned him an arts scholarship to Howard University.

Anderson currently lives in Los Angeles. He is married to his college sweetheart, and they have two children.

Thank You

We owe huge thanks to all our contributors. We know that you poured your hearts and souls into the thousands of stories that you shared with us. We appreciate your unselfish willingness to open up your lives to other Chicken Soup for the Soul readers and share your own experiences of forgiveness, no matter how personal. Many of you said this was the first time you were sharing your story, so we thank you for letting our readers be your confidants.

We could only publish a small percentage of the stories that were submitted, but every single one was read by our senior editor Barbara LoMonaco and even the ones that do not appear in the book had an influence on us and on the final manuscript. I need to thank our assistant publisher D'ette Corona, who chose most of the inspirational quotes that start off each story. She also worked with all the contributors to make sure they approved our edits, a particularly important job considering the emotional content in these stories. Managing editor Kristiana Pastir and senior editor Barbara LoMonaco performed their normal masterful proofreading job.

We also owe a very special thanks to our creative director and book producer, Brian Taylor at Pneuma Books, for his brilliant vision for our covers and interiors.

~Amy Newmark

Sharing Happiness, Inspiration, and Wellness

R eal people sharing real stories, every day, all over the world. In 2007, *USA Today* named *Chicken Soup for the Soul* one of the five most memorable books in the last quarter-century. With over 100 million books sold to date in the U.S. and Canada alone, more than 200 titles in print, and translations into more than forty languages, "chicken soup for the soul" is one of the world's best-known phrases.

Today, twenty-one years after we first began sharing happiness, inspiration and wellness through our books, we continue to delight our readers with new titles, but have also evolved beyond the bookstore, with wholesome and balanced pet food, delicious nutritious comfort food, and a major motion picture in development. Whatever you're doing, wherever you are, Chicken Soup for the Soul is "always there for you™." Thanks for reading!

Share with Us

We all have had Chicken Soup for the Soul moments in our lives. If you would like to share your story or poem with millions of people around the world, go to chickensoup.com and click on "Submit Your Story." You may be able to help another reader, and become a published author at the same time. Some of our past contributors have launched writing and speaking careers from the publication of their stories in our books!

We only accept story submissions via our website. They are no longer accepted via mail or fax.

To contact us regarding other matters, please send us an e-mail through webmaster@chickensoupforthesoul.com, or fax or write us at:

Chicken Soup for the Soul
P.O. Box 700
Cos Cob, CT 06807-0700
Fax: 203-861-7194

One more note from your friends at Chicken Soup for the Soul: Occasionally, we receive an unsolicited book manuscript from one of our readers, and we would like to respectfully inform you that we do not accept unsolicited manuscripts and we must discard the ones that appear.

Special Bonus!

2 Extra Stories about the power of forgiveness

Reboot Your Life

101 Stories about Finding a New Path to Happiness

Amy Newmark
and Claire Cook

Meeting Mom

Fortunately analysis is not the only way to resolve inner conflicts.
Life itself remains a very effective therapist.
~Karen Horney

"So, what does poison ivy look like?" my mom asked with a nervous laugh. I could hear her picking her way gingerly through the bramble—over rocks, around prickly bushes. As she followed me over a fallen tree, I realized that some part of me was purposefully choosing the toughest, most overgrown path and, amazingly, she was following nearly without complaint.

As we trudged through the damp weeds and clambered over a jutting rock, I felt the years melt away... I was no longer an out-of-shape teacher in her late twenties leading her overweight fifty-year-old mother down into an abandoned ravine choked with debris and runaway weeds. I was twelve again and, for the first time ever I was sharing a childhood exploration with my mom.

A lump rose in my throat and I blinked hard, silently chastising myself: Don't cry now, she'll never understand. The tears came anyway and so I tucked my head down and pressed further into the overgrowth.

"What did you and Cyd do down here?" my mother puffed as she struggled to keep up.

"You'll see, if we ever manage to find the creek under all these weeds."

As a kid I had been as familiar with this ravine as I was with the path that ran from my house to Cyd's, but it hadn't been so overgrown then. It used to be so open and pretty, and when I had stood at the mouth of the ravine with my best friend and looked down, it was like staring into our own private Land of the Lost.

We had made it to the base of the ravine by now and I caught a glimpse of the creek's dark water beneath the branches of a fallen tree. I climbed out and balanced precariously on the limb that served as a tenuous bridge between the two banks. "See? I told you it was here."

I stepped off onto the other bank and slipped off my shoes. The water felt just like I remembered, so cold my feet were numb to the squishy mud between my toes. On her side, my mom leaned tentatively against the fallen tree and untied her muddied shoes, which only fifteen minutes ago had been as white as her linen sheets. Then she was in the water with me, her pants delicately rolled up halfway to her knees.

At first she fretted about getting her clothes wet or cutting her foot on a rock submerged in the dark water, but soon she was staring in awe at the untouched wilderness around her. I wished I knew what she was thinking—I could see her face lighten, the worries and stresses being carried toward the river on the creek's cool current.

She spotted a crayfish in a shallow pool near me. As she leaned toward the water for a better view, I couldn't restrain myself. I knew it would break the spell and ruin the moment, possibly the whole afternoon, but I just couldn't keep my hands from doing it.

Maybe I was trying to punish her for withholding this moment from me when I was twelve years old and desperately yearning for my mom's affection. Maybe it was just one of those childish pranks revived from my twelve-year-old mind, the ones that had irritated even Cyd.

Either way, it could not be stopped.

My hands did the unthinkable—they scooped up the ice cold water and flung it at my mom. It wasn't a lot of water—more than a splash, but less than a dousing. Just enough to soak her neatly pressed pants.

She looked up astonished. "What...?" Her voice trailed off and her eyes took on a strange cast, almost devilish. Next thing I knew, I was drenched head to toe, and my mother's look of surprise had been replaced with one of feigned innocence. I was flabbergasted. How could she do that? I knew I splashed first, but...

Then it occurred to me how we must look: two grown women standing knee-deep in a creek, fully dressed and dripping wet, make-up melting into rivulets down our faces.

My mom must have been thinking the same thing, because suddenly she tilted her head back and laughed, a sweet beautiful laugh rising from her heart and startling the birds from the treetops. It was a sound so foreign to the small dark house in which we had tiptoed around each other for all those years that now it collected in my throat like forgotten sadness and I swallowed until I could feel the weight of it in my chest. Her laughter, so light and sudden in the abandoned ravine, made me realize something that had never occurred to me before: Maybe it wasn't me who had been deprived all those years that she wasn't part of my life. Maybe while my mother sat alone in her dark room, locked within the prison of her depression, she dreamed of today and a daughter who would insist that she live... even if it meant dragging her kicking and screaming into the sunlight.

Later, as we trekked home trailing wet weeds behind us, I almost asked her. I could feel the heat of the unspoken question, the challenge I had carried for the last fifteen years: "Mom, where were you?"

I smiled as I realized that I didn't have to voice that question.

You're here now, Mom.

Thank you.

~Katherine Higgs-Coulthard

Forgiveness
and Freedom

Forgiveness does not change the past, but it does enlarge the future.
~Paul Boese

The dream startled me so much that I woke up gasping, my hand clutching the comforter. My husband's gentle snore and the familiar shapes in our darkened bedroom reassured me that what I'd seen wasn't real.

Even so, the image of my father wearing a red shirt, lying on his back on my living room sofa, would not go away. Nor would the words he'd said—one short sentence that I could not forget.

The clock on the nightstand told me I needed to go back to sleep but I hesitated to close my eyes. I feared the dream might continue, that Dad would once again say, "You haven't forgiven me yet." Five words that made my stomach churn.

The next day, I told myself it was ridiculous to allow a dream to unsettle me so. And it was only a dream. Dad had died in 1995, so suddenly that there had been no time to say anything to him. We'd had no final moments together. In life, my father would never have worn a red shirt or a red tie, not a red anything. He would also never have asked for forgiveness.

My father had been a complicated man, and during all of my adult years, I had a love/hate relationship with him. He provided the necessities of life in my growing-up years. He was fun to be with some of the time. My three brothers and I knew he loved us, but we also knew that he could turn from loving father to a man who belittled and verbally abused us if we moved outside the lines he'd drawn. We were to believe only what he believed, there was no discussion, no difference of opinion, no respect for our thoughts. It was a love so conditional that we lived with a tiny thread of fear every day.

He verbally and emotionally abused my mother even while loving her deeply. Having to watch silently hurt me. None of us suffered physical abuse from him, but we bore the scars of the cutting words hurled at us during his flares of temper.

He raged like a bull in a Spanish bullring when I wanted to leave the Midwest and teach in California. He disowned my youngest brother because the young college student had the nerve to fall in love with someone of a different race. The bitterness I harbored against my father sat inside me like a weighty rock for many years.

When he died, I had conflicting emotions—sadness that I'd lost my father, the man who loved me, sang songs to me when I was a little girl, who made special foods to cajole me to eat. Another part of me felt only relief that I would never again have to listen to him rant and rave, nor would I have to stand by and watch as he verbally abused my mother. Along with the relief came shame that I would feel this way. I never spoke about it to my mother or my husband. Instead, I carried it with me for the next fifteen years.

The dream brought it all to the surface. All that day, whenever I passed through my living room, I saw my father in the red shirt lying on the sofa and I shivered inwardly. Why now? What made this pop up so many years later? My sensible self knew he wasn't really there. I only imagined it.

Days, and then weeks, passed and I still had trouble looking at my sofa. No way would I sit on it! I churned inside. Why the dream? Why the red shirt? Why was he asking for my forgiveness? I couldn't put it together, didn't know what I should do, and it felt like a wound that refused to heal.

One afternoon, I needed a break while cleaning house, so I fixed a cup of steaming hot tea, grabbed a freshly-baked sugar cookie and sank into my favorite chair. Suddenly, Dad appeared on the sofa, and, yes, he had on that same red shirt. "You still haven't forgiven me," he said so softly I had to strain to hear the words.

Then began an epiphany. Instead of all the negative memories about my father that I'd harbored for so many years, I thought about the positives. My Girl Scout troop sponsored a Father-Daughter Dance and Dad escorted me, beaming with pride. He taught me to be loyal, to love my country and to believe in God. He encouraged me to go to college when our family really could not afford it.

As I sipped my tea, I remember the wonderful support Dad gave me when my first child was born with severe birth defects. I had a vision of the secondhand bike he'd fixed up like new as a birthday gift for me. I thought about my wedding day when he'd walked me down the aisle while I held on to his strong, steady arm.

I set my cup of tea on the end table and silently forgave him for all the hurt he'd inflicted over the years. It was time to bring some balance to my memories. Besides that, I finally realized that my forgiving him would afford both of us peace of mind. What good, I asked myself, did holding a grudge all these years do? It didn't help anyone, most of all, me. Once it was done, Dad disappeared from the sofa. I never saw him or his red shirt again.

What significance the red shirt had, I still do not know. But now, the good times about my life with Dad are remembered more than the dark ones. He came to ask my forgiveness, but the one who felt cleansed and free of bitterness turned out to be me.

~Nancy Julien Kopp

Chicken Soup
for the Soul

Changing your life one story at a time®
www.chickensoup.com